# WORDPERFECT WIZARDRY

## Advanced Techniques and Applications

Paul Garrison

Wordware Publishing, Inc.

**Library of Congress Cataloging-in-Publication Data**

Garrison, Paul.
    WordPerfect wizardry : advanced techniques and applications / by Paul Garrison.
       p.     cm.
  ISBN 1-55622-183-5 : $21.95
    1. WordPerfect (Computer program)   2. Word processing.   I. Title.
Z52.5.W65G388   1990
652.5'536—dc20                                                  90-12905
                                                                                 CIP

Copyright © 1991, Wordware Publishing, Inc.

All Rights Reserved

1506 Capital Avenue
Plano, Texas 75074

No part of this book may be reproduced in any form or by any means
without permission in writing from Wordware Publishing, Inc.

Printed in the United States of America

ISBN 1-55622-183-5
10 9 8 7 6 5 4 3 2 1
9011

WordPerfect 5.0 and 5.1 are trademarks of WordPerfect Corporation.
Sidekick and Superkey are trademarks of Borland International.
HiJaak and InSet are trademarks of Inset Systems, Inc.

All inquiries for volume purchases of this book should be addressed to Wordware Publishing, Inc., at the above address. Telephone inquiries may be made by calling:

(214) 423-0090

# CONTENTS

INTRODUCTION . . . . . . . . . . . . . . . . . . . . . . . . . . . . . . . . . . . . . . . . x
    What this book is all about

## PART ONE
## 50 Ways of Exploring the
## Hidden Features of WordPerfect

CHAPTER 1  **Macros and Characters** . . . . . . . . . . . . . . . . . . . . 1

CHAPTER 2  **Database Management, Part I** . . . . . . . . . . . . . 5
    Developing a simple database. Adding and retrieving data.

CHAPTER 3  **Database Management, Part II** . . . . . . . . . . . . 8
    Adjusting the database to be used with the Merge function.

CHAPTER 4  **Database Management, Part III** . . . . . . . . . . . 14
    Sorting and selecting records by different parameters.

CHAPTER 5  **Base Fonts** . . . . . . . . . . . . . . . . . . . . . . . . . . . . . . . . . 19
    The font selections available with different printers. Manipulating selected fonts.

CHAPTER 6  **Page Formatting, Part I** . . . . . . . . . . . . . . . . . . . 23
    Designing several memo formats. Designing a letter format.

CHAPTER 7  **Page Formatting, Part II** . . . . . . . . . . . . . . . . . . 31
    Designing an invoice format. Using the Merge function to simplify using preprinted documents.

CHAPTER 8  **Newspaper Columns** . . . . . . . . . . . . . . . . . . . . . . 41
    Using the Math/Columns function to produce multiple columns.

CHAPTER 9  **Parallel Columns** . . . . . . . . . . . . . . . . . . . . . . . . . . 45

CHAPTER 10  **Spreadsheet Columns** . . . . . . . . . . . . . . . . . . . . 47
    Using the math functions.

Contents

**CHAPTER 11 Page Formatting, Part III** .................... 52
Formatting the first page of chapters, magazine articles, etc.

**CHAPTER 12 Labels** .................................... 55
Using macros to produce three-across labels in WordPerfect 5.0 and 5.1.

**CHAPTER 13 Business Cards and Disk Labels** ............. 59
A macro that prints six business cards on a page. A macro for printing disk labels.

**CHAPTER 14 Styles - Part I** ............................ 66
Creating style formats for chapter headings and for blocks of text.

**CHAPTER 15 Styles - Part II** ........................... 72
Creating a memorandum style and using the LETTER.STY file provided by WordPerfect.

**CHAPTER 16 Headers and Footers** ........................ 78
Creating headers and footers and macros for that purpose.

**CHAPTER 17 Footnotes and Endnotes** ..................... 82
Creating footnotes and endnotes and macros for that purpose.

**CHAPTER 18 Automatic References** ....................... 87
Referring on one text page to some item on another text page. Creating a macro for that purpose.

**CHAPTER 19 Indenting and Outdenting** ................... 90
Centering text horizontally and vertically on the page.

**CHAPTER 20 Line Numbering** ............................. 95
Using line numbering to count items in lists, or to keep track of the number of lines typed. Also, adjusting column width to specified numbers of characters.

**CHAPTER 21 Drawing Lines** .............................. 100
Using the two line-draw options. Creating macros that draw lines.

**CHAPTER 22 Comment Boxes** .............................. 105
Creating comment boxes for a letter format and for a purchase order.

**CHAPTER 23 Using Two Screens** .......................... 115
Alternating between two screens. Using two document windows simultaneously.

CHAPTER 24  **List Files Option** . . . . . . . . . . . . . . . . . . . . . . 117
   Creating and editing document summaries.

CHAPTER 25  **Multiple Fonts** . . . . . . . . . . . . . . . . . . . . . . . . . 124
   Discovering how your printer handles different font styles and sizes.
   Converting WordPerfect files to generic and ASCII text files.

CHAPTER 26  **Editing Parallel Columns** . . . . . . . . . . . . . . . . 129
   Creating macros that delete individual columns in multicolumn
   documents.

CHAPTER 27  **Slide Shows** . . . . . . . . . . . . . . . . . . . . . . . . . . . 134
   Using the WordPerfect graphics capabilities to produce macros that run
   slide shows.

CHAPTER 28  **Graphics** . . . . . . . . . . . . . . . . . . . . . . . . . . . . . 140
   Using the Figure, Table, Text box, and User-defined box options.

CHAPTER 29  **Screen Capture Programs - Part I** . . . . . . . . . . 150
   Activating and using GRAB.COM.

CHAPTER 30  **Screen Capture Programs - Part II** . . . . . . . . . 154
   Using the HiJaak and InSet programs to capture text screens and convert
   them to WordPerfect-compatible graphics files.

CHAPTER 31  **Comparing Documents** . . . . . . . . . . . . . . . . . 156
   Displaying differences between a document on screen and one on disk.
   Writing a macro to delete redline and strikeout codes.

CHAPTER 32  **Master Documents and Hyphenation** . . . . . . . 159
   Combining several documents into a single file.

CHAPTER 33  **Tables of Contents** . . . . . . . . . . . . . . . . . . . . . 163
   Using WordPerfect functions to generate tables of contents.

CHAPTER 34  **Indexes** . . . . . . . . . . . . . . . . . . . . . . . . . . . . . 166
   Using WordPerfect functions to generate indexes automatically. Creating
   macros to simplify producing indexes.

CHAPTER 35  **Concordance Files** . . . . . . . . . . . . . . . . . . . . . 171
   The pros and cons of using concordance files for frequently occurring
   words and phrases.

CHAPTER 36  **Widows, Orphans, and Conditional End-Of-Page Features** . . . 173
   Also using the block-protect feature.

## Contents

**CHAPTER 37 Running DOS Programs** . . . . . . . . . . . . 176
    The limitations based on available RAM.

**CHAPTER 38 Math and Scientific Symbols in WordPerfect 5.0** . . . . . . . . 178
    Using Exact to insert special characters into WordPerfect documents.

**CHAPTER 39 Math and Scientific Symbols in WordPerfect 5.1** . . . . . . . . 181
    Using the Equation option available with this version of WordPerfect.

**CHAPTER 40 Converting Word Processing Files** . . . . . . . . . . 184

**CHAPTER 41 Using Asterisk (*) in LIST FILES** . . . . . . . . . . . 188
    Creating a macro that copies each day's work to a floppy disk before shutting down.

**CHAPTER 42 Mouse Operation with WordPerfect 5.0** . . . . . . . . . 190
    The source code used to program the Logitech C7 mouse for use with WordPerfect 5.0.

**CHAPTER 43 Mouse Operation with WordPerfect 5.1** . . . . . . . . . 196
    Cursor movement, menus and submenus resulting from mouse operation.

**CHAPTER 44 DrawPerfect Clip-Art** . . . . . . . . . . . . . . 199
    Using the Library and importing clip-art files from other external clip-art libraries.

**CHAPTER 45 Writing Program Source Code** . . . . . . . . . . . 201
    Converting such code to ASCII format for actual use.

**CHAPTER 46 The Library Shell** . . . . . . . . . . . . . . . 204
    Edit Macros, Notebook, DOS Command, Program Editor, Beast Game.

**CHAPTER 47 The Library Appointment Calendar** . . . . . . . . . . 207
    Entering an appointment and using the alarm function.

**CHAPTER 48 The Library Calculator** . . . . . . . . . . . . . 209
    Figure the future value of an amount, based on interest rates and compounding periods. Figure the surface area of a ball.

**CHAPTER 49 The Library File Manager** . . . . . . . . . . . . 211

**CHAPTER 50 Using External Programs** . . . . . . . . . . . . 212
    Importing graphics and font files from external software.

## PART TWO
## Features and Functions Reference

CHAPTER 51 **Function Keys** . . . . . . . . . . . . . . . . . . . . . 217
 A complete alphabetical list of all function-key commands, menus and submenus, with explanations of the results obtained.

CHAPTER 52 **Additional Features and Functions** . . . . . . . . . . . 251
 An alphabetical list of the additional features available with keystrokes other than those involving the function keys.

## PART THREE
## Macro and Style Libraries

CHAPTER 53 **Utility Macro Library** . . . . . . . . . . . . . . . . . 261
 A collection of useful macros.

CHAPTER 54 **Utility Style Library** . . . . . . . . . . . . . . . . . 265
 A collection of a few useful styles.

## APPENDIXES

APPENDIX A  **Extended ASCII Codes** . . . . . . . . . . . . . . 271
 ASCII Code used in programming the Logitech Mouse to work with WordPerfect 5.0.

APPENDIX B  **List of Macros** . . . . . . . . . . . . . . . . . . 273
 Macros described in this book.

APPENDIX C  **Glossary** . . . . . . . . . . . . . . . . . . . . . 275

INDEX  . . . . . . . . . . . . . . . . . . . . . . . . . . . . . 277

# INTRODUCTION

This book deals with the many unusual features and functions available with WordPerfect 5.0 and 5.1. Quite a few of these go considerably beyond what can normally be expected of a word processor. Depending on the type of work you commonly do with your computer, some of the features described may be particularly useful and others less so.

To make it easy for you to decide which specific subject is of interest at any given time, Part One of the book is divided into a large number of short chapters. Each chapter deals with a specific feature or function and each includes step-by-step instructions, showing exactly what to enter to achieve the desired result.

Basically WordPerfect is simply a word processor, much like any other, designed primarily to generate text. But versions 5.0 and 5.1 include a wealth of less obvious features that make it one of the most versatile software programs on the market today. To give some examples:

- It can produce sophisticated **database** programs that can be accessed and manipulated in a variety of ways.
- You can develop **spreadsheets** that perform mathematical functions automatically.
- You can include all manner of **graphics** in text documents, both those provided as part of the WordPerfect software packages and those produced by external programs.
- WordPerfect produces **tables of contents** and automatically alphabetized **indexes** for documents of just about any size.
- It generates **headers, footers, footnotes,** and more.
- It can even produce complete **slide shows**, to be operated either manually from the keyboard, or timed for automatic operation in conjunction with recorded commentary.
- The program includes an application that can take "snapshots" of screen images produced by other programs to be included in WordPerfect documents.

There is much more, as you'll see when you read on.

The book is written with the assumption that you are familiar with the basic operation of WordPerfect. The book is not intended as a word-processing tutorial. Rather, it concentrates entirely on the more obscure uses of the program.

*Introduction*

Nearly all of the subjects covered in this book can be executed with WordPerfect 5.0 as well as WordPerfect 5.1. The primary differences between the two versions are few. Version 5.1 can be operated with a mouse, but as is shown in Chapter 42, you can easily program a mouse to operate effectively with the 5.0 version. The later version includes a means of generating math and science symbols. With the earlier version you have to use an external program to achieve the same result. Version 5.1 lets you import or link spreadsheet files produced by Lotus 1-2-3 or other spreadsheet programs. The new version simplifies printing labels, but that isn't particularly difficult with the earlier version.

On the negative side, version 5.1 is somewhat larger, more complicated, and a bit more difficult to master. Because of its increased size, it is slower than earlier versions and it includes a few unpleasant peculiarities, such as the fact that text is illegible in the double-size view-document mode.

A few of the chapters in this book deal with using WordPerfect in conjunction with other software. It is not necessary to own the specific software programs described. The principles described work with any other software that performs comparable tasks.

**Acknowledgement**: I want to express my appreciation to Qume Corporation for the use of the CrystalPrinter Series II Laser printer for printing the manuscript and screen captures.

Paul Garrison

# PART ONE

# 50 Ways of Exploring the Hidden Features of WordPerfect

# Chapter 1
# MACROS AND CHARACTERS

One of WordPerfect's most useful features, and of major importance in most of the exercises described in this book, is its *macro* capability. A macro is a miniature program that, when called up by one or two keystrokes, causes a lengthy series of steps to be performed automatically. Thus macros are time savers as they eliminate the need to remember all the keystrokes necessary to produce a given result. This chapter explains how to create macros. It then illustrates their use in creating foreign language characters.

WordPerfect permits the use of three different types of macros. Two of these, once created, are saved and thus remain available until intentionally erased. The third type is temporary. It remains in RAM as long as the computer is turned on and WordPerfect remains active.

The first type of macro is created by using the **Alt** key in combination with any one of the 26 letters of the alphabet as the filename, with the extension **.WPM** being supplied automatically by WordPerfect. In the file directory these macros are displayed as **ALTA.WPM, ALTB.WPM**, etc. The steps involved in getting ready to write this type of macro are:

1. Press **Ctrl-F10** which produces the following display on the status line: **Define macro:** asking that the macro name be entered.
2. Press **Alt-A** (or use any other letter of your choice) to produce a macro called ALTA.WPM. You can use uppercase or lowercase letters. It makes no difference.
3. The status line now changes to **Description:** providing an opportunity to add a description of the macro. Such descriptions are useful when trying to remember what each macro is designed to do.
4. Press **Enter** and the macro is ready to be written to.

The second macro group have filenames of eight or less letters and are saved as **FILENAME.WPM** files. To produce such a macro, the steps are identical to the ones described above except that, instead of pressing Alt and a letter, you key in a filename and press Enter as before.

*Chapter 1*

The third type of macro is useful if a document uses a given word, phrase, or sentence with great frequency. To demonstrate, let's take the word **WordPerfect** which appears here repeatedly. To have the program type it automatically, the steps are:

1. Press **Ctrl-PgUp** which produces the prompt **Variable:** on the status line. It requires that any integer number (0 through 9) be typed as the macro name. Type a number.
2. The status line changes to prompt **Value:**. Type **WordPerfect** and press **Enter**. The status line message disappears, and the macro is saved.
3. Press **Alt-0** (or whatever number you used) and instantly the program will type **WordPerfect**.

This type of macro disappears when the computer is turned off or WordPerfect is deactivated.

For demonstration purposes, follow the steps outlined below, writing a macro that can be used to change regular type to *italic*. Call it **ALTI.WPM** and perform the following steps:

1. Press **Ctrl-F10** (Macro define) and then press **Alt-I**.
2. For the **Description:** type **Italics** and press **Enter**. The status line now flashes **Macro Def**, meaning that it is ready to accept the keystroke sequence.
3. Press **Ctrl-F8** (Font) and type **2** and then **4**.
4. Press **Ctrl-F10** (Macro define) to terminate the process.

From now on, at any time, if you press **Alt-I**, the font style changes from whatever you've been using to *italics*.

To see what this macro looks like, follow these steps:

1. Press **Ctrl-F10** followed by **Alt-I** and the status line reads:
   `ALTI.WPM is Already Defined. 1 Replace; 2 Edit: 0.`
2. Type **2** and the display changes to the one shown in Fig. 1-1.

The **{DISPLAY OFF}** command is added automatically to prevent having each step displayed on the screen while the macro is executed. The **{Font}** was produced by pressing **Ctrl-F8** and the **24** represents pressing the **2** and **4** keys.

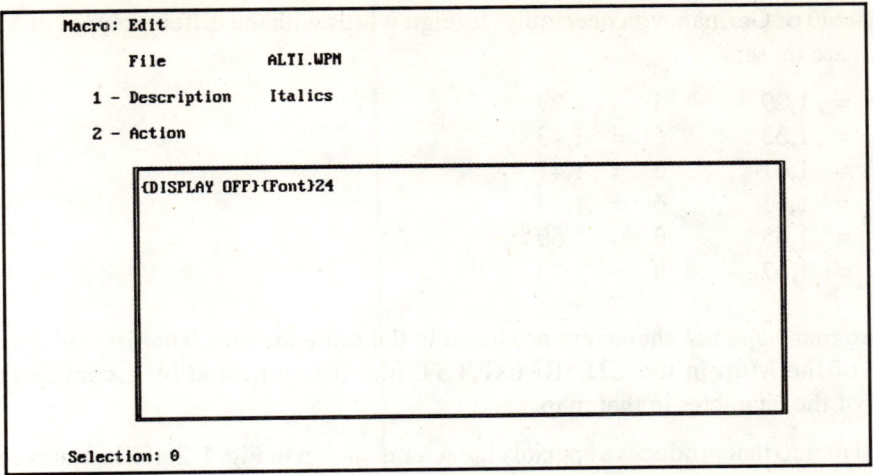

Figure 1-1

WordPerfect can produce a great number of odd and unconventional characters, which are included here to illustrate the use of macros. Some printers will actually print only a limited number of those available. To find out what your printer will or will not print, WordPerfect includes a file called **CHARMAP.TST**. Print it and the result shows you which of these characters you can use. The ones that you think you might be using with any degree of frequency can be called up through macros.

When a document is being prepared that requires the use of German words, many may include umlauts.

The steps required to produce an ä are:

1. Press **Ctrl-V** which results in **Key** = as a prompt on the status line.
2. Type **1,31** and press **Enter** and the ä appears at the cursor position.

To create ö change step 2 above to **1,63** and press **Enter**; to produce the ü, change those steps to **1,71** and **Enter**. Uppercase versions of these letters can also be created:

Ä = 1,30
Ö = 1,62
Ü = 1,70

## Chapter 1

Or, if instead of German, you need other foreign words with the different types of accents, the steps are these:

| | | | | | |
|---|---|---|---|---|---|
| â | = | 1,29 | á | = | 1,27 |
| à | = | 1,33 | ê | = | 1,43 |
| é | = | 1,41 | è | = | 1,47 |
| ô | = | 1,61 | ó | = | 1,59 |
| ò | = | 1,65 | û | = | 1,69 |
| ú | = | 1,67 | ù | = | 1,73 |

There are many special characters produced in the same manner. The first number is the number of the **Map** in the **CHARMAP.TST** file. It is followed by a comma and the number of the character in that map.

A typical macro that produces a special character is shown in Fig. 1-2. It illustrates a macro called **A.WPM** that causes the umlaut to be typed at the cursor position whenever you press **Alt-F9**, type **A**, and press **Enter**. To produce such macros, follow the steps described above.

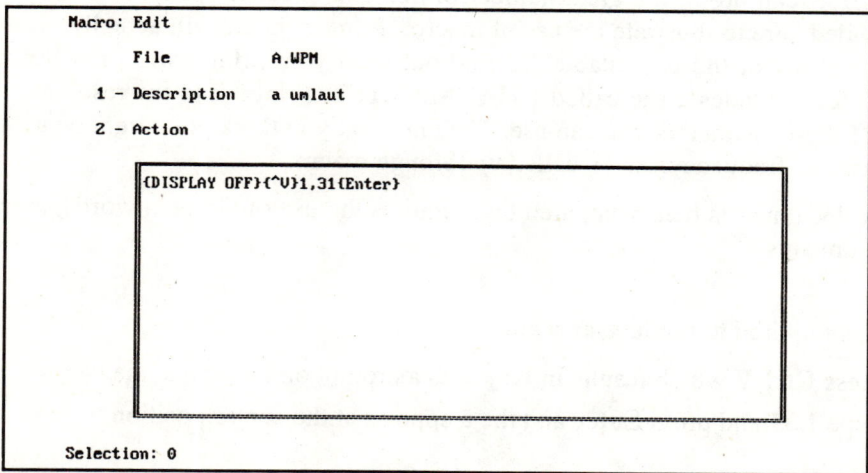

Figure 1-2

# CHAPTER 2
# DATABASE MANAGEMENT — PART I

As a general rule, when thinking in terms of databases, it would seem that a program like dBASE III Plus or IV is needed to do an efficient job. Not necessarily so. It is perfectly possible to construct eminently satisfactory databases using WordPerfect. Granted, dBASE and comparable programs offer specialized capabilities that are not available with WordPerfect, but for most everyday use, the databases discussed here are easy to create and easy to use.

Simply stated, a database is a list of related data; the sort of thing that, in precomputer days, was represented by card files. To start, create the format for a name-and-address list by typing names and addresses like the following:

```
John W. Smith
ABC Computer Stores, Inc.
123 Main Street
Anytown, AA, 12345-6789
========================================================
Robin Preston
ABC Construction, Inc.
P.O. Box 1234
Atlanta, GA, 12345-6789
========================================================
```

Do not type the double lines at the end of each record. They represent **hard page breaks** (press **Ctrl-Enter**). In this manner you can enter hundreds of names and addresses and retrieve them selectively with ease. If these names and addresses are to be used on envelopes and in letters, a series of simple keystrokes produces the desired result. Save the database file as ADDRESS.LST for the following procedure.

The most convenient way to use this database is to create two macros, each serving a different purpose. Fig. 2-1 shows a macro called **ENVELOPE.WPM**, used to address regular #10 business envelopes; and Fig. 2-2 shows a second macro called **LETTER.WPM**, used to enter the address block into letters using preprinted stationary. To create the two macros, one at a time, first press **Ctrl-F10** (Macro) and create the macro by typing name and description. Then exit (press **Ctrl-F10**) and repeat the above step, this time typing **2** when told that the macro already exists. Then type **2** again to move the cursor into the macro for editing. Then press **Ctrl-F10** to enter the macro editing mode and follow that with the following steps.

Chapter 2

In the **ENVELOPE.WPM** macro the steps are these:

1. **{DISPLAY OFF}** is entered automatically by the program. Press **Shift-F8** (Format) to create **{Format}** and select **1 Line**, select **7 Left/Right Margins**, and type **4** for four inches from the left edge of the envelope. Press **Enter Enter F7** (Exit).
2. Press **Shift-F8** (Format) again and select **2 Page** and **5 Margins Top/Bottom**. Type **2** for two inches from the top of the paper. Press **Enter Enter F7** (Exit).
3. Press **Ctrl-F9** (Merge/Sort) and type **2** to select Sort. Then type the name of the database file, **ADDRESS.LST**, and press **Enter Enter**. Now select **7 Type of sort**, **3 Paragraph**, and **4 Select**.
4. Press **Ctrl-End** (Delete to end of line) which clears away any previously used data. Type **keyg=** where the **g** stands for global.
5. Press **Ctrl-PgUp**, move the highlighting to **{PROMPT}message~**, and press **Enter**. Type the prompt message you want to appear on the status line followed by a tilde sign (~). For example, type **Type the name. Then press F7 (Exit) and 1~**.
6. Press **Ctrl-PgUp** again and move the highlighting to **{PAUSE}** and press **Enter**.
7. Press **Ctrl-F10** to exit the **Macro editing** function. Press **F7** (Exit) to save you work and the macro is ready to use.

```
Macro: Edit
        File            ENVELOPE.WPM
   1 - Description      First Class #10 from ADDRESS.LST
   2 - Action

        {DISPLAY OFF}{Format}174{Enter}
        {Enter}
        {Exit}{Format}252{Enter}
        {Enter}
        {Exit}{Merge/Sort}2ADDRESS.LST{Enter}
        {Enter}
        734{Del to EOL}keyg={PROMPT}Type·the·name··Then·press·F7·(Exit)·and·
        1~{PAUSE}




Selection: 0
```

Figure 2-1

Place an envelope in the printer, press **Alt-F10** (Macro), type **ENVELOPE** (or envelope), and press **Enter**. The computer now works for a second or so and then the status line reads: **Type the name Then press F7 (Exit) and 1**. Type anything that is unique in the address block to be used, a last or first name, company name, city, the zip code — anything that is likely to appear only once in the database — and press **F7**. The display changes to the bottom half of the Sort screen with **keyg=name** (or whatever you typed) under the

6

word **Select**. Select **1 Perform Action** and a line at the bottom of the screen counts out the records being examined. Then it changes to **1 Records Transferred** and the selected record appears at the top of the screen. The status line identifies its position as **Ln 2" Pos 4"**.

Now press **Shift-F7** (Print) and type either **1** or **2** and the address is printed onto the envelope. (If more than one record is displayed because what you typed happens to be included in more than one record, erase the record(s) you don't want to use.)

The **LETTER.WPM** macro is quite similar, except for some added steps:

1. The number of initial **{Enter}**s to use depends on how far from the top of the page the date is to appear. After that press **Shift-F5** (Date/Outline) and type **2** and press **Enter Enter**. Each time this macro is used, it automatically enters the current date.
2. Press **Ctrl-F9** (Merge/Sort), select **2 Sort** and type the name of the database file followed by **Enter Enter**.
3. Select **7 Type of sort**. Select **3 Paragraph** and **4 Select**.
4. Repeat steps 4 through 7 above and your macro is ready for use.

```
Macro: Edit
        File            LETTER.WPM
    1 - Description     Stationary using ADDRESS.LST
    2 - Action

        {DISPLAY-OFF}{Enter}
        {Enter}{Enter}{Enter}{Enter}{Enter}
        {Enter}{Enter}{Enter}
        {Date/Outline}2{Enter}
        {Enter}
        {Merge/Sort}2ADDRESS.LST{Enter}
        {Enter}
        734{Del to EOL}keyg={PROMPT}·Type·the·name··Then·press·F7·(Exit)·and
        ·1~{PAUSE}


Selection: 0
```

Figure 2-2

Place a piece of stationary in the printer, press **Alt-F10**, and type **LETTER** (or letter) and press **Enter** which is followed by action identical to that described previously. The current date followed by the address record appears on the screen. You can now either type your letter or, if a form letter is to be used, use the **Shift-F10** (Retrieve) function to insert it into the letter and then print the final result in the usual manner.

The next chapter looks at several different database formats and varying ways in which they can be used to extract individual data selectively.

## CHAPTER 3
# DATABASE MANAGEMENT — PART II

The previous chapter examined how WordPerfect can be used to create a simple database from which individual records or groups of records can be retrieved at random. This chapter takes that database concept one step further.

Originally the individual records were entered just the way they are finally to be used. By adding some **merge codes** it becomes possible to retrieve only selected portions of these records.

Fig. 3-1 shows three records, divided into five **fields**. Each field is concluded with a ^R merge code. The record as a whole is terminated by a ^E merge code that automatically adds the **hard page break** represented by the double-dashed line.

```
James MacDonald^R
Mexican Foods, Inc.
P.O. Box 1234
Albuquerque, NM 87109-1234^R

Jim^R

(505) 555 5678 Ext.: 23^R

September 28^R
^E
================================================================================
Marianne Johnson^R
Empire Decorating Corp.
87 Park Avenue
New York, NY 10016^R

Marianne^R

(212) 555 9876 Ext.: 12^R

April 30^R
^E
================================================================================
Peter W. Adams^R
Business Software Corp.
55 Washington Circle
Dallas, TX 75003^R

Mr. Adams^R

(214) 555 4321 Ext.: none^R

September 9^R
^E
================================================================================
```

Figure 3-1

**NOTE**

**Merge codes** are different in WordPerfect 5.1. Check the details in Chapter 51.

The first field is created by typing the addressee's name followed by pressing **F9** (Merge R). The second field, consisting of the company name and address, is typed in the usual manner, followed by pressing **F9** (Merge R). The third field is the type of salutation, either using simply the first name (Dear Jim:) or using the more formal Mr. (Dear Mr. Adams:), again followed by pressing **F9** (Merge R). The fourth field is the phone number complete with area code and extension, followed by **F9** (Merge R). And the last field represents the birth date, just in case that is to be included, also followed by **F9** (Merge R).

After all fields have been typed, press **Shift-F9** (Merge Codes) and type **E** (or **e**). The ^E appears, followed by the **hard page break**. Enter as many records in this manner as you like and save the file as **RECORD.SF** where the .SF is used to denote that this is the **secondary file** during subsequent **merge** operations. (Any other extension can also be used.)

The **primary files** used in conjunction with the above determine which fields of the records are retrieved. The steps below create four such primary files:

1. Press **Shift-F9** (Merge Codes). Type **F** and **1** and press **Enter**. Then press the **Spacebar** and press **Shift-F9** (Merge Codes), type **F** and **4**, and press **Enter**. The result is ^F1^ ^F4^. Now save this as **DB1.PF** where the PF stands for primary file (any other extension is OK).

2. Press **Shift-F9** (Merge Codes). Type **F** and **1** and press **Enter**. Press the **Spacebar** and press **Shift-F9**, type **F** and **5**, and press **Enter** which results in ^F1^ ^F5^. Save this as **DB2.PF**.

3. Press **Shift-F9** (Merge Codes). Type **F** and **2** and press **Enter**. Press the **Spacebar** and **Shift-F9** (Merge Codes), type **F** and **4**, and press **Enter** which results in ^F2^ ^F4^. Save this as **DB3.PF**.

4. Press **Shift-F9** (Merge Codes), type **F** and **1**, and press **Enter** twice. Press **Shift-F9** (Merge Codes), type **F** and **2**, and press **Enter**, which results in ^F1^ ^F2^ (on separate lines).

Save this as **DB4.PF**. Fig. 3-2 shows the four primary files.

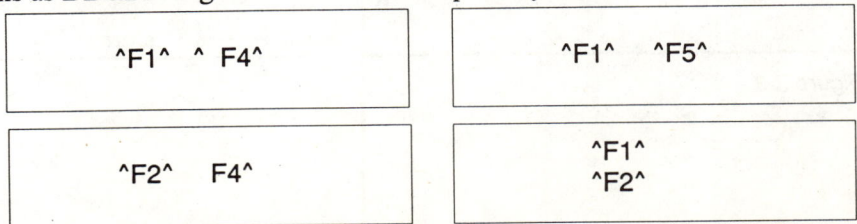

Figure 3-2

*Chapter 3*

Next create four macros designed to use these files. The contents of these macros look like this:

**{Merge/Sort}1db1.pf{Enter}**
**record.sf{Enter}** saved as **DB1.WPM**

**{Merge/Sort}1db2.pf{Enter}**
**record.sf{Enter}** saved as **DB2.WPM**

**{Merge/Sort}1db3.pf{Enter}**
**record.sf{Enter}** saved as **DB3.WPM**

**{Merge/Sort}1db4.pf{Enter}**
**record.sf{Enter}** saved as **DB4.WPM**

Each of these calls up the **Merge/Sort** feature and selects **1 Merge** after which it calls up one of the four primary files (db1.pf through db4.pf) and then the secondary file (record.sf).

If you have entered the files and created the macros as shown here, pressing **Alt-F10** (Macro), typing **DB1** (or db1), and pressing **Enter** results in Fig. 3-3. Pressing **Alt-F10** (Macro), typing **DB2** (or db2), and pressing **Enter** results in Fig. 3-4. Then try pressing **Alt-F10** (Macro), typing **DB3** (or db3), and pressing **Enter**. It results in Fig. 3-5. Pressing **Alt-F10** (Macro), typing **DB4** (or db4), and pressing **Enter** results in Fig. 3-6.

```
James MacDonald
(505) 555 5678 Ext.: 23
================================================================================
Marianne Johnson
(212) 555 9876 Ext.: 12
================================================================================
Peter W. Adams
(214) 555 4321 Ext.: none
================================================================================




                                                      Doc 1 Pg 3 Ln 1.16" POS 1"
```

Figure 3-3

```
James MacDonald
September 28
================================================================
Marianne Johnson
April 30
================================================================
Peter W. Adams
September 9
================================================================
```

Figure 3-4

```
Mexican Foods, Inc.
P.O. Box 1234
Albuquerque, NM 87109-1234
(505) 555 5678 Ext.: 23
================================================================
Empire Decorating Corp.
87 Park Avenue
New York, NY 10016
(212) 555 9876 Ext.: 12
================================================================
Business Software Corp.
55 Washington Circle
Dallas, TX 75003
(214) 555 4321 Ext.: none
================================================================
```

Figure 3-5

```
James MacDonald
Mexican Foods, Inc.
P.O. Box 1234
Albuquerque, NM 87109-1234
================================================================
Marianne Johnson
Empire Decorating Corp.
87 Park Avenue
New York, NY 10016
================================================================
Peter W. Adams
Business Software Corp.
55 Washington Circle
Dallas, TX 75003
================================================================
```

Figure 3-6

The last file is, of course, a new database, identical to the one that was created in the preceding chapter. It can now be saved and used with the macro that was created in Chapter 2.

Chapter 3

The type of database that includes the merge codes is also useful in producing form letters. Fig. 3-7 is a greatly abbreviated form letter that can serve as a demonstration. It includes the date code (press **Shift-F9** (Merge Codes) and type **D** which places the **^D** code into the desired position); the name and address codes (**^F1^** and **^F2^**); and the greeting code (**^F3^**) twice, once at the beginning of the letter, and once in the body text. It is saved as **DB5.PF**. Next, one more macro is needed. Called **DB5.WPM**, it is identical to the ones above, but it accesses the **DB5.PF** file. Now, pressing **Alt-F10** (Macro), typing **DB5** (or db5), and pressing **Enter** results in one form letter for each record in the file, as in Fig. 3-8. This demonstrates how the greeting code embedded in the text of the letter results in either just a first name or a more formal format. (Actually, each letter is printed on a separate sheet of paper as each includes a hard page break.)

The methods discussed here can be applied to any type of database such as inventories, customer records, lists of books, publications, manufacturers, software . . . you name it.

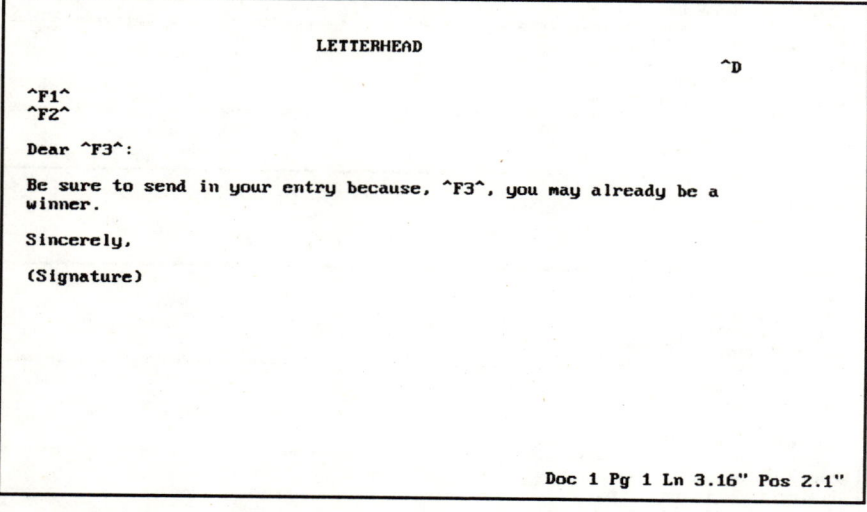

Figure 3-7

12

```
                    LETTERHEAD
                                        November 6, 1990

James MacDonald
Mexican Foods, Inc.
P.O. Box 1234
Albuquerque, NM 87109-1234

Dear
Jim:

Be sure to send in your entry because, Jim, you may already be a
winner.

Sincerely,

(Signature)
==============================================================================
                    LETTERHEAD
                                        November 6, 1990

Marianne Johnson
Empire Decorating Corp.
87 Park Avenue

Dear
Marianne:

Be sure to send in your entry because, Marianne, you may already
be a winner.

Sincerely,

(Signature)
==============================================================================
                    LETTERHEAD
                                        November 6, 1990

Peter W. Adams
Business Software Corp.
55 Washington Circle

Dear
Mr. Adams:

Be sure to send in your entry because, Mr. Adams, you may already
be a winner.

Sincerely,

(Signature)
==============================================================================
```

Figure 3-8

## CHAPTER 4
# DATABASE MANAGEMENT — PART III

This chapter deals with manipulating a database and its data in a variety of ways. Records are sorted alphabetically by last name, company name, state and city, and by zip code. Considering that a database called RECORD.SF is available:

1. Press **Shift-F10** (Retrieve), type **RECORD.SF**, and press **Enter**, and after a moment the name-and-address database from Chapter 3 (Fig. 3-1) appears on the screen.

2. Press **Ctrl-F9** (Merge/Sort), select **2 Sort**, and press **Enter** and **Enter** again to select **Screen** as both input and output file. The screen is now divided into two windows, where the upper window shows part of the file and the lower window offers a variety of options as in Fig. 4-1.

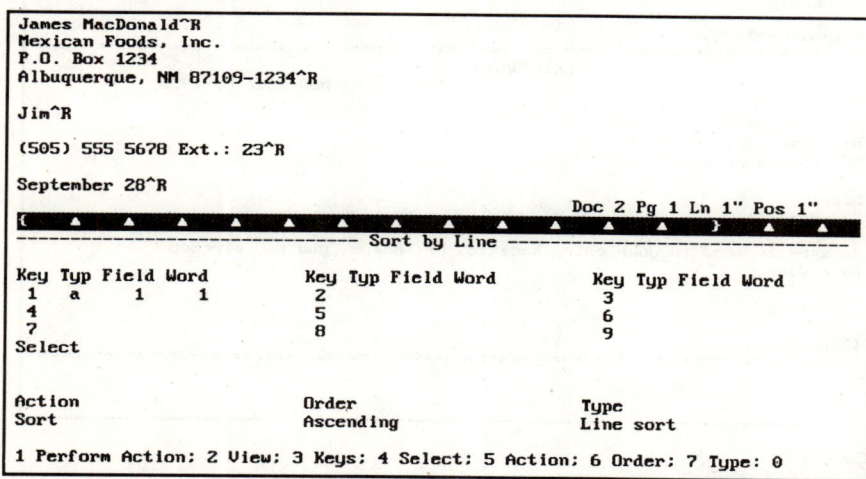

Figure 4-1

3. First select **7 Type** and **1 Merge sort** and then select **3 Keys** because the data that you enter for one or several keys determines the manner in which the records are sorted. Selecting **3 Keys** places the cursor under the **a** in the first **Key** field. There are only two choices for **Type**: either **a** for alphanumeric or **n** for numeric. In nearly all cases the alphanumeric default setting should be retained. (Numeric sorts are used when sorting is done by numbers of unequal lengths.)

*Database Management — Part III*

4. In this first try you want to sort the records alphabetically by the last names. Use **Right Arrow** to move the cursor to the **Field** and retain the number **1**, as the names are in the first field. Move the cursor to **Line** and again retain the **1**, as this field only has one line. Finally, move the cursor to **Word**. Now you have a problem. Some of the persons listed in the database have more than one first name. Therefore, you can't simply specify the second word. To always select the last name, you want to identify the first word reading from right to left. To accomplish this, change the **1** to **−1**.
5. Press **F7** (Exit) to tell WordPerfect that the key selection is complete. Then select **1 Perform Action** and after a moment the reformatted list of records is displayed in ascending alphabetical order.

You can combine the above steps into a macro if you want to repeat the action without having to remember all those keystrokes. Fig. 4-2 shows a macro containing all the steps described above. Fig. 4-3 shows another macro that pauses while you enter the name of the file to be retrieved and sorted.

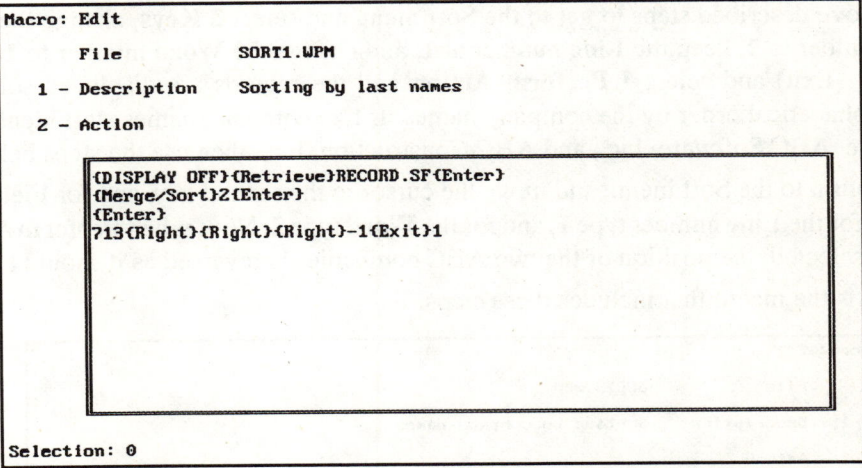

Figure 4-2

Chapter 4

```
Macro: Edit
        File            SORT2.WPM
   1 - Description     Sorting by last names
   2 - Action

    {DISPLAY OFF}When you are prompted, type the file name. Now press
    {Bold}Enter{Bold}{PAUSE}{Retrieve}{PAUSE}{Enter}{Merge/Sort}2{Enter}
    {Enter}713{Right}{Right}{Right}-1{Exit}1
```

Figure 4-3

6. Next you can sort the records in alphabetical order by company name. Follow the above described steps to get to the Sort menu and select **3 Keys,** change the **Field** number to **2**, keep the **Line** number at **1**, and change the **Word** number to **1**. Press **F7** (Exit) and select **1 Perform Action** and the records are displayed sorted in alphabetical order by the company names. If two company names start identically, like ABC Software, Inc., and ABC Construction, Inc., then use the steps below.

7. Return to the Sort menu, and move the cursor to the second key, and for **Field** type **2,** for the **Line** number type **1**, and for the **Word** type **2**. Now, when **Perform Action** is selected, the position of the two ABC companies is reversed as it should be.

Fig. 4-4 is the macro that includes these steps.

```
Macro: Edit
        File            SORT3.WPM
   1 - Description     Sorting by company names
   2 - Action

    {DISPLAY OFF}When you are prompted, type the file name. Now press
    {Bold}Enter{Bold} {Retrieve} {Enter}{Merge/Sort}2{Enter}
    {Enter}3{Right}2{Right}1{Right}1{Exit}1




Selection: 0
```

Figure 4-4

16

8. How about sorting by state? Return to the Sort menu and select the following key settings:

   | Key | Typ | Field | Line | Word |
   |-----|-----|-------|------|------|
   | 1   | a   | 2     | 3    | –2   |

   | Key | Typ | Field | Line | Word |
   |-----|-----|-------|------|------|
   | 2   | a   | 2     | 3    | 1    |

   where the first key finds the two-letter state ID as the second word from the end on line 3 in field 2, and the second key finds the name of the city as the first word in line 3 in field 2. When the sort is performed it displays the records sorted by states and within each state alphabetically by city.

Fig. 4-5 shows the macro that includes these steps.

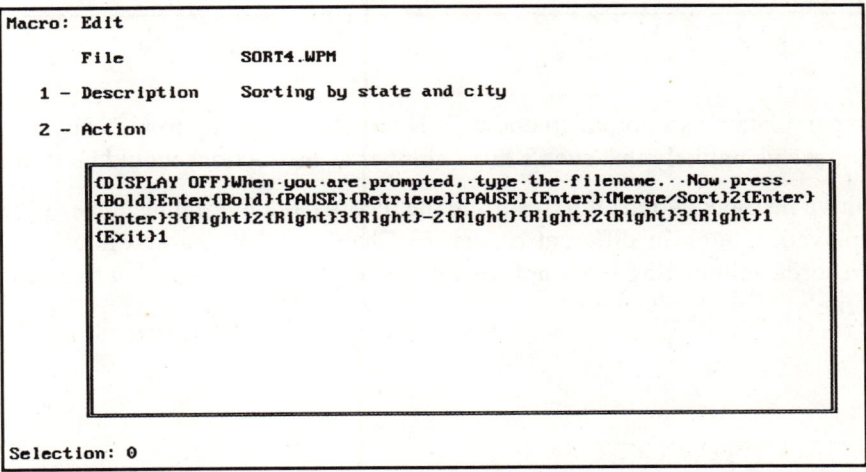

Figure 4-5

9. Finally, sort by zip code which, in certain types of mailings, saves money. Return to the Sort menu and select these key settings:

   | Key | Typ | Field | Line | Word |
   |-----|-----|-------|------|------|
   | 1   | a   | 2     | 3    | –1   |

   where the zip code is the last word on line 3 in field number 2. When the sorted records are displayed they are arranged in ascending order by zip codes regardless of the five-digit or nine-digit variety as long as, in the latter case, the numbers are connected with a hyphen (87504-1234). In that case they are regarded by WordPerfect as one word.

Fig. 4-6 shows the macro that performs these functions.

Chapter 4

```
Macro: Edit

        File              SORT5.WPM
1 - Description     Sorting by zip codes
2 - Action

   {DISPLAY OFF}When you are prompted, type the filename. Now press
   {Bold}Enter{Bold}{PAUSE}{Retrieve}{PAUSE}{Enter}{Merge/Sort}2{Enter}
   {Enter}3{Right}2{Right}3{Right}-1{Exit}1




Selection: 0
```

*Figure 4-6*

For some complicated sorting instructions, it is possible to use up to nine keys; though, off hand, it seems unlikely that such a huge number of instructions would be needed.

So far you've restricted yourself to resorting the records, but in each instance, all records were displayed, though in different orders. In Chapter 3 you learned how to display selected records, eliminating those not needed without actually removing them from the database file.

# CHAPTER 5
# BASE FONTS

WordPerfect offers means by which to select, change, or manipulate the font styles and sizes. There are the base fonts, the ones available as standard font styles and sizes. They depend to a considerable degree on the printer being used, or the printer selection when more than one printer is installed with the program. You can look at the font selection that is available to you by pressing **Ctrl-F8** (Fonts) and selecting **4 Base Font**. A list of font styles and sizes is displayed.

As an example the version of WordPerfect being used at this writing includes four printer options, as in Fig. 5-1. The list of available printers is displayed when **S** is typed from the Print menu. Selecting the Standard printer from the printer list shows that only the one font, Courier 10 Pitch, is available as in Fig. 5-2. Selecting the Hewlett-Packard LaserJet Series II printer (or its emulation by other printers, such as the Qume CrystalPrint Series II) offers the somewhat greater, but still limited selection in Fig. 5-3. Selecting the Epson LQ-800 printer presents the fairly large selection in Fig. 5-4. Finally, selecting the Epson LQ-2500 printer presents the list in Fig. 5-5.

```
Print: Select Printer

   Epson LQ-2500
 * Epson LQ-800 Enhanced
   HP LaserJet Series II
   Standard Printer
```

Figure 5-1

```
Base Font

 * Courier 10 Pitch
```

Figure 5-2

Chapter 5

```
Base Font

* Courier 10 pitch (PC-8)
  Courier 10 pitch (Roman-8/ECMA)
  Courier Bold 10 pitch (PC-8)
  Courier Bold 10 pitch (Roman-8/ECMA)
  Line Draw 10 pitch
  Line Printer 16.66 pitch (PC-8)
  Line Printer 16.66 pitch (Roman-8/ECMA)
  Solid Line Draw 10 pitch




1 Select; N Name search: 1
```

*Figure 5-3*

```
Base Font

  Roman ( 5 CPI)
  Roman ( 6 CPI)
  Roman ( 7.5 CPI) 8pt
  Roman ( 8.5 CPI)
  Roman (10 CPI)
  Roman (12 CPI)
  Roman (15 CPI) 8pt
  Roman (17 CPI)
  Roman (20 CPI)
* Roman (PS)
  Roman (PS) Condensed
  Roman (PS) Double Width
  Sans_serif ( 5 CPI)
  Sans_serif ( 6 CPI)
  Sans_serif ( 7.5 CPI) 8pt
  Sans_serif ( 8.5 CPI)
  Sans_serif (10 CPI)
  Sans_serif (12 CPI)
  Sans_serif (15 CPI) 8pt
  Sans_serif (17 CPI)
  Sans_serif (20 CPI)

1 Select; N Name search: 1
```

*Figure 5-4*

You can determine which of the available font options you want to select as the one that is active automatically when WordPerfect is started. You do that by selecting **S Select printer** from the Printer menu. You then select **3 Edit** and several options are displayed. Now select **6 Initial font** and the list of available fonts is displayed. Use the cursor keys to highlight the one you want and select **1 Select**. Then press **F7** (Exit) as many times as necessary to exit. From now on, the font that you selected, Roman (Proportional Spacing) in the illustration, is the one that will always be active when WordPerfect is started.

```
Base Font

   Courier  05 Pitch
 * Courier  10 Pitch
   Courier  15 Pitch
   Courier  17 Pitch
   Courier Italic 05 Pitch
   Courier Italic 10 Pitch
   Courier Italic 15 Pitch
   Courier Italic 17 Pitch
   Prestige 06 Pitch
   Prestige 12 Pitch
   Prestige 20 Pitch
   Prestige Italic 06 Pitch
   Prestige Italic 12 Pitch
   Prestige Italic 20 Pitch
   Roman 05 Pitch
   Roman 10 Pitch
   Roman 15 Pitch
   Roman 17 Pitch
   Roman 9 pt. PS
   Roman Italic 05 Pitch
   Roman Italic 10 Pitch

1 Select; N Name search: 1
```

*Figure 5-5*

You can change that base font at any time while working on a document by pressing **Ctrl-F8** (Font). It displays the options shown in Fig. 5-6. You can use **4 Base font** and **1 Select** to change the base font by making a selection from the displayed options.

```
1 Size: 2 Appearance: 3 Normal: 4 Base Font: 5 Print Color: 0
```

*Figure 5-6*

To change the appearance or size of the selected base font, you can press **Ctrl-F8** (Font) and select **1 Size** and the selection line in Fig. 5-7 is displayed across the bottom of the screen. Those options are more or less self-explanatory. They retain the base font that is currently in use, but change the manner in which that font is printed. Not all options may work with your printer. If in doubt, experiment.

```
1 Suprscpt: 2 Subscpt: 3 Fine: 4 Small: 5 Large: 6 Vry Large: 7 Ext Large: 0
```

*Figure 5-7*

Pressing **Ctrl-F8** (Font) and selecting **2 Appearance** produces the options in Fig. 5-8. Again, most are obvious, and many are printer dependent.

```
1 Bold 2 Undln 3 Dbl Und 4 Italc 5 Outln 6 Shadw 7 Sm Cap 8 Redln 9 Stkout: 0
```

*Figure 5-8*

Selecting **3 Normal** at the font menu returns you to the original base font.

The last option, **5 Print Color,** produces the menu shown in Fig. 5-9. This is only useful if you have a color printer. If you do, you can control the color in which the next text is printed. With black and white printers this option has no effect. For a detailed examination of the different font manipulation options, see FONTS in Chapter 51.

```
Print Color
                          Primary Color Mixture
                          Red     Green    Blue
          1 - Black       0%      0%       0%
          2 - White       100%    100%     100%
          3 - Red         67%     0%       0%
          4 - Green       0%      67%      0%
          5 - Blue        0%      0%       67%
          6 - Yellow      67%     67%      0%
          7 - Magenta     67%     0%       67%
          8 - Cyan        0%      67%      67%
          9 - Orange      67%     25%      0%
          A - Gray        50%     50%      50%
          N - Brown       67%     33%      0%
          O - Other

          Current Color   0%      0%       0%




Selection: 0
```

*Figure 5-9*

The various versions of WordPerfect include a file called PRINTER.TST. It includes all font and formatting options available. Print it to find out what your printer will and will not support.

The many ways in which WordPefect permits using different font styles, sizes, and options with reference to manipulating each of the available fonts is why WordPerfect can be instrumental in producing exceptionally effective documents.

## CHAPTER 6
# PAGE FORMATTING — PART I

In this chapter you develop formats for a letter, a memo, envelopes, and address labels. The letter and the memo formats include an automatic display of the current date and other data. The first step is to create the basic memo format.

**MEMO FORMAT**

1. Press **Shift-F6** (Center). Type **Memorandum** and press **Enter**.
2. Press **Enter** several times to create some empty lines.
3. Press **F6** (Bold), type **To:**, and press **F6** (Bold) to cancel Bold. Press **Tab** and press **Enter** twice again.
4. Press **F6** (Bold), type **From:**, press **F6** (Bold) followed by **Tab**, and press **Enter** twice again.
5. Press **F6** (Bold) and type **Date:**, press **F6** (Bold), **Tab**, and press **Enter** twice again. Press **F6** (Bold), type **Subject:**, press **F6** (Bold) followed by **Tab**, and press **Enter**.
6. Add a line using the WordPerfect **repeat** feature: press **Shift-F6** (Center) to center the line. Press **Esc** and the prompt in the status line at the left bottom corner of the screen reads **Repeat Value: 8**. Type **50** and then type **~** (the tilde) as the sign to be repeated 50 times and the centered line of 50 ~s appears instantly. The screen should now look like Fig. 6-1.

```
                        Memorandum


   To:

   From:

   Date:

   Subject:  _____











                                        Doc 1 Pg 1 Ln 2.66" Pos 6.7"
```

*Figure 6-1*

23

Chapter 6

7. Before saving the memo form, first enter a command that would produce the current date whenever the file is retrieved for use. Place the cursor on the word "Date:" and press **End** to move it to the end of the line. Press **Shift-F5** (Date/Outline) and select **2 Date Code** and the current date appears.

8. Press **F7** (Exit) and type **y** to save the file. Type **MEMO.6A** for the filename, press **Enter**, and then type **n** to clear the screen.

While the memorandum in this format would be perfectly usable, it is a nuisance to move the cursor manually from one space to the next. WordPerfect includes the necessary commands to perform all of these steps automatically.

1. Press **Shift-F10** (Retrieve) to retrieve the memo saved as **MEMO.6A** and the screen will redisplay the memo with the current date as in Fig. 6-2.

```
                        Memorandum

        To:

        From:

        Date:     November 6, 1990
        Subject: _____




        C:\WP50\MEMO.6A                      Doc 1 Pg 1 Ln 1" POS 1"
```

Figure 6-2

2. Move the cursor to "To:" and press **End** and **Tab** to place the cursor in a position that horizontally is equal to a space to the right of the colon (:) in the "Subject:" line.

3. Press **Shift-F9** (Merge Codes) and type **C** which places a ^C at the cursor position. Move the cursor to that same horizontal position to the right of the "From:" line and repeat the above.

### NOTE

The **Merge Codes** are different in WordPerfect 5.1. See Chapter 51.

4. Place the cursor at the end of the displayed date and press **Backspace** to delete all of it. Then press **Shift-F9** (Merge Codes) and type **D** to place a ^D on the "Date:" line.

*Page Formatting —Part I*

5. Repeat step 3 for the "Subject:" line and then move the cursor to the far left about two lines below the line of tildes (~) and repeat step 3 again. Your screen should now look like Fig. 6-3.

```
                      Memorandum

    To:        ^C
    From:      ^C
    Date:      ^D
    Subject:   ^C_____

    ^C




```

Figure 6-3

6. Press **F10** (Save) and save this version of the memo using the filename **MEMO.6D**.

7. As one final convenience, produce a macro that eliminates the need for a series of keystrokes. Press **Ctrl-F10** (Macro Define) and type **MEMO** as the macro name and press **Enter**.

8. Type a description and press Enter or ignore the Description, and with Macro Def prompt flashing, press **Ctrl-F9** (Merge/Sort), select **1 Merge**, type **MEMO.6D**, and press **Enter**. In reply to the prompt for the secondary file, type the filename and press **Enter**; then press **Ctrl-F10** (Macro Define) to terminate the macro definition process. From now on, pressing **Alt-F10** and typing **MEMO** produces the memo ready for use. If you want to print more than one copy of the memorandum, BEFORE activating the macro, press **Shift-F7** (Print) followed by **n** or **N** and the number of copies and press **Enter**. Then activate the macro to print the copies.

9. If memoranda are habitually printed on paper of a size different from standard (8.5" x 11"), retrieve **MEMO.6D**, press **Shift-F8** (Format), and select **2 Page**. Then select **8 Page Size/Type** and either select the appropriate option or type **o Other** and enter the dimension of the paper you'd normally be using.

10. If the memorandum macro is used by a number of persons who may not know how to enter data correctly (such as pressing **F9** rather than **Enter** at the end of a line or subject), it is a good idea to display prompt lines at the bottom of the screen. In that case you have to write a secondary file and make some changes in the primary file. Then create a new macro including the edited primary and new secondary file.

25

## Chapter 6

11. Write a file that looks like the one shown in Fig. 6-4 with the ^O and ^C characters created by pressing **Shift-F9** (Merge Codes) and typing **O** and **C**. The ^R character is created by simply pressing **F9** (Merge R). Save the file as **MEMO.6PR**.

```
^OEnter addressee(s)  (Press F9)^O^C^R
^OEnter name of sender (Press F9)^O^C^R
^OEnter subject description (Press F9)^O^C^R
^OPress F9 to start printing^O^C^R
```

Figure 6-4

12. Retrieve file **MEMO.6D** and replace the **^C** characters with **^F1^**, **^F2^**, **^F3^**, and **^F4^**, each of which is created by pressing **Shift-F9** (Merge Codes), typing **F**, and in reply to the **Field:** prompt, typing appropriate number and pressing **Enter**. The revised file should look like Fig. 6-5. Save it as **MEMO.6D** (or another letter if you want to save the earlier version.

```
                    Memorandum

    To:       ^F1^

    From:     ^F2^

    Date:     ^D

    Subject:  ^F3^
              ~~~~~~~~~~~~~~~~~~~~~~~~~~~~~~~~~~~~~~~~~~~~~~~

    ^F4^
```

Figure 6-5

13. Now write a new macro. Call it **MEMOX**. Press **Ctrl-F10** (Macro Define) and type **MEMOX**. Press **Enter**. Type a description or ignore the Description prompt and press Enter. With the Macro Def prompt flashing, press **Ctrl-F9** (Merge/Sort) followed by **1 Merge**. For the primary file enter **MEMO.6D** and for the secondary file enter **MEMO.6PR**. Press **F7** (Exit). Fig. 6-6 shows the new macro. Type **n n** and after the screen is cleared, press **Alt-F10**, type **MEMOX**, and press **Enter**. The new memorandum format is displayed with the first prompt line across the bottom of the screen.

```
        File              MEMOX.WPM
1 - Description      Memo with prompt lines
2 - Action

    {DISPLAY OFF}{Merge/Sort}1MEMO.6D{Enter}
    MEMO.6PR{Enter}
```

Figure 6-6

You can use a similar routine to prepare personal stationery automatically, printing the current date whenever it is activated and including a series of prompts telling you what to do next.

Before going on, create a print macro that is used repeatedly later on.

1. Press **Ctrl-F10** and use **print** as the macro name.
2. In the Macro def stage press **Shift-F7** and type **1**.
3. Press **F7** and type **nn**.
4. Press **Ctrl-F10** to save the new macro.

With this macro available for future use, take the next steps.

1. Press **Shift-F6** (Center) and press **F6** (Bold). Type your name or the name of your company and press **F6** (Bold) again. Press **Enter** and **Shift-F6** (Center). Type the address, city, state ID and zip code; press **Enter** and **Shift-F6** (Center) for the area code and phone number.
2. Press **Enter** three times followed by **Shift-F9** (Merge Codes) and type **D** to place the date code into its proper place. Press **Enter Enter**. This has created three empty

Chapter 6

lines after the letterhead and two empty lines after the date. Next comes the addressee's name and address:

3. Press **Shift-F9** (Merge Codes) and type **F**. In reply to the **Field:** prompt type **1** and press **Enter Enter**.
4. Press **Shift-F9** (Merge Codes) and type **F**. For the **Field:** type **2** and press **Enter Enter**.
5. Press **Shift-F9** (Merge Codes) and type **F**, and for the **Field:** type **3** followed by pressing **Enter Enter**.
6. Again press **Shift-F9** (Merge Codes) and again type **F**, and for the **Field:** type **4** followed by pressing **Enter**.
7. Type a comma (,) and press the **Spacebar**, then press **Shift-F9** (Merge Codes). Type **F** and **5** and press **Enter**.
8. Press the **Spacebar** and for one final time press **Shift-F9** (Merge Codes), type **F** and **6**, and press **Enter** which concludes the addressee's name and address block.
9. Press **Enter** twice for one blank line and then type **Dear**, press the **Spacebar**, press **Shift-F9** (Merge Codes), type **F** and **7**, press **Enter**, and type a colon (:). Press **Enter** twice for another blank line.
10. Press **Shift-F9** (Merge Codes), type **F** and **8**, and press **Enter Enter**.
11. Now type **Sincerely yours,** press **Enter** four times, and type your company name. Press **Enter** and type your name.
12. Now, assuming that you like the date and the signature block flush right, place the cursor ahead of ^D and press **Alt-F6** (Flush Right) and the ^D will jump to the right edge. Now do the same with the Sincerely Yours, company, and name lines and they will line up on the right side of the page.
13. Now press **Home Home Down Arrow** to get to the bottom of the file and press **Enter**. Then press **Shift-F9** (Merge Codes), type **F** and **9**, and press **Enter**.
14. Press **Shift-F9** (Merge Codes), type **G**, and then type **print** which is the name of the macro that you created earlier.
15. Press **Shift-F9** (Merge Codes) and type **G** and press **Enter**.
16. You're now ready to save your work. Press **F10** (Save) and type **LETTER.SF** as the filename. If you now examine the file on the screen, it should look like Fig. 6-7.
17. Now we must create the prompt file. Clear the screen and, using the same routine that was described earlier, produce a nine-line file similar to the one shown in Fig. 6-8. When that is done, save it as **LETTER.PF**.

```
                    ABC SOFTWARE, INC.
         P.O. Box 1234  Santa Fe, NM 87504
                    (505) 555-1234

                                                    ^D

^F1^
^F2^
^F3^
^F4^, ^F5^ ^F6^

Dear ^F7^:

^F8^
                                         Sincerely yours,


                                         ABC Software, Inc.
                                         Peter McBride, President

^F9^^Gprint^G
```

*Figure 6-7*

```
^OEnter addressee name (Press F9)^O^C^R
^OEnter company name (Press F9)^O^C^R
^OEnter address/P.O. Box (Press F9)^O^C^R
^OEnter city (Press F9)^O^C^R
^OEnter state ID (Press F9)^O^C^R
^OEnter zip code (Press F9)^O^C^R
^OEnter greeting name (Press F9)^O^C^R
^OEnter body text (Press F9)^O^C^R
^OTo print press F9^O^C^R
```

*Figure 6-8*

18. Clear the screen once more and press **Ctrl-F10** (Macro Define). For the macro name type **LETHEAD** and press **Enter Enter** to bypass the description. Press **Ctrl-F9** (Merge/Sort) and select **1 Merge**. For the primary file enter **LETTER.PF**, for the secondary file enter **LETTER.SF**, and press **Ctrl-F10** (Macro Define) again to tell WordPerfect that the macro is complete. Fig. 6-9 is the finished macro.

Chapter 6

```
        File          LETHEAD.WPM
  1 - Description

  2 - Action

     {Merge/Sort}1LETTER.PF{Enter}
     LETTER.SF{Enter}




Selection: 0
```

*Figure 6-9*

19. Press **Alt-F10,** type **LETHEAD,** and press **Enter**. The letter format appears on the screen with the date line flush right and the cursor on the place where ^F1^ had been placed. The prompt across the bottom of the page displays the prompt **Enter addressee name (Press F9),** as in Fig. 6-10. After each entry, the prompt line changes to the next, and as you type the body of the letter, the **Sincerely yours,** line moves down one line each time an additional line of text is typed.

```
                      ABC SOFTWARE, INC.
              P.O. Box 1234   Santa Fe, NM 87504
                        (505) 555-1234

                                              November 22, 1990

  ^F2^
  ^F3^
  ^F4^, F5^ ^F6^

  Dear ^F7^:

  ^F8^



                                              Sincerely, yours


                                              ABC Software, Inc.
                                              Peter McBride, President
  ^F9^^Gprint^G
  Enter addressee name (Press F9)
  C:\WW\WW6-10.TXT                      Doc 1 Pg 1 Ln 1" Pos 1"
```

*Figure 6-10*

30

## Chapter 7
# PAGE FORMATTING — PART II

This time the subject is one of the ways in which an invoice format can be designed, printed, and then written to. This operation makes use of some of the graphics capabilities of WordPerfect and assumes that you have a printer that will print graphics.

The first step involves developing the basic invoice format that can subsequently be manipulated for use in a number of different ways. Fig. 7-1 is an invoice format developed strictly for demonstration with reference to this exercise. It utilizes a graphic image, included in the files comprising the WordPerfect system, as a logo. It also includes horizontal and vertical lines produced by one of WordPerfect's graphics functions. The steps to create this invoice form are as follows:

1. Press **Shift-F8** (Format), select **3 Document** and **3 Initial font,** and move the highlighting to **ROMAN (10 CPI)** to select the initial font. (If your printer does not include this font, use another 10 CPI font.)
2. Press **Alt-F9** (Graphics) and select **1 Figure, 1 Create,** and **1 Filename.** With **Enter filename:** on the status line, type **THINKER.WPG** or the name of any other graphics file you want to use as a logo. Press **Enter.**
3. After WordPerfect loads the graphics file, select **3 Type** and **2 Page.**
4. Select **5 Horizontal Position, 3 Set Position**, type **1**, and press **Enter.**
5. Select **6 Size, 1 Width Auto height,** type **0.75**, and press **Enter.**
6. Press **F7** (Exit).

This series of keystrokes has placed the logo into the upper left-hand corner of the page with one-inch margins top and left. After pressing **Enter** the position of the graphic image is indicated on the screen by a line outlining it.

7. Place the cursor next to the bottom right-hand corner of the line outlining the graphic image so that it is aligned with the bottom of the logo. Press **Alt-F6** (Flush Right). Press **Ctrl-F8** (Font), select **2 Appearance** and **5 Outline,** and press **Ctrl-F8** (Font) again, followed by **1 Size** and **5 Large.** Type the name of the company and press **End Enter.**
8. The cursor is now located just below the logo and the status line reads **Pos 1".**

*Chapter 7*

ABC Computer Corporation

1157 Capitol Avenue        Anytown, XX   12345-1234        (123) 555-1234

INVOICE

Purchase Order :

| Product Description | Units Ordered | Units Shipped | Unit Price | Subtotal |
|---|---|---|---|---|
| | | | | |

Totals

Comments:

*Figure 7-1*

9. Press **Ctrl-F8** (Font) and select **3 Normal**. Press **F6** (Bold) and type the address and phone number, spacing the items manually to create a pleasing look. Press **Enter**.
10. Press **Alt-F9** (Graphics) and select **5 Line** and **1 Horizontal line**. Now select **1 Horizontal Position** and **5 Set position** and accept the default values that are displayed by pressing **Enter** and **F7** (Exit). This places a horizontal line under the address data line.
11. Press **Enter** ten times. Press **Shift-F6** (Center) and **Ctrl-F8** (Font). Select **2 Appearance** and **5 Outline**, press **Ctrl-F8** (Font), and select **1 Size**, and **5 Large**. Type **INVOICE** and press **End** and **Enter**. Press **Ctrl-F8** (Font) and select **3 Normal**.
12. Repeat step 10.
13. Press **Enter**. Press **Alt-F6** (Flush right). Type **Purchase Order:** and press **Enter Enter**.
14. Press **Shift-F8** (Format) and select **1 Line 8 Tab** to select the tab setting option. Press **Home Home Left Arrow** and press **Ctrl-End** to erase all preset tabs. Type **3.18** and press **Enter**. Type **4.5** and press **Enter**. Type **5.83** and press **Enter**. Type **6.76** and press **Enter**. Press **F7** (Exit) twice and type **Product Description**. Press **Tab** and type **Units Ordered**. Press **Tab** and type **Units Shipped**. Press **Tab** and type **Unit Price**. Press **Tab** and type **Subtotal**. Press **Enter**.
15. Repeat step 10.
16. Press **Enter** repeatedly until the status line reads **Ln 7.75"** or something close to it.
17. Repeat step 10.
18. Press **Enter**. Type **Totals** and press **Enter** twice.
19. Repeat step 10.
20. Press **Enter** and type **Comments:**.

This sequence of steps has entered the copy and the horizontal lines. What remains is to enter the four vertical lines. Move the cursor to a spot below the "Product Description" line.

21. Press **Alt-F9** (Graphics) and select **5 Line** and **2 Vertical line**.
22. Select **1 Horizontal Position**, type **4** and **3.04**, and press **Enter**.
23. Select **2 Vertical Position**, type **5**, and press **Enter**.
24. Select **3 Length of Line**, type **3.5**, and press **Enter** and **F7 Exit**.
25. Repeat step 21.
26. Type **1**, **4**, and **4.37** and press **Enter**.
27. Repeat steps 23 and 24 and 21.

28. Type **1, 4,** and **5.69** and press **Enter**.
29. Repeat steps 23 and 24 and 21.
30. Type **1, 4,** and **6.7** and press **Enter**.
31. Repeat steps 23 and 24.

That completes the task of designing the invoice format. Be sure to save your work at repeated intervals. Now you're ready to print the work. Some printers print graphics and text simultaneously. Others do a better job printing graphics (or text) first and then, after the paper has been repositioned, printing the remaining material. Fig. 7-1 is the finished invoice format.

There are a number of different ways in which a predesigned form like this can be utilized. The simplest and most obvious is to run off a number of copies (or use the original as camera-ready copy and have a fast-print shop run off as many as you think you might need) and then type into it. WordPerfect includes a function that makes it possible to use the keyboard in the manner of an ordinary typewriter. The option is called *Type Through* and it can be activated by these steps:

1. Press **Shift-F7** (Print) and select **5 Type Through**.
2. The status line now reads **Type Through by: 1 Line; 2 Character**.

(This option is not available with all printers.)

The first choice means that you can type an entire line of up to 200 characters, and the entire line (after editing, if needed) is sent to the printer when **Enter** is pressed. The second choice causes each character to be sent to the printer as soon as it is typed. In this mode the up/down arrow keys are used to move the carriage one line up or down and the left/right arrow keys are used to move the print head one character space to the left or right.

This method is designed to be used primarily with preprinted documents, but to use it effectively, the printer must be positioned in such a way that you can see the position of the print head at all times.

While that is a reasonably satisfactory method of using predesigned forms, there are several alternatives that may be better.

The first alternate method deals with printing the invoice form and all the data that need to be entered as one continuous operation:

1. Press **Shift-F10** (Retrieve) and type **INVOICE.FRM** to retrieve the completed invoice form into memory.
2. Using the arrow keys, move the cursor to where the date is to be entered and type the date. **Do NOT press Enter!**
3. Again using the arrow keys move the cursor to the starting position of the first line of the address.
4. Type the address one line at a time, using **Down Arrow** to move to the next line. (If at any time during the data entry process the Enter key is pressed accidentally, press Del to reverse its effect.)
5. Move the cursor to the right of the colon after **Purchase Order:** and type the number (if any).
6. Move the cursor to two lines below the P in **Product Description** and enter the name of the product.
7. Move the cursor on the same line to the position below the U in **Units Ordered** and fill in the number.
8. Move the cursor on the same line to the position below the U in **Units Shipped** and fill in the number.
9. Move the cursor on the same line to the position below the U in **Unit Price** and fill in the amount.
10. Move the cursor on the same line to the position below the S in **Subtotal** and fill in the amount. Use **Down Arrow** to move to the next line.
11. Repeat steps 6 through 10 for each product to be added.
12. Use the arrow keys to move the cursor to the line on which **Totals** appears and fill in the totals for the second, third, and fifth column.
13. If desired, move the cursor to the **Comments:** line and enter any additional data.

Fig. 7-2 shows what the result of this effort might look like. There is nothing much wrong with it, except that moving the cursor to the right positions on the screen where the horizontal and vertical lines are invisible is a bit of a nuisance. There is a better way.

Chapter 7

ABC Computer Corporation

1157 Capitol Avenue     Anytown, XX   12345-1234     (123) 555-1234

May 19, 1990

Mr. Harry Brown  
Apex Software Corp.  
11 Washington Circle  
Dallas, TX 75001

INVOICE

Purchase Order :12345

| Product Description | Units Ordered | Units Shipped | Unit Price | Subtotal |
|---|---|---|---|---|
| Widgets | 15 | 10 | $17.68 | $176.80 |
| Gadegets | 15 | 9 | $10.05 | $ 90.45 |
| Totals | 30 | 19 | | $267.25 |

Comments:   Sales Tax @ 6.75% : 18.04   Total: $285.29

Thank you

Figure 7-2

*Page Formatting—Part II*

This time use the WordPerfect **Merge** function to always cause the cursor to automatically be moved to the correct position for data entry.

As before, during the following **Do NOT press Enter!**

1. Press **Shift-F10** (Retrieve) and type **INVOICE.FRM** again to place the invoice format into RAM.
2. Use the arrow keys to place the cursor two lines below the address, one line below the invisible horizontal line (approximately at Ln 2.59" Pos 7.29" position). Press **Shift-F9** (Merge Codes) and type **D**, which produces a ^D at the cursor position. This code causes the current date to be displayed automatically whenever the file is activated.
3. Move the cursor to the **Ln 2.51" Pos 1"** position, press **Shift-F9** (Merge Codes), and type **F**. Reply to the **Field:** prompt on the status line by typing **1**, which results in ^F1^ at the cursor position.
4. Move the cursor successively to **Ln 2.84" Pos 1", Ln 3.01" Pos 1", Ln 3.18" Pos 1"**, and **Ln 3.34" Pos 1"**. Each time press **Shift-F9** and use successive numbers (2, 3, 4) for the **Field:** prompts. (These measurements may have to be adjusted when different font sizes or spacings are used.)
5. Move the cursor to **Ln 4.18 Pos 6.24"** and follow the same steps to produce ^F5^ at the cursor position.
6. Move the cursor to **Ln 4.86"** and successively to positions **Pos 1", 3.18", 4.47", 5.75"**, and **6.78"**. Each time produce the merge codes as before, using field numbers 6 through 10.
7. Move the cursor to **Ln 7.7"** and successively to positions **3.18", 4.47"**, and **6.78"** adding merge codes 11, 12 and 13.
8. Finally, move the cursor to **Ln 8.22" Pos 1.8"** to add merge code 14.
9. Press **F10** (Save) to save the completed work as **INVOICE3.FRM**.

If you want to, you can now print this new file and it will look like Fig. 7-3.

Remember: **Merge Codes** look different in WordPerfect 5.1. See Chapter 51.

Chapter 7

ABC Computer Corporation

**1157 Capitol Avenue**        **Anytown, XX   12345-1234**            **(123) 555-1234**

^D

^F1^
^F2^
^F3^
^F4^

INVOICE

Purchase Order :^F5^

| Product Description | Units Ordered | Units Shipped | Unit Price | Subtotal |
|---|---|---|---|---|
| ^F6^ | ^F7^ | ^F8^ | ^F9^ | ^F10^ |
| Totals | ^F11^ | ^F12^ | | ^F13^ |

Comments:^F14^

*Figure 7-3*

But you're not finished. Fig.7-4 is the next file that is needed. Here the ^O and ^C codes are produced by pressing **Shift-F9** (Merge Codes) and typing **O** or **C**. The ^R code is produced by simply pressing **F9** (Merge R). When the data have been typed exactly as shown, save the file as **INVOICE3.TXT**.

```
^OEnter name of addressee Press F9^O^C^R
^OEnter company of addressee Press F9^O^C^R
^OEnter address or P.O. Box Press F9^O^C^R
^OEnter city, state ID, zip Press F9^O^C^R
^OEnter purchase order # Press F9^O^R^C^R
^OEnter product description Press F9^O^C^R
^OEnter number units ordered Press F9^O^C^R
^OEnter number units shipped Press F9^O^C^R
^OEnter unit price Press F9^O^C^R
^OEnter subtotal (+:dn arrw) Press F9^O^C^R
^OEnter total units ordered Press F9^O^C^R
^OEnter total units shipped Press F9^O^C^R
^OEnter total price Press F9^O^C^R
^OEnter comments or simply Press F9^O^C^R
```

Figure 7-4

Finally you need to create a macro that uses the two newly created files:

1. Press **Ctrl-F10** (Macro Define) and call it **INVOICE** (the .WPM extension is added automatically) and describe it as **Invoice Format**. Press **Ctrl-F10** twice again and then select **2** twice. Your cursor is now inside the macro window.

2. Press **Ctrl-F9** (Merge/Sort) followed by typing **1** and **invoice3.frm**. Now press **Ctrl-F10** to activate the macro editing function and press **Enter**. Type **invoice3.txt** and press **Enter**.

3. Press **Ctrl-F10** to deactivate the macro editing function and press **F7** (Exit) twice to return to the document screen.

Now press **Alt-F10** (Macro). Type **invoice** and press **Enter**. After a moment the invoice form appears on the screen with the current date already in place and the cursor having replaced the ^F1^ code and with the status line reading: "Enter name of addressee. Press F9." Each time **F9** is pressed after some data have been typed, the cursor moves automatically to the next ^F^ code position and the status line changes to a new set of instructions. To enter more then one product, use **Down Arrow** to go to the next line and use **Tab** to move from column to column. After the last product entry, press **F9** again and the cursor moves to the ^F11^ position. Fig. 7-5 is the macro that prints the invoice.

Chapter 7

```
Macro: Edit
        File            INVOICE.WPM
    1 - Description     Invoice format
    2 - Action

        {DISPLAY OFF}{Merge/Sort}1invoice3.frm{Enter}invoice3.txt{Enter}
```

Figure 7-5

Finally, there's still another way. Instead of entering the codes on the invoice form itself, they can be entered as a separate file by using steps 2 through 8 above (the routine that creates all those ^D and ^F^ codes) and then saving it as, say, **INVOICE5.FRM**. Now change the macro to the one shown in Fig. 7-6, naming it **INVOICE5** for argument's sake.

```
Macro: Edit
        File            INVOICE5.WPM
    1 - Description     Invoice format
    2 - Action

        {DISPLAY OFF}{Merge/Sort}1invoice5.frm{Enter}invoice3.txt{Enter}
```

Figure 7-6

This method is ideal if you have had a number of the invoice forms preprinted. Insert one of the preprinted forms into the printer and press **Alt-F10** (Macro). Type **INVOICE5** and press **Enter**. You are prompted for data input as before, but you do not see the invoice on the screen. Then, when the result is printed, the entered data appear in exactly the right places.

## CHAPTER 8
# NEWSPAPER COLUMNS

Most average word processing involves typing text across the entire page from the left margin to the right one. This is fine for letters, memos, magazine articles, books and such. But there are times when it becomes important to use two or more columns. In *newspaper*-type columns the text runs from the top to the bottom of one column and then continues at the top of the next. Fig. 8-1 is an example of two columns and Fig. 8-2 is the same basic text reformatted into three. It becomes immediately apparent that narrow columns should be avoided if possible because they tend to be excessively ragged with the varying length of words in the text. Or they produce unpleasant spaces if the text is justified.

```
        CHAPTER 28                    4.  For the moment ignore
        GRAPHICS                      Filename and Caption and
                                      accept the defaults for
This chapter examines the             everything except the Vertical
various aspects of                    position. Select 4 Vertical
WordPerfect's graphics                Position, type 2, and press
capabilities. WordPerfect is          Enter. The measurement is
not actually a full-fledged           changed to 2".
desktop publishing program.
Still, it does include a              5.  Press F7 (Exit) to return
sufficient number of functions        to the document screen. The
to make it not only possible,         text has remained unchanged
but relatively easy to produce        and there is no sign of the
simple documents such as              box that is supposed to have
letterheads, newsletters,             been created.
pamphlets, announcements and
the like, without having to           6. Use Down Arrow to scroll
resort to an actual desktop           the cursor down across the
publishing program.                   document and suddenly the box
                                      does appear, as in Fig. 28-2.
Your computer must be equipped
with some type of graphics            7. Press Shift-F7 (Print) and
adapter (CGA, EGA, Hercules,          select 6 View Document and you
C:\WP50\CH28.TXT                                  Col 1 Doc 1 Pg 1 Ln 1" Pos 3"
```

*Figure 8-1*

## Chapter 8

```
CHAPTER 28              a graphics adapter    supposed to have
  GRAPHICS              is installed, you     been created.
                        can always use the
This chapter            View Document         6. Use Down Arrow
examines the            feature to see        to scroll the
various aspects of      what your printed     cursor down across
WordPerfect's           page would look       the document and
graphics                like.                 suddenly the box
capabilities.                                 does appear, as in
WordPerfect is not      First place an        Fig. 28-2.
actually a full-        empty box onto the
fledged desktop         page with text and    7. Press Shift-F7
publishing              have WordPerfect      (Print) and select
program. Still, it      wrap the text         6 View Document
does include a          around the box:       and you see your
sufficient number                             full page with the
of functions to         1. Press Shift-       box positioned two
make it not only        F10 (Retrieve) and    inches down the
possible, but           type the name of      page flush with
relatively easy to      any text file.        the right margin.
produce simple
documents such as       2. Press Alt-F9       INSERT GRAPHIC
letterheads,            (Graphics).           IMAGE AND ADD A
C:\WP50\CH28.TXT                              CAPTION
                                              Col 1 Doc 1 Pg 1 Ln 1" Pos 2.41"
```

*Figure 8-2*

First use an existing text file that was entered in the normal single-column manner and observe how such a file can be formatted into several column formats.

1. Press **Shift-F10** (Retrieve) and type the name of any text file that you want to use, possibly preceded by disk or directory path information if the file is not contained on the logged disk or directory.

2. The text is now displayed on your screen. Press **Alt-F7** (Math/Columns) and from the options select **4 Column Def**. This results in the screen in Fig. 8-3, used to define the number and type of columns. Accept the default data shown. Press **F7** (Exit) to return to the document screen.

```
Text Column Definition

    1 - Type                                  Newspaper

    2 - Number of Columns                     2

    3 - Distance Between Columns

    4 - Margins

        Column    Left      Right     Column    Left      Right
          1:      1"        4"          13:
          2:      4.5"      7.5"        14:
          3:                             15:
          4:                             16:
          5:                             17:
          6:                             18:
          7:                             19:
          8:                             20:
          9:                             21:
         10:                             22:
         11:                             23:
         12:                             24:

Selection: 0
```

*Figure 8-3*

3. The **Math/Columns** status line is still displayed at the bottom of the screen. Select **3 Column On/Off** and then press **Home Home Down Arrow**. The status line displays **Repositioning**, and after a moment the text file is displayed in the form of two columns as in Fig. 8-1.

4. Unless you want to save the file in this form, press **F7** (Exit) and type **n n** to clear the screen. Now retrieve the same text file and press **Alt-F7** (Math/Columns). From the options select **4 Column Def.** which displays a column definition screen. Select **2 Number of Columns**, type **3**, and press **Enter**. Select **3 Distance Between Columns** and accept the default (0.5) by pressing **Enter**. Fig. 8-4 is that screen. Press **F7** (Exit) to return to the document screen.

```
Text Column Definition

    1 - Type                              Newspaper

    2 - Number of Columns                 3

    3 - Distance Between Columns          0.5"

    4 - Margins

    Column    Left      Right     Column    Left      Right
      1:      1"        2.83"       13:
      2:      3.33"     5.16"       14:
      3:      5.66"     7.5"        15:
      4:                            16:
      5:                            17:
      6:                            18:
      7:                            19:
      8:                            20:
      9:                            21:
     10:                            22:
     11:                            23:
     12:                            24:

Selection: 0
```

Figure 8-4

5. Select **3 Column On/Off** and then press **Home Home Down Arrow** and the status line displays **Repositioning**. After a moment the text file is displayed in the form of three columns as in Fig. 8-2.

If you decide that you want the text in your columns to be right justified, move the cursor to the top of the file.

1. Press **Shift-F8** (Format) and select **1 Line** and **3 Justification**. Change it to **yes** if necessary.

2. Press **Enter** and **F7** (Exit) to return to your document screen.

3. Press **Home Home Down Arrow**. On the screen absolutely nothing seems to happen.

4. Press **Shift-F7** (Print), select **6 View Document**, and then type **3** to see your document in the full-page format. You now see that your text is, in fact, justified as in Fig. 8-5, even though the editing screen does not show it.

*Chapter 8*

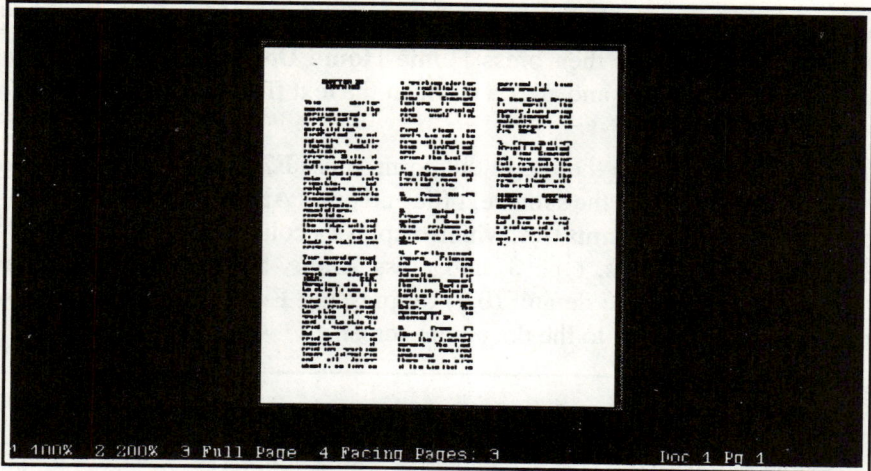

*Figure 8-5*

In addition to newspaper-type columns there are **parallel** columns in which the item in the first column is related to the item(s) in the other column(s). They are used to produce inventory lists, price lists, lists of phone numbers, and so on. Chapter 9 deals with parallel columns in detail.

# CHAPTER 9
# PARALLEL COLUMNS

Begin by creating a short file with three parallel columns in which the left column is used for the name, the center column for the address, and the right column for the phone number.

1. Press **Alt-F7** (Math/Columns) and select **4 Column Def**. Then select **1 Type** and **2 Parallel**. Select **2 Number of Columns**, type **3**, and press **Enter**. Select **3 Distance Between Columns** and accept the default (0.5) by pressing **Enter**. Fig. 9-1 shows the result. Press **F7** (Exit) to return to the document screen and select **3 Columns On/Off** to remove the menu at the bottom of the screen which should now be blank.

```
Text Column Definition

    1 - Type                            Parallel

    2 - Number of Columns               3

    3 - Distance Between Columns        0.5"

    4 - Margins

        Column    Left      Right       Column    Left      Right
          1:      1"        2.83"        13:
          2:      3.33"     5.16"        14:
          3:      5.66"     7.5"         15:
          4:                              16:
          5:                              17:
          6:                              18:
          7:                              19:
          8:                              20:
          9:                              21:
         10:                              22:
         11:                              23:
         12:                              24:

Selection: 0
```

*Figure 9-1*

2. Type a name followed by **Ctrl-Enter** (hard page break) which moves the cursor to the second column. Type an address which may occupy several lines. Now press **Ctrl-Enter** (hard page break) and the cursor jumps to the top of the third column. Type a phone number and press **Ctrl-Enter** to return to the first column. The cursor automatically goes to the line below the last line in the address column. Repeat the procedure with a few more names, just for practice. The result is similar to Fig. 9-2.

Chapter 9

```
John F. Brady         XYZ Construction,        (213) 555 4321
                      Inc.
                      77 Sunset Boulevard
                      Los Angeles, CA 90046

Sarah W. Fisher       QuickPrint Co., Inc.     (505) 555 9876
                      67 Plaza Drive
                      Santa Fe, NM 87501

Xavier W. Corder      Apex Advertising,        (212) 555 7000
                      Inc.
                      500 Fifth Avenue
                      New York, NY 10010




                                          Col 3 Doc 1 Pg 1 Ln 2.5" Pos 7.23"
```

Figure 9-2

The ability to enter related data occupying a different number of lines into columns like this is extremely useful. But it must always be remembered that **Ctrl-Enter** is used to jump from column to column and to advance to the next group of data. Pressing **Enter** can only be used inside each column to advance to the next line.

# Chapter 10
# SPREADSHEET COLUMNS

**NOTE**

This chapter refers to the use of WordPerfect 5.0 only. Version 5.1 includes a **Table** feature (Alt-F7) with many options that can be used to produce spreadsheet-style columns with ease.

In this chapter you create an entirely different type of file consisting of four parallel columns that interact with one another, but this time the columns are created using Tab settings rather than the Column Def. function.

1. Press **F7** (Exit), type **n n** to clear the screen, and press **Shift-F8** (Format). From it select **1 Line** and then select **8 Tab Set**. Clear away the default tabs (**Home Home Left Arrow Ctrl-End**). Type **4.8** and press **Enter**, type **6.3** and press **Enter**, and type **7.4** and press **Enter**. Press **F7** (Exit) twice to return to the document screen.

2. Press **Shift-F6** (Center) and **F6** (Bold) and type **INVENTORY**. Press **Enter** and **Shift-F6** (Center) and type the date. Press **Enter Enter** and type **Description of Item**, press **Tab**, type **Cost**, press **Tab**, type **Quantity**, press **Tab**, type **Total**, and press **Enter Enter**. This finishes the headings for each column. (Depending on the font size and spacing being used, you may have to adjust the Tab settings or margins.)

3. Press **Alt-F7** (Math/Columns) and select **2 Math Def.** which produces a display used to define the different columns as in Fig. 10-1. The A through X represent the maximum 24 columns. The 2s in the Type line represent a numeric type of column. The ( in the Negative Numbers line means that negative values are displayed in parentheses. And the bottom line of 2s represents the number of digits to the right of the decimal point.

4. The far left column is ignored by this math function. Thus **A** is column 2 (Cost), **B** column 3 (Quantity), and **C** column 4 (Total). You want columns 2 and 3 to be numeric, but column 4 should display the result of a calculation. Move the cursor to the 2 under C and type **0** (Calculation). This produces a C after Calculation 1 and the cursor is to the right of it. Type **A*B** because you want A to be multiplied by B. Now move the cursor to the 2 in the Number of Digits line under B and type **0** because you don't want decimal digits used in the QUANTITY column. Fig. 10-2 is that screen. Press **F7** (Exit) to return to the document screen. Select **3 Columns On/Off** to remove the menu line from the bottom of the screen.

Chapter 10

```
Math Definition          Use arrow keys to position cursor
Columns                  A B C D E F G H I J K L M N O P Q R S T U V W X
Type                     2 2 2 2 2 2 2 2 2 2 2 2 2 2 2 2 2 2 2 2 2 2 2 2
Negative Numbers         ( ( ( ( ( ( ( ( ( ( ( ( ( ( ( ( ( ( ( ( ( ( ( (
Number of Digits to      2 2 2 2 2 2 2 2 2 2 2 2 2 2 2 2 2 2 2 2 2 2 2 2
  the Right (0-4)
Calculation    1
  Formulas     2
               3
               4
Type of Column:
     0 = Calculation    1 = Text      2 = Numeric    3 = Total
Negative Numbers
     ( = Parentheses (50.00)        - = Minus Sign  -50.00

Press Exit when done
```

*Figure 10-1*

```
Math Definition          Use arrow keys to position cursor
Columns                  A B C D E F G H I J K L M N O P Q R S T U V W X
Type                     2 2 0 2 2 2 2 2 2 2 2 2 2 2 2 2 2 2 2 2 2 2 2 2
Negative Numbers         ( ( ( ( ( ( ( ( ( ( ( ( ( ( ( ( ( ( ( ( ( ( ( (
Number of Digits to      2 0 2 2 2 2 2 2 2 2 2 2 2 2 2 2 2 2 2 2 2 2 2 2
  the Right (0-4)
Calculation    1     C     A*B
  Formulas     2
               3
               4
Type of Column:
     0 = Calculation    1 = Text      2 = Numeric    3 = Total
Negative Numbers
     ( = Parentheses (50.00)        - = Minus Sign  -50.00

Press Exit when done
```

*Figure 10-2*

5. Press **Alt-F7** (Math/Columns) and select **1 Math On**. Place the cursor at the far left edge, two lines below "Description..." (if it is not already there), and type the name of a product.

6. Press **Ctrl-F6** (Tab Align) to move the cursor to the next tab stop. Type a price figure. (Do not use Tab. The Tab Align feature is used to align numerical data by the decimal point.)

7. Press **Ctrl-F6** (Tab Align) to move the cursor to the next tab stop. Type a quantity figure.

*Spreadsheet Columns*

8. Press **Tab** to move the cursor to the final column where a **!** automatically appears, indicating that WordPerfect calculates the value for this column. (In this case Tab must be used and not Tab Align.)
9. Repeat steps 5 through 8 several times with different product descriptions, price, and quantity figures. The interim result is shown in Fig. 10-3.

```
                         INVENTORY
                        January 1990

Description of Item             Cost         Quantity    Total

Widgets                        17.45            72         !
Gadgets                        48.83           104         !
Gimmicks                      102.68            29         !
```

Figure 10-3

10. When finished, press **Enter Enter** and type **Totals**, press **Ctrl-F6** (Tab Align) and type **+**, and press **Ctrl-F6** (Tab Align) again and type **+**. Press **Tab**, delete the **!**, and replace it with **+**. Press **Enter**.
11. Press **Alt-F7** (Math/Columns), select **2 Calculate**, and the status line displays * Please Wait * for a moment, after which the display includes the total data that were calculated by WordPerfect, as in Fig. 10-4. Save the result (**F10** (Save)).

```
                         INVENTORY
                        January 1990

Description of Item             Cost         Quantity    Total

Widgets                        17.45            72      1,256.40!
Gadgets                        48.83           104      5,078.32!
Gimmicks                      102.68            29      2,977.72!

Totals                        168.96+          205+     9,312.44+
```

Figure 10-4

49

Chapter 10

The reason for replacing the last **!** with a **+** is that you don't want the total for Price to be multiplied by the total for Quantity. That would produce an inaccurate result. You want the different subtotals to be added to produce the grand total.

You can also use a document like this to demonstrate a different type of calculation just to show that there is a variety of formulas that WordPerfect can use.

1. Press **F7** (Exit) and type **n n** to clear the screen and retrieve the previous file (or, if you did not clear the screen, go to the top of it).
2. Change the heading to **INFLATION**, the second line to **The rate of inflation over a period of 12 months**, and the category headings to **Previous Price**, **Next Price**, and **Percentage Change**.
3. Press **Alt-F7** (Math/Columns) and select **2 Math Def**. Change the 2 in the top line of 2s in column C to **0**, and for the Calculation formula type **B−A/A*100**. Press **F7** (Exit) to save the settings shown in Fig. 10-5. Select **3 Columns On/Off** to remove the menu line from the bottom of the screen.

```
Math Definition            Use arrow keys to position cursor
Columns                    A B C D E F G H I J K L M N O P Q R S T U V W X
Type                       2 2 0 2 2 2 2 2 2 2 2 2 2 2 2 2 2 2 2 2 2 2 2 2
Negative Numbers           ( ( ( ( ( ( ( ( ( ( ( ( ( ( ( ( ( ( ( ( ( ( ( (
Number of Digits to        2 2 2 2 2 2 2 2 2 2 2 2 2 2 2 2 2 2 2 2 2 2 2 2
    the Right (0-4)
Calculation   1    C       B-A/A*100
  Formulas    2
              3
              4
Type of Column:
      0 = Calculation    1 = Text      2 = Numeric    3 = Total
Negative Numbers
      ( = Parentheses (50.00)          - = Minus Sign  -50.00

Press Exit when done
```

Figure 10-5

4. Press **Alt-F7** (Math/Columns) and select **1 Math On**. Now change the values in the second column to new ones, somewhat greater than those listed in the Previous Price column. After entering each value, press **Tab** to place an **!** into the last column. Then press **End** and type **%**.
5. Press **Alt-F7** (Math/Columns) and select **2 Calculate** and after a moment the results of the various calculations are displayed on the screen, as in Fig. 10-6.

```
                       INFLATION
           The rate of inflation over a period of 12 months
Description of Item        Previous      Next       Percentage
                           Price         Price      Change

Widgets                    17.45         23.91      37.02!%
Gadgets                    48.83         57.48      17.71!%
Gimmicks                   102.68        115.03     12.03!%

Totals                     168.96+       196.42+    16.25!%




Math                                     Doc 1 Pg 1 Ln 2.83" Pos 0.5"
```

Figure 10-6

If this chapter gave you the idea that WordPerfect is capable of being a full-fledged spreadsheet program, that is, in fact, not the case. It can perform some limited mathematical functions, but these are too limited to be used for true spreadsheets. For those, you are better advised to use a program like Quattro or Lotus 1-2-3.

WordPerfect 5.1 includes a Spreadsheet Import and Spreadsheet Link feature that allows Lotus 1-2-3, Quattro, PlanPerfect, and other spreadsheet files to be combined with WordPerfect documents.

# CHAPTER 11
# PAGE FORMATTING — PART III

The subject of this chapter is a macro that formats the first page of a chapter in a book. With minor modifications it can also be used for the first pages of magazine articles or short stories.

The macro establishes a header, then stops to have you enter a chapter number and an optional chapter description into it. After pressing **Enter** it goes through a number of steps and then displays the available font styles and sizes, waiting for you to decide on the one that is to be used. It then moves the cursor halfway down the page and activates Bold, ready for you to add the chapter heading. You're then ready to start writing body text.

Figure 11-1 is the macro. It is quite lengthy and is best produced in the macro editing mode.

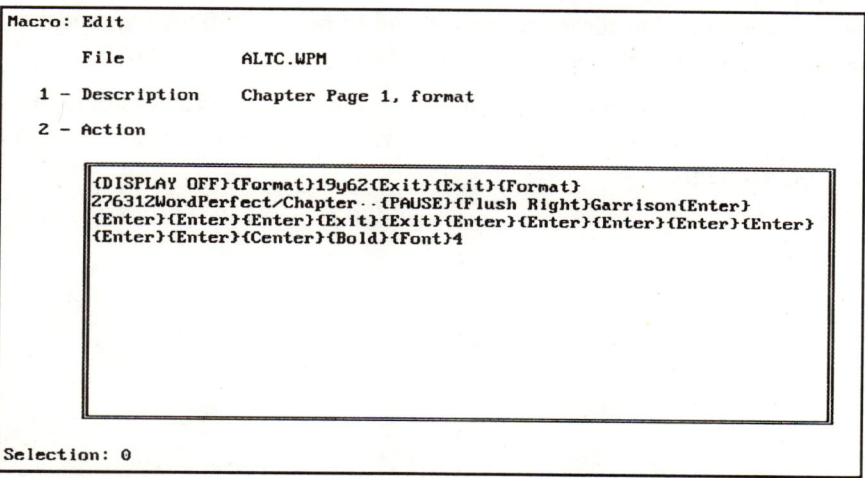

Figure 11-1

1. Press **Ctrl-F10** (Macro define).
2. Press **Alt-C** if that is the name you want to use for the macro.
3. For the description, type one of your choice.
4. Press **Ctrl-F10** (Macro define) to save the as-yet empty macro.

*Page Formatting — Part III*

5. Press **Ctrl-F10** (Macro define) and **Alt-C**. When asked whether to 1 Replace or 2 Edit type **2** twice which places the cursor inside the macro frame.
6. Press **Ctrl-F10** which at this stage activates the **Macro editing** mode, indicated on the status line. This is necessary to enter such commands as F7 (Exit) which otherwise would simply terminate the macro editing session.

Press **End** to move the cursor to the right of **{DISPLAY OFF}**. You can now enter the actual keystrokes that make up the complete macro. They are listed here in consecutive order:

1. **Shift-F8** (produces **{Format}**)
2. **1** (Line)
3. **9** (Widow/Orphan Protection)
4. **y** (yes)
5. **6** (Line spacing)
6. **2** (2)
7. **F7 F7** (produces **{Exit}{Exit}**)
8. **Shift-F8** (produces **{Format}**)
9. **2** (Page)
10. **7** (Page numbering)
11. **6** (Bottom center)
12. **3** (Headers)
13. **1** (Header A)
14. **2** (Every page)
15. **WordPerfect/Chapter** (or your own header text)
16. **Spacebar Spacebar** (produces .. (2 dots))
17. **Ctrl-F10** (temporarily exits the macro editing mode)
18. **Ctrl-PgUp** (accesses the macro command list)
19. Highlight **{PAUSE}** and press **Enter** (produces **{PAUSE}** which causes macro execution to halt until Enter is pressed.
20. **Alt-F6** (produces **{Flush Right}**)
21. **Garrison** (the author's name)
22. **Ctrl-F10** (returns to the macro editing mode)
23. **Enter** four times (produces **{Enter}{Enter}{Enter}{Enter}**)
24. **F7 F7** (produces **{Exit}{Exit}**)

*Chapter 11*

25. **Enter** seven times (produces **{Enter}{Enter}{Enter}{Enter}{Enter}{Enter}{Enter}**)
26. **Shift-F6 F6** (produces **{Center}{Bold}**)
27. **Ctrl-F8** and **4** (produces **{Font}4**)
28. **Ctrl-F10** (deactivates the **Macro editing** mode)
29. **F7 F7** (saves the finished macro)

From now on, pressing **Alt-C** or whatever name you gave that macro automatically executes all those steps and leaves the cursor in the Ln 4.33" Pos 4.65" position with Bold active. By using this macro for the first page of all chapters in a book, you achieve a uniformity otherwise not readily available.

# CHAPTER 12
# LABELS

Using WordPerfect 5.0 to produce mailing labels can present a minor problem if your label sheets have three self-adhesive labels placed in a row. It is necessary to make sure that the text for each label is printed on the label itself. It also requires printing from the very top of the page to the very bottom.

The best way to accomplish this is to use the **Parallel columns** feature that was discussed in Chapter 9.

Setting everything up so that the results are satisfactory requires a series of steps best represented by a macro, since macros, once tested, don't make mistakes. The keystrokes, step by step, are:

1. Press **Ctrl-F10** (Macro define).
2. Type **LABEL** (or any other name) and press **Enter**.
3. Type a description and press **Enter**.
4. Press **Shift-F8** (Format) and select **1 Line**.
5. Select **7 Margins Left/Right**.
6. Type **0.25** and press **Enter**; type **0.25** and press **Enter**.
7. Press **F7** (Exit).
8. Press **Shift-F8** (Format) and select **2 Page**.
9. Select **5 Margins Top/Bottom**.
10. Type **0.2** and press **Enter**; type **0.2** and press **Enter**.
11. Press **F7** (Exit).
12. Press **Alt-F7** (Math/Columns) and select **4 Column Def**.
13. Select **1 Type** and **2 Parallel**.
14. Select **2 Number of columns**, type **3**, and press **Enter**.
15. Select **3 Distance between columns**, type **0.25**, and press **Enter**.
16. Press **F7** (Exit).
17. Select **3 Column On/Off**. Then press **Ctrl-F10** (Macro define) to end the macro generating process.

Chapter 12

You now have a macro that should look like Fig. 12-1. To try it out, press **F7** (Exit) and type **n n** to be sure that your screen is clear. Press **Alt-F10**, type **LABEL** (or label), and press **Enter**. The cursor should be in the top left corner of the screen and the status line should read: **Col 1 Doc 1 Pg 1 Ln 0.2" Pos 0.25"**. If it does, fine. If it does not, you made a mistake.

```
Macro: Edit

        File              LABEL.WPM

    1 - Description       Labels, three in a row

    2 - Action

        {DISPLAY OFF}{Format}170.25{Enter}0.25{Enter}
        {Exit}{Format}250.2{Enter}
        0.2{Enter}{Exit}{Math/Columns}41223{Enter}
        30.25{Enter}{Exit}3




Selection: 0
```

Figure 12-1

You can now start entering name and address data. Use up to four lines and then press **Ctrl-Enter** to jump to the next column. Use **Enter** only to move to the next line within the individual columns. Fig. 12-2 is an example, consisting of nine name-and-address records. To make sure things are working the way they are supposed to, enter a row or two of such records and print them. Then check what you have printed against the position of the labels on your label sheets. If they don't match exactly, try experimenting with the column width and spaces between the columns in the **Math/Columns** (Alt-F7) screen.

*Labels*

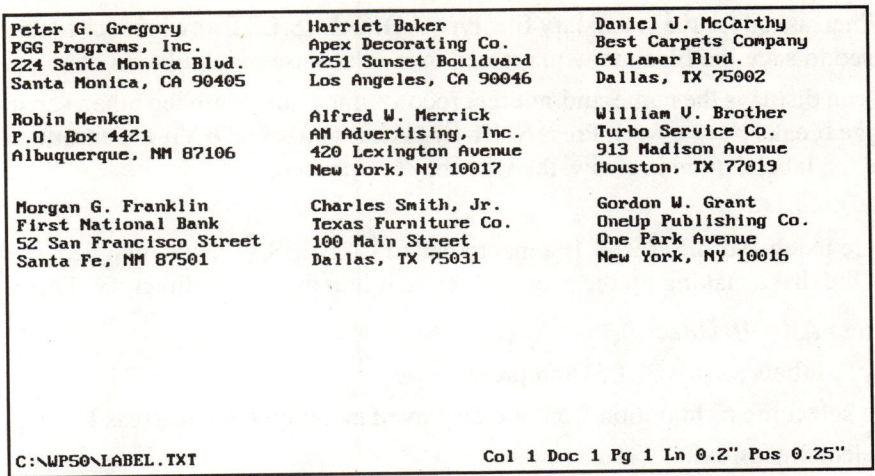

*Figure 12-2*

WordPerfect 5.1 has a special **Labels** feature that you can use instead of the routine described above. The steps involved are:

1. Press **Shift-F8** (Format), select **2 Page**, and select **7 Paper Size/Type**.
2. Observe the menu at the bottom of the screen. Select **2 Add**.
3. Select **4 Labels** which returns you to the Edit Paper Definition menu.
4. Select **8 Labels** and type **y**. The Labels menu is displayed.
5. Accept the default settings. Press **Enter**.
6. The Edit Paper Definition menu is displayed. Select **4 Prompt to Load** and type **y**.
7. Select **5 Location** and **3 Manual**.
8. Press **F7** (Exit) three times to return to the editing screen.
9. Press **F7** (Exit) and type **n n** to clear the screen.
10. Press **Shift-F8** (Format) and select **3 Document**. Select **2 Initial Codes**.
11. Press **Shift-F8** (Format) and select **2 Page**. Select **7 Paper Size/Type**.
12. Select **1 Select**. Press **F7** (Exit) three times to return to the document screen.
13. Press **Shift-F9** (Merge Codes), select **1 Field**, and type **1**.
14. Press **Enter** to start a new line.
15. Press **Shift-F9** (Merge Codes), select **1 Field**, press **Enter**, and type **2**.
16. Press **F7** (Exit) and type **y**. Type **LABELS.PR** as the name for the primary file. Type **n** to clear the screen.
17. Press **Ctrl-F9** (Merge/Sort) and select **1 Merge**.
18. When asked for the primary file, type **LABELS.PR**.

*Chapter 12*

19. When asked for the secondary file, type **ADDRESS.LST** or whatever filename you used to save the files that you created in the database manipulation chapters.

The screen displays the name-and-address records one underneath the other, separated by hard page breaks (=======). Press **Shift-F7** (Print) and select **6 View document**. There you see the labels, three in a row, the way they are printed.

If you are using WordPerfect 5.1, a macro called LABELS.WPM is included among the files on the disks making up the program. Load it into the active directory. Then:

1. Press **Alt-F10** (Macro).
2. Type **labels** (or LABELS) and press **Enter**.
3. To select the right option from the displayed menu type **g** and press **Enter**.
4. Select **3 Manual**.
5. To be prompted to load a new sheet of labels, select **Yes**.
6. Press **Enter** to return to the document screen.

You're now ready to use the normal merge option to enter your name-and-address records onto 30-label sheets.

## Chapter 13
# BUSINESS CARDS AND DISK LABELS

In this chapter you start by creating a macro that automatically produces six business cards on a single page, ready to be printed. Since this involves a large number of steps, it would be best to experiment with the project before using the macro-define option:

1. Type the text that you want on the business card in the approximate layout you want to use. Quite probably this may have to be adjusted later, but for the moment any halfway sensible layout, such as the one in Fig. 13-1, will do.

```
John Smith                    (505) 555-1234




P.O. Box 4321
Middletown, NM 87304-4321
```

*Figure 13-1*

2. Press **F10** (Save) and type a filename (CARD.TXT). Press **F7** and type **n n** to clear the screen.
3. Press **Shift-F8** (Format) and select **1 Line**.
4. Select **7 Margins** and type **0.1** for the left and right margins. Otherwise there is insufficient room to get two 3.5-inch wide business cards onto the page. Press **Enter** twice.
5. Press **F7** (Exit) to return to the document screen.
6. Press **Alt-F9** (Graphics) and select **1 Figure** and **1 Create**.
7. From the graphics menu select **1 Filename**, type **CARD.TXT** (or whatever filename you used), and press **Enter**.
8. Select **5 Horizontal Position** and **1 Left**.
9. Select **6 Size** and **3 Both Width and Height**. For the width type **3.5** and press **Enter**, and for the height type **2** and press **Enter**.

Chapter 13

10. Press **Enter** to return to the document screen.
11. Press **Shift-F7** (Print) and select **6 View Document** to see what the first business card looks like. You are likely to find that the text placement is not quite right and you might want to rearrange it and save it again. Press **F7** to return to the document screen.
12. Press **Alt-F9** (Graphics) and select **1 Figure** and **2 Edit**.
13. Be sure that **Figure 1** is displayed on the status line. If not, change the number to **1** and press **Enter**.
14. From the graphics menu select **1 File Name** and the old filename is displayed on the status line. Press **Enter** to accept it and type **y** in reply to the question whether the old entry is to be replaced.
15. Return to the document screen. Repeat step 11 to see if the layout is now satisfactory. If it is, fine. If it is not, fix the text and repeat steps 12, 13, and 14. Once the layout is right, it's time to define the macro.

To define the macro, perform the following steps.

1. Press **Ctrl-F10** (Macro Define) and for the name type **CARD**. For the description type **6 business cards on one page** and press **Enter**.
2. Press **Shift-F8** (Format) and select **1 Line**.
3. Select **7 Margins** and type **0.1** for the left margin and **0.1** for the right margin.
4. Press **Enter F7** (Exit) to return to the document screen.
5. Press **Alt-F9** (Graphics) and select **1 Figure** and **1 Create**.
6. From the graphics menu select **1 Filename** and type **CARD.TXT** or whatever filename you are using. Then press **Enter**.
7. Select **5 Horizontal Position** and select **1 Left**.
8. Select **6 Size** and **3 Both Width and Height**. For the width type **3.5** and press **Enter**, and for the height type **2** and press **Enter**.
9. Press **Enter** to return to the document screen.
10. Press **Alt-F9** (Graphics) and select **1 Figure** and **1 Create**.
11. Select **1 Filename** and type **CARD.TXT** (or whatever). Then press **Enter**.
12. Select **6 Size** and **3 Both Width and Height**. For the width, type **3.5** and press **Enter**, and for the height type **2** and press **Enter**.
13. Press **Enter** to return to the document screen.
14. Press **Alt-F9** (Graphics), select **1 Figure**, **1 Create**, **1 Filename** and type **CARD.TXT** (or your filename) and press **Enter**.
15. Select **4 Vertical Position**, type **3.16**, and press **Enter**.

*Business Cards and Disk Labels*

16. Repeat steps 7 through 11.
17. Select **4 Vertical Position**, type **3.16**, and press **Enter**.
18. Repeat steps 12 through 13.
19. Press **Alt-F9** (Graphics), select **1 Figure, 1 Create, 1 Filename** and type **CARDTST.WW** (or your filename).
20. Select **4 Vertical Position**, type **6.32**, and press **Enter**.
21. Repeat steps 7 through 11.
22. Select **4 Vertical Position**, type **6.32**, and press **Enter**.
23. Repeat steps 12 through 13.
24. Press **Ctrl-F10** (Macro Define) to end the macro definition process. Return to the document screen.
25. Press **Alt-F10** (Macro), type **CARD**, and press **Enter**. Now the status line reads * Please Wait * for a little while. When it disappears use the **View Document** option to see your page with its six business cards as in Fig. 13-2.

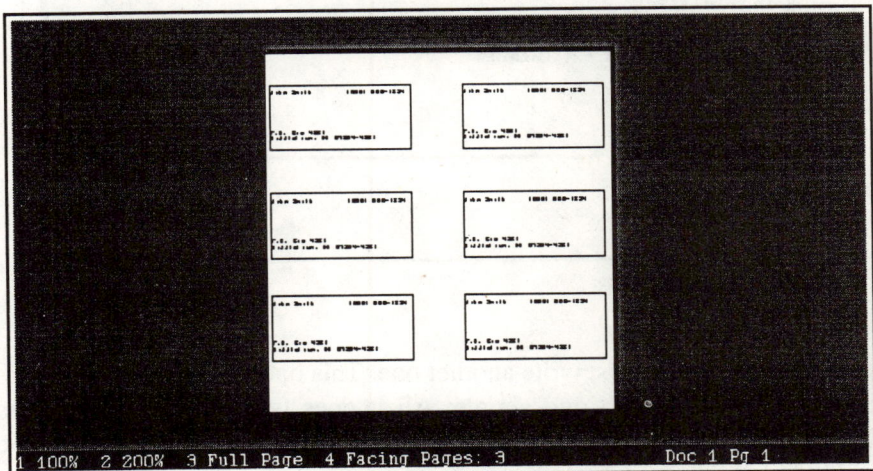

Figure 13-2

If you want to see what your macro looks like:

1. Press **Ctrl-F10** (Macro Define) and from the options on the status line select **2 Edit**.
2. From the macro editing menu select **2 Action** to place the cursor inside the box.
3. Use the arrow keys to scroll to the end of the macro and you are seeing each step you took along the way shown in Fig. 13-3.

You can save the result of using this macro and whenever that file is retrieved, there are your six business cards ready to be printed.

## Chapter 13

```
Macro: Edit
        File            CARD.WPM
  1 - Description       6 business cards on one page
  2 - Action
        {DISPLAY OFF}{Format}170.1{Enter}
        0.1{Enter}
        {Enter}
        {Exit}{Graphics}111card.txt{Enter}
        51633.5{Enter}
        2{Enter}
        {Enter}
        {Graphics}111card.txt{Enter}
        633.5{Enter}
        2{Enter}
        {Enter}
        {Graphics}111card.txt{Enter}
        43.16{Enter}
        51633.5{Enter}
        2{Enter}
        {Enter}
        {Graphics}111card.txt{Enter}
        43.16{Enter}
        633.5{Enter}
        2{Enter}
        {Enter}
        {Graphics}111card.txt{Enter}
        46.32{Enter}
        51633.5{Enter}
        2{Enter}
        {Enter}
        {Graphics}111card.txt{Enter}
        46.32{Enter}
        633.5{Enter}
        2{Enter}
        {Enter}

Selection: 2
```

*Figure 13-3*

While on the subject of macros, write another one. This one, designed to print labels for 5.25-inch disks, is quite short and simple. All it does is merge two short files: one containing the label format and the other the prompts displayed on the status line, telling the user what to type next:

1. To create the secondary file press **Shift-F9** (Merge Codes) and type **O** which prints a ^O.

2. Type **Enter disk content  (Press F9)**. Press **Shift-F9** (Merge Codes) and type **O**, press **Shift-F9** (Merge Codes) and type **C**, and press **F9** (Merge R), which prints as ^O^C^R.

3. Press **Shift-F9** and type **O**. Type **Enter disk #  (Press F9)**. Press **Shift-F9** (Merge Codes), and type **O**. Press **Shift-F9** (Merge Codes) and type **C**. Press **F9** (Merge R). The result prints as ^O^C^R.

4. Press **Shift-F9** and type **O**. Type **Enter number of disks in group** (**Press F9**). Press **Shift-F9** (Merge Codes) and type **O** and press **Shift-F9** (Merge Codes) and type **C**. Press **F9** (Merge R), which prints as ^O^C^R.

5. Press **Shift-F9** and type **O**. Type **Enter starting command** (**Press F9**). Press **Shift-F9** (Merge Codes) and type **O**. Press **Shift-F9** (Merge Codes) and type **C**. Press **F9** (Merge R).

6. Press **Shift-F9** and type **O**. Type **To print press F9**. Press **Shift-F9** (Merge Codes) and type **O**. Press **Shift-F9** (Merge Codes) and type **C**. Press **F9** (Merge R). Fig. 13-4 is the result.

7. Press **F10** (Save) and for the filename type **LABEL1.PF**.

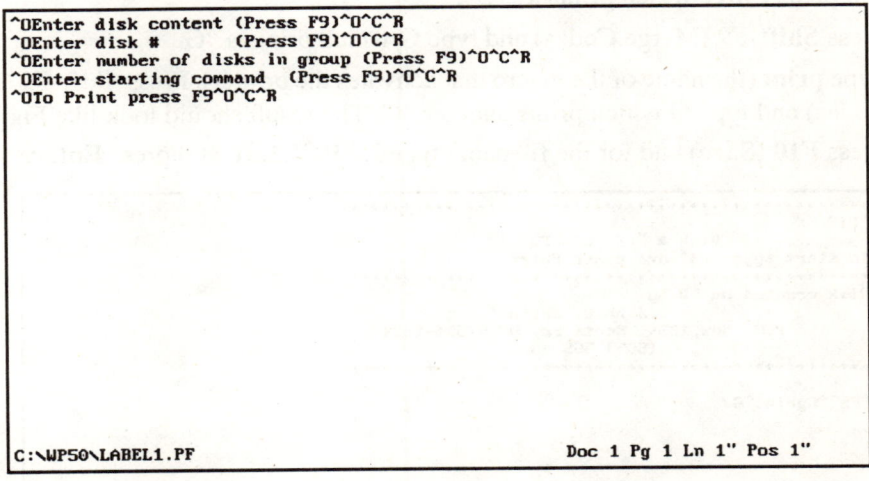

Figure 13-4

Next produce the secondary file, the one containing the format for the disk label:

1. Press **Esc** (Repeat) and type **50 +** which places a line of 50 +s onto the screen. Press **Enter** to move the cursor down one line.

2. Press **Shift-F9** (Merge Codes) and type **F**. For the field number type **1** and press **Enter**.

3. In approximately the center of the next line type **Disk #** and press **Shift-F9** (Merge Codes). Press **F** and for the field number type **2** and press **Enter**.

4. Type **of** preceded and followed by a space, press **Shift-F9** (Merge Codes), and type **F**. For the field number type **3** and press **Enter**.

5. Type **To start type** plus one space and press **Shift-F9** (Merge Codes). Type **F**, and for the field number type **4** and press **Enter**. Type **and press Enter** and press **Enter**.

Chapter 13

6. Press **Esc** (Repeat) and type **50+** which places a line of 50 **+**s onto the screen. Move the cursor down one line.
7. Type **Disk created on** and press **Shift-F9** and type **D** which prints a ^D. Press **Spacebar**. Type **by** and press **Enter**.
8. Press **Shift-F6** (Center). Type your name and press **Enter**.
9. Press **Shift-F6** (Center). Type your address and press **Enter**.
10. Press **Shift-F6** (Center). Type your phone number and press **Enter**.
11. Press **Esc** (Repeat) and type **50 +** which places a line of 50 **+**s onto the screen.
12. Press **Enter Enter**, press **Shift-F9** (Merge Codes), and type **F**. For the field type **5** and press **Enter** which prints a ^F5^.
13. Press **Shift-F9** (Merge Codes) and type **G** which prints a ^G.
14. Type **print** (the name of the macro that activates the printer). Press **Shift-F9** (Merge Codes) and type **G** which prints another ^G. The result should look like Fig. 13-5.
15. Press **F10** (Save) and for the filename type **LABEL2.SF** and press **Enter**.

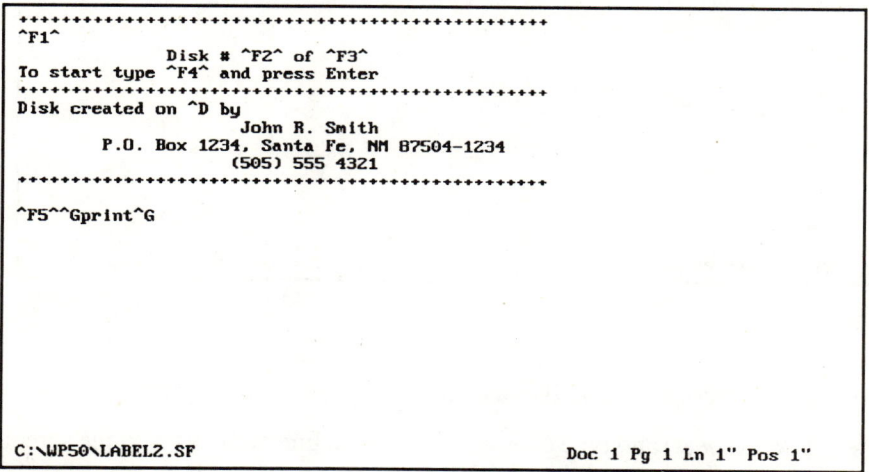

Figure 13-5

### NOTE

The Merge Codes function produces different codes in WordPerfect 5.1. See Chapter 51.

# Business Cards and Disk Labels

The ^Gprint^G is a command asking that the macro named PRINT be executed. If you have not done so earlier, you have to create it:

1. Press **Ctrl-F10** (Macro define), for the name type **PRINT**, and for the description type **To activate the printer**. Press **Enter**.
2. With the **Macro Def** prompt flashing, press **Shift-F7** (Print) and type **1**.
3. Press **Ctrl-F10** (Macro define) to end the definition process.

Finally, create the macro that controls the execution and printing of the label:

1. Press **Ctrl-F10** (Macro define), for the name type **DISKLBL**, and for the description type **Labels for 5.25-inch disks**. Press **Enter**.
2. With the **Macro Def** prompt flashing press **Ctrl-F9** (Merge/Sort) and select **1 Merge**.
3. For the primary file type **label1.pf** and press **Enter**.
4. For the secondary file type **label2.sf** and press **Enter**.
5. Press **Ctrl-F10** (Macro define) to end the macro definition process. Fig. 13-6 is the result.

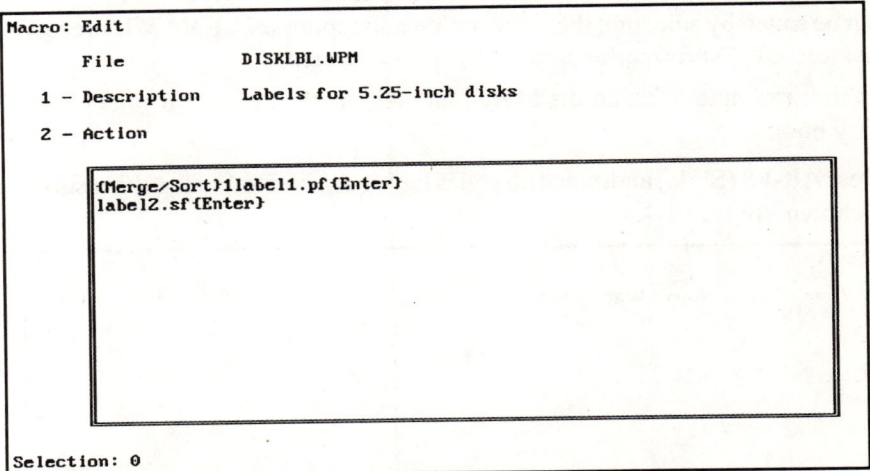

Figure 13-6

Now all the pieces are ready for use:

1. Press **Alt-F10** (Macro), type **DISKLBL**, and press **Enter**. The display shows the blank label format with the status line reading Enter disk content (Press F9).
2. From here on follow the instructions on the status line, and when finished, the printer prints your label.

# CHAPTER 14
# STYLES — PART I

In addition to using macros for predetermined sequences of keystrokes and commands, WordPerfect includes a Style function to automate the formatting of documents. Use this function to create Styles for your documents that can be used over and over, thus saving time and keystrokes needed to create and manipulate text.

Before **Styles** are created, you may want to set up a directory where they are stored:

1. Press **Shift-F1** (Setup) and select **7 Location of Auxiliary Files**.
2. Select **6 Style-Library Filename** and type something like **C:\WW\LIB.STY** if you're using a hard disk, or something like **B:\LIB.STY** if you want to use the floppy disk in drive B:. Or you can simply place them into you work disk or directory by typing **C:\WW** or **B:**.
3. Press **Enter** and **F7** (Exit) to save the information. Any style created from now on can be saved by selecting the **Save** option and typing **\FILENAME** preceded by the disk/directory information used in the previous step.

As your first example of using the **Style** function, create a format for the chapters in an imaginary book:

1. Press **Alt-F8** (Style) and, since no styles have been created so far, the resulting screen is shown in Fig. 14-1.

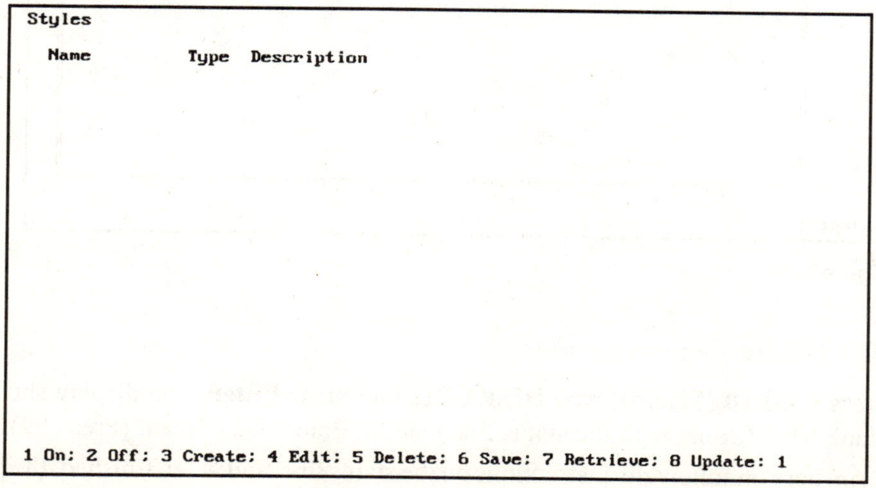

```
Styles
   Name        Type  Description













 1 On; 2 Off; 3 Create; 4 Edit; 5 Delete; 6 Save; 7 Retrieve; 8 Update: 1
```

Figure 14-1

*Styles —Part I*

2. Select **3 Create**, then select **1 Name**, type **Chapters**, and press **Enter**.
3. Select **2 Type Paired** which produces two options, 1 Paired and 2 Open. Select **2 Open**.
4. Select **3 Description**. Type **Format for the chapters of a book** and press **Enter**. Fig. 14-2 is the result.

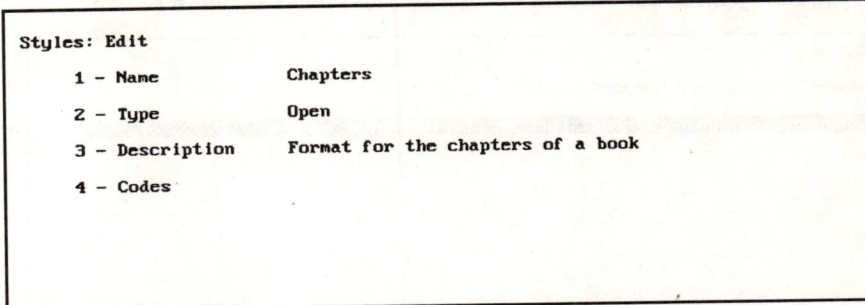

Figure 14-2

5. Select **4 Codes** and the screen changes to the familiar **Reveal Codes** format.
6. Now it's time to enter the style codes and text. Press **Shift-F8 1 6 2 Enter 8 Home Home Left Arrow Ctrl-End 1.5 Enter 2 Enter 2.5 Enter F7 9 y Enter 2 3 1 2 WordPerfect/Chapter Alt-F6 Author's name Enter Enter Enter Enter F7 7 6 Enter F7 Enter Enter Enter Enter Enter Enter Shift-F6 F7**. These are all the steps needed to produce a useful style for the chapters of a book. The screen displays all steps in the **Reveal codes** format as in Fig. 14-3.

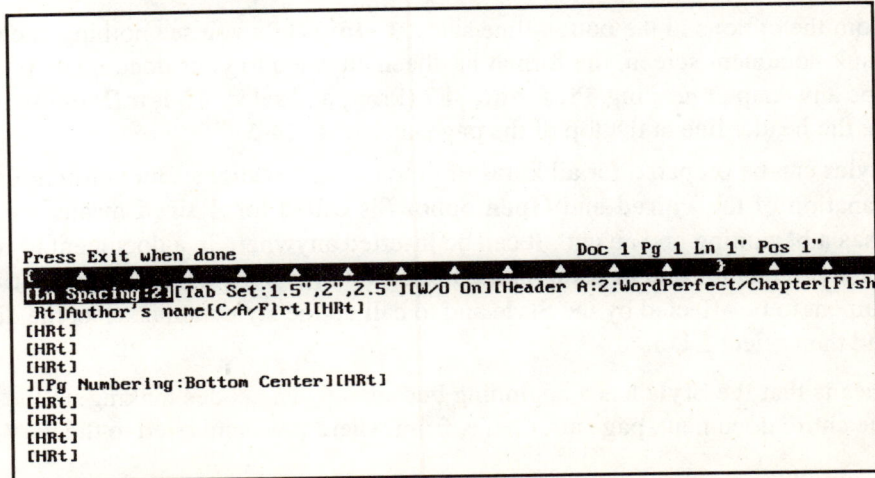

Figure 14-3

Chapter 14

These steps produce double spacing, three tab stops, widow/orphan protection, a header with the book title, chapter info, and author's name flush right plus four blank lines, page numbering bottom center, six additional blank lines, and cursor centered.

7. At this point **F7** returns you to the previous **Styles** menu as in Fig. 14-4. Select **6 Save**. When asked for a filename, type **C:\WW\CHAPTER** or whatever disk/directory information you want to use, and press **Enter F7**.

```
Styles
  Name          Type   Description
  Chapters      Open   Format for the chapters of a book




















1 On; 2 Off; 3 Create; 4 Edit; 5 Delete; 6 Save; 7 Retrieve; 8 Update: 1
```

Figure 14-4

8. With a blank document screen, press **Alt-F8** (Style). The screen displays your previously saved **Style** name and description.

9. From the options in the bottom line select **1 On**. While you see nothing except the blank document screen, the format has been attached to your document. To see it, type any chapter heading. Press **Shift-F7** (Print) and select **6 View Document**. You see the header line at the top of the page, as in Fig. 14-5.

Such **Styles** can be prepared for all kinds of practical applications. But before going on, an explanation of the **Paired** and **Open** options is called for. **Paired** means the **Style** format has a beginning and an end. It can be inserted anywhere in a document to format a single paragraph or group of paragraphs. The best way is to **Block** define the portion of the document to be affected by the **Style** and to call up the style menu, select the desired style, and then select **1 On**.

**Open** means that the **Style** has a beginning but no end. The codes making up the **Style** affect the entire document, page after page, from where it was invoked to the very end.

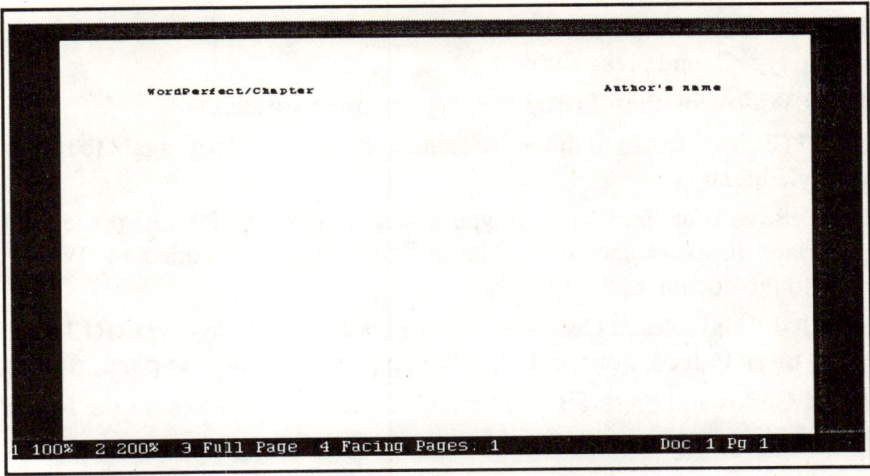

*Figure 14-5*

For the next demonstration, retrieve any convenient text document and create two **Styles**. Use them to change the appearance of individual paragraphs.

1. Press **Shift-F10** (Retrieve). Type the path information and filename of the text document you want to use.
2. Press **Alt-F8** (Style) and select **3 Create**. For the **1 Name** type **SPACING**. Retain the **2 Type** as **Paired**. For the description, type **Change spacing in one paragraph** as in Fig. 14-6

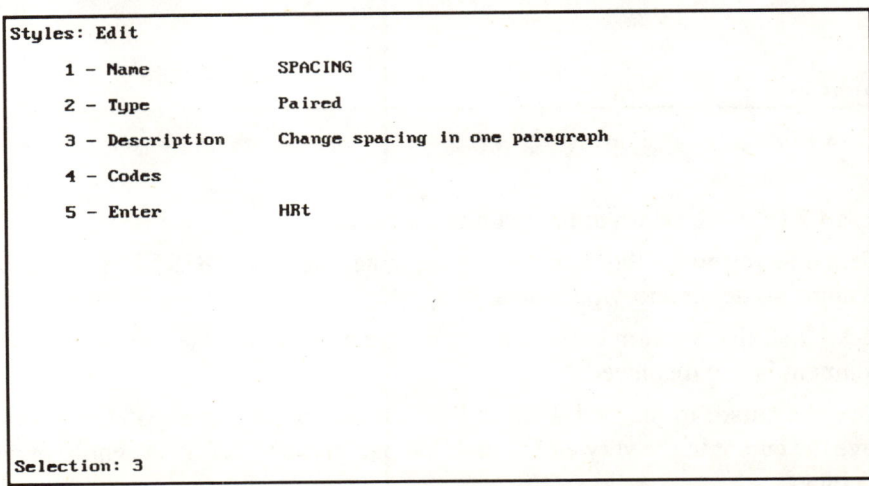

*Figure 14-6*

Chapter 14

3. Select **4 Codes**. Press **Shift-F8** (Format) and select **1 Line**. Then select **6 Line spacing,** type **2,** and press **Enter**.
4. Select **9 Widow/orphan Protection,** type **y,** press **Enter**.
5. Press **F7** (Exit) to return to the **Style** menu and press **F7** (Exit) again to return to the main style menu.
6. Select **6 Save**. For the filename type a name, such as **SPACE,** preceded by the appropriate directory/path data. The **.STY** extension is added by WordPerfect. Return to the document screen.
7. Press **Alt-F8** and select **3 Create** again. For the **1 Name** type **UNDERLINE**. Retain the **2 Type** as **Paired**. For the description, type **Underline one paragraph**.
8. Select **4 Codes** and press **F8** (Underline). Press **F7** (Exit) to save the format as in Fig. 14-7.

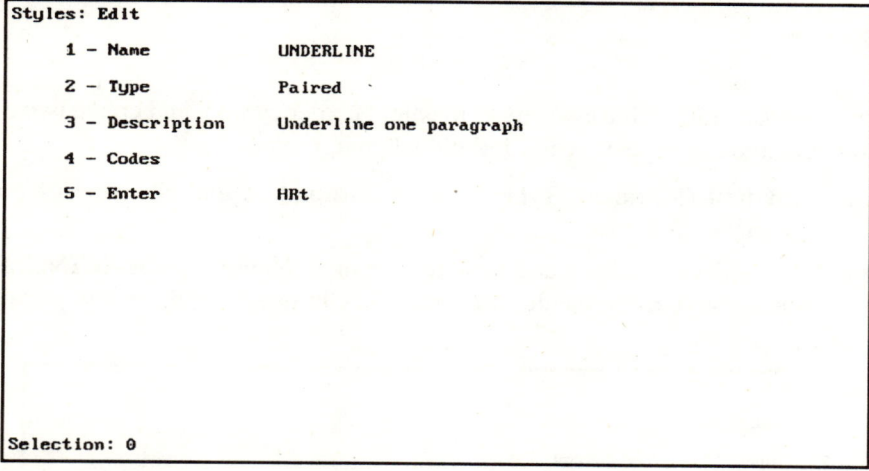

Figure 14-7

9. Press **F7** (Exit) to return to the main Style menu.
10. Select **6 Save** and for the filename type a name, such as **UNDRLINE,** preceded by the appropriate directory/path data.
11. Press **F7** (Exit) to return to the document screen on which the previously retrieved document is still displayed.
12. Move the cursor to the first word in the first paragraph. Press **Alt-F4** (Block) and move the cursor to the very end of that first paragraph to define the entire paragraph as a block.

*Styles —Part I*

13. Press **Alt-F8** (Style), move the highlighting to **Spacing**, and from the options at the bottom line select **1 On**. You're immediately returned to the document screen where the first paragraph is now double spaced as in Fig. 14-8.

```
Every once in a while it would be kind of fun to know roughly how

long it would take to double a given amount of investment,

based on currently available annual interest rates and applicable

compounding periods.

The simplest method involves something that we might refer to as
a "magic number," which must be divided by the interest rate in
order to produce the time period in terms of years and decimal
fractions of years that will be involved in doubling the
investment. For instance, if the compounding period is daily then
the "magic number" is 69. Assuming the available interest rate
is 7.75% then the equation would be:
                        69 / 7/75 = 8.9
which means that it would take eight years and approximately 11
months to double the initial amount.

The magic numbers are:
  69    if the interest is anywhere from 5% to 19.9% and the
compounding period is daily.
  70    if the interest is anywhere from 5% to 19.9% and the
compounding periods are monthly or quarterlly.
                                            Doc 1 Pg 1 Ln 2" Pos 3"
```

Figure 14-8

14. Move the cursor to the first letter of the first word in the second paragraph. Press **Alt-F4** (Block) and move the cursor to somewhere in the middle of that paragraph.
15. Press **Alt-F8** (Style), move the highlighting to **Underline**, and again select **1 On**. Depending on the monitor, no actual underline may be shown in the display. Then the portion of the paragraph is highlighted.
16. Press **Shift-F7** (Print) and select **6 View Document**. You see that the second paragraph is now underlined while the third and fourth paragraphs have remained quite unaffected.

After you have used WordPerfect to create all manner of personal or business documents, you're likely to have created a considerable library of Style formats. Since it is often difficult to remember the filenames used, it is a good idea to use adequate descriptions during the process of creating a Style file.

## CHAPTER 15
# STYLES — PART II

In an earlier chapter a combination of the **macro** and **merge** options produced a form for memos. This time the idea is to use a **Style** file to produce the same results:

1. With the document screen blank, press **Alt-F8** (Style) and select **3 Create**.
2. Select **1 Name** and type **MEMO**. Press **Enter**. Select **2 Type** and from the displayed options select **2 Open**.
3. Select **3 Description**, type **Format for an inter-office memo,** and press **Enter**. Fig. 15-1 is the current screen.

```
Styles: Edit
       1 - Name            MEMO
       2 - Type            Open
       3 - Description     Format for an inter-office memo
       4 - Codes




Selection: 0
```

Figure 15-1

4. Select **4 Codes,** press **Shift-F6** (Center) and **F6** (Bold), type **INTER-OFFICE MEMO,** and press **Enter Enter**.
5. Type **Date:**, press **Tab** twice, press **Shift-F9,** and type **D**.
6. Press **Enter Enter,** type **From:**, press **Tab** twice, press **Enter Enter** again and type **To:,** and press **Enter Enter**.
7. Press **Esc** and type **70** and a hyphen (-) to add a line of hyphens.
8. Press **Enter Enter,** type **Subject:**, press **Tab** twice, press **F6** (Bold), and press **F7** (Exit) twice. Fig. 15-2 is the Reveal Codes screen with the codes that you entered.

*Styles — Part II*

```
                    INTER-OFFICE MEMO
Date:          ^D

From:

To:
_____

Subject:
Press Exit when done                    Doc 1 Pg 1 Ln 1" Pos 1"
{     ▲    ▲    ▲    ▲    ▲    ▲    ▲   }  ▲    ▲
[Cntr][BOLD]INTER[-]OFFICE MEMO[C/A/Flrt][HRt]
[HRt]
Date:[Tab][Tab]^D[HRt]
[HRt]
From:[Tab][Tab][HRt]
[HRt]
To:[Tab][Tab][HRt]
[HRt]
[-][-][-][-][-][-][-][-][-][-][-][-][-][-][-][-][-][-][-][-][-][-][-[
-][-][-][-][-][-][-][-][-][-][-][-][-][-][-][-][-][-][-][-][-][-][-][
-]
```

*Figure 15-2*

9. With the **Style** main menu up, select **6 Save** and type **MEMO** preceded by the appropriate directory/path information.
10. Select **1 On** and your memo form instantly appears on the document screen with the current date displayed in the **Date:** line, as in Fig. 15-3.

```
                    INTER-OFFICE MEMO
Date:      November 22, 1990

From:

To:
_____

Subject:




                                    Doc 1 Pg 1 Ln 1.67" Pos 2"
```

*Figure 15-3*

## Chapter 15

WordPerfect includes a fair amount of ready-to-use files. Take a few moments to look at them with an eye toward the possibility of modifying them for your own use. One group of such style files may be located on the Learning disk/directory under the file names LETTER.STY, NEWS.STY, and LIBRARY.STY. For the moment, look at the LETTER.STY files. These, because they are styles, cannot be retrieved in the usual manner.

1. Press **Alt-F8** (Style) and you are probably faced by a document screen with a style menu at the top and a status line at the bottom similar to the following:

```
Styles
  Name         Type   Description












1 On; 2 Off; 3 Create; 4 Edit; 5 Delete; 6 Save; 7 Retrieve; 8 Update: 1
```

2. Select **7 Retrieve**, type **C:\WP50\LEARN\LETTER.STY**, and press **Enter** (or whatever disk/directory path information is appropriate). Your document screen changes to the one in Fig. 15-4. **Closing, Letterhead, Second,** and **Settings** are the files saved under LETTER.STY.

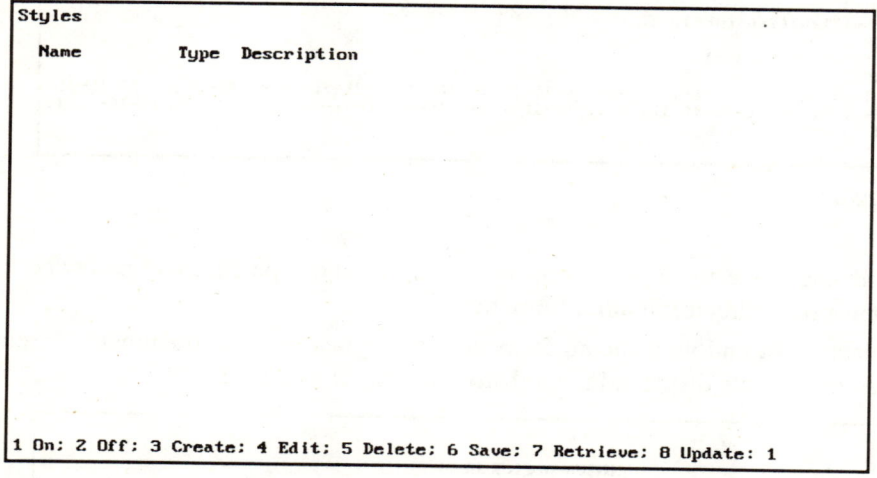

Figure 15-4

74

*Styles — Part II*

Since **Letterhead** is the one in the group to be used first, look at what it consists of.

3. Select **4 Edit** and the document screen displays:

```
Styles: Edit
    1 - Name           Letterhead
    2 - Type           Open
    3 - Description    Letterhead format for first page
    4 - Codes
```

4. Select **4 Codes** and the document screen changes to the **Reveal Codes** screen, displaying the codes in Fig. 15-5.

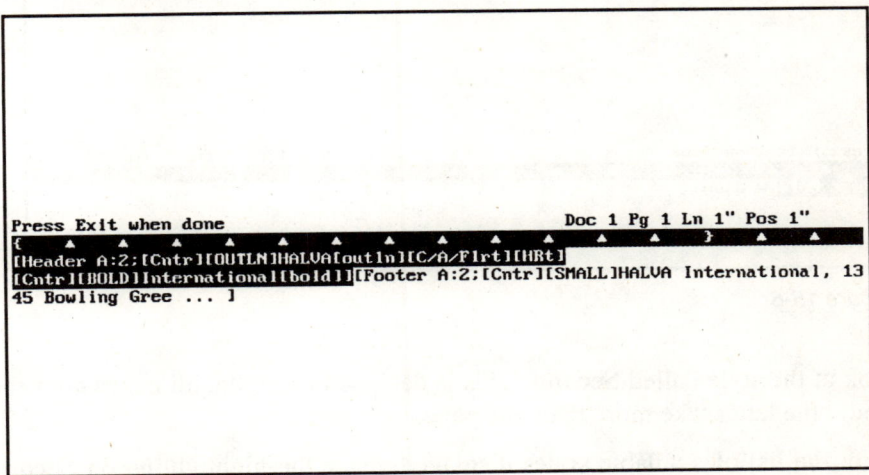

Figure 15-5

5. Press **F7** (Exit) to return to the previous screen and press **F1** (Cancel) to return to the list of **Style** files.
6. Highlight the **Letterhead** file and select **1 On**. Actually nothing happens. That is, nothing that you can see. On the other hand, something did happen.
7. Press **Shift-F7** and select **6 View Document** and you see that there is a letterhead where the top two lines are the company names:

**HALVA**
**International**

and the bottom line is the address:

**HALVA International, 1345 Bowling Green Ave., Manhattan, NY 10004**

*Chapter 15*

Even though there is nothing on the screen, if you now press **Shift-F7** (Print) and select **1 Full Document** the printer prints a blank letter format.

If you want to use this letterhead style, use the **Alt-F8** (Style) function and select **4 Edit** to edit it by replacing HALVA International and the address with your own name or company name and address.

Now look at the next file in the group of **style** files. This one is called **Settings**.

1. With the list of available styles displayed, place the highlighting on **Settings** and press **Enter**.
2. Select **4 Edit** and the Reveal Codes screen displays the codes shown in Fig. 15-6 which turn **Justification** to **Off** and activate the **Widow/Orphan** protection feature.

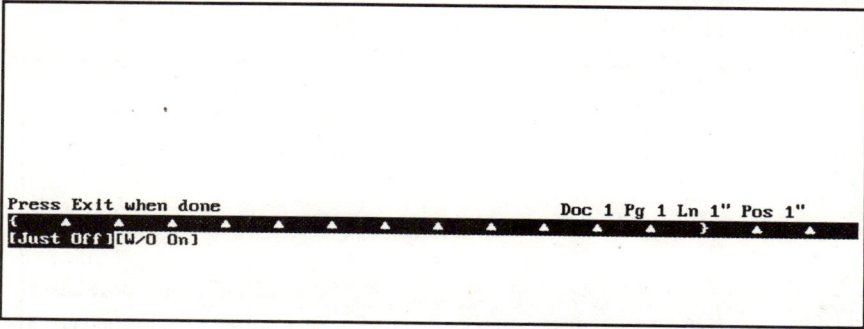

*Figure 15-6*

Next look at the style called **Second**. This is designed to format all pages after the first one, should the letter take more than one page.

1. With the list of available styles displayed, place the highlighting on **Second** and press **Enter**.
2. Select **4 Edit**. The screen displays the codes shown in Fig. 15-7.

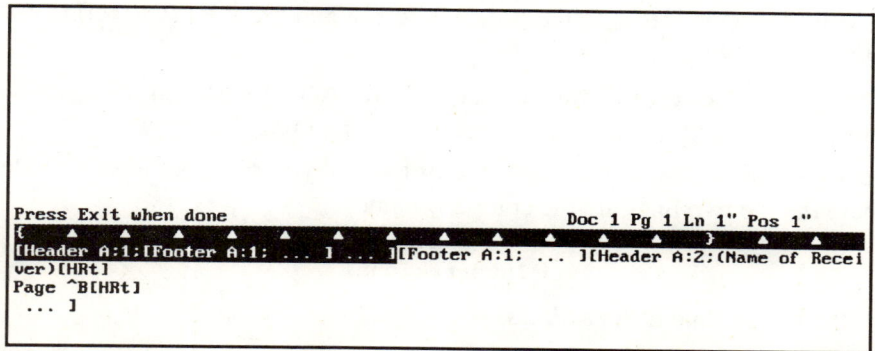

*Figure 15-7*

Again, nothing appears on the screen, but using the **View Document** option you see that it displays:

```
Page 2
February 20, 1991
```

or whatever is applicable.

Next look at the Style file called **Closing**.

1. With the available style files displayed, place the highlighting on **Closing** and press **Enter**.
2. Select **4 Edit** to reveal the codes in that file, shown in Fig. 15-8.

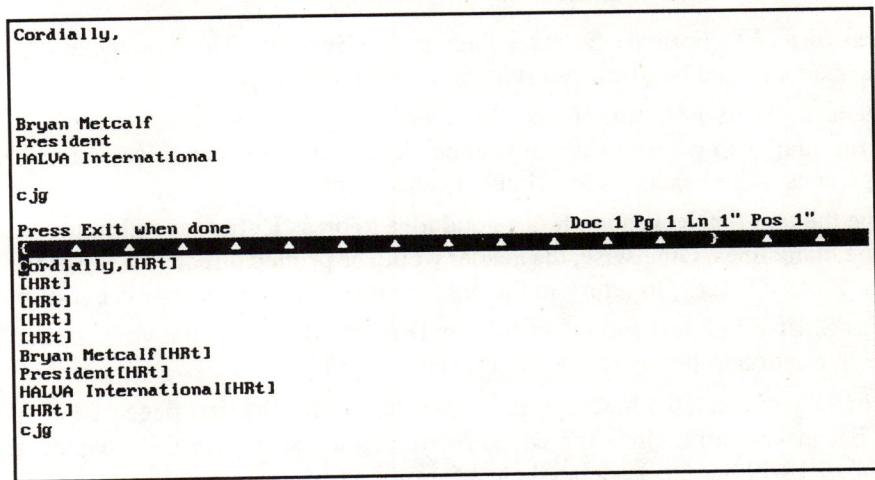

Figure 15-8

3. Press **F7** (Exit) twice and select **1 On**. This time something does happen. The letter closing is actually printed.

It might be pointed out that whatever is accomplished by style files can as easily be accomplished with macros. But the advantage of using **styles** is that they are saved along with the document that used them. Whenever such a document is retrieved, the style is automatically formatted correctly. This is of no great value with individual letters as they are rarely retrieved after they have been sent. But with documents that have repeat value, this function does come in handy.

## CHAPTER 16
## HEADERS AND FOOTERS

Headers are lines of copy appearing at the top of all pages or at the top of selected pages. For instance, when writing articles or chapters for books, the manuscript always includes certain information at the top of the page, such as the name of the author, the title of the article or book, and chapter information.

1. Press **Shift-F8** (Format). Select **2 Page** and **3 Headers**. This is done at the top of your document to be displayed starting with the first page.
2. Select **1 Header A** and from the succeeding option select the one that is representative of where you want your headers used. For instance, selecting **2 Every Page** causes the header to be printed on each page.
3. Type the text for the header. It is a good idea to press **Enter** several times to create some blank lines. Otherwise, the header would be printed directly on top of the body text. Press **F7** (Exit) to return to the document screen. The header is not displayed.
4. Press **Shift-F7** (Print) and select **6 View Document** to see what your header looks like in relation to the rest of the text when it is printed.

In Chapter 11 you created a macro to produce a format for the first page of a chapter or article. That macro did include the codes producing a header. For this chapter, simply create a header without the associated page formatting.

1. Press **Ctrl-F10** (Macro define). Type **HEADER** for the name and enter any description.
2. Press **Enter**.
3. Press **Shift-F8** (Format).
4. Select **2 Page** and **3 Headers**.
5. Select **1 Headers** and **2 Every page**.
6. Type the book or article title and type **Chapter #**.
7. Press **Ctrl-PgUp**. Select **1 Pause**.
8. Press **Alt-F6** (Flush right) and type the author's name.
9. Press **Enter** four times to insert three blank lines.
10. Press **F7** (Exit) **F7** (Exit) to exit the **Format** screen.
11. Press **Ctrl-F10** to end macro definition.

Fig. 16-1 is the complete macro, ready for use.

*Headers and Footers*

```
Macro: Edit

        File              HEADER.WPM
   1 - Description        Create a header
   2 - Action
       ┌────────────────────────────────────────────────────┐
       │ {PAUSE}{Format}2312Book/Article·title/Chapter·#{PAUSE}│
       │ {Flush Right}Author's·name{Enter}                  │
       │ {Enter}                                            │
       │ {Enter}                                            │
       │ {Enter}                                            │
       │ {Exit}{Exit}                                       │
       └────────────────────────────────────────────────────┘

Selection: 0
```

*Figure 16-1*

When you press **Alt-F10**, type **HEADER** (or header), and press **Enter,** the line that you typed is displayed at the top of the screen and macro execution is halted, waiting for you to type a chapter number and related information. Press **Enter** and macro execution continues. Type a letter or a word to indicate the initial cursor position. Press **Shift-F7** (Print) and select **6 View Document** and **1 100%**. Fig. 16-2 is the top of the page.

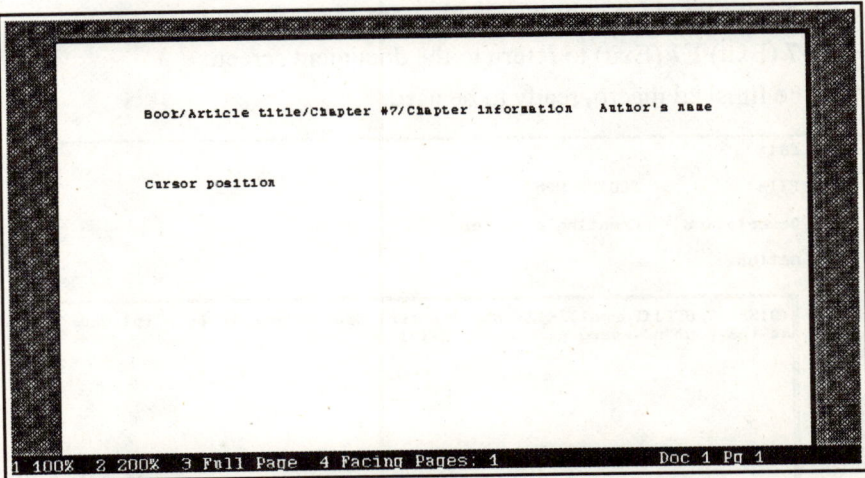

*Figure 16-2*

Chapter 16

## FOOTERS

A footer is the same as a header, but it is printed at the bottom of the page.

1. Press **Shift-F8** (Format). Select **2 Page** and **4 Footers**. Do this with the cursor in page 1 of your document to display the footer starting with the first page.
2. Select **1 Footer A**. From the succeeding option select the one representative of where you want your footer used. For instance, selecting **2 Every Page** causes the footer to be printed on each page.
3. Type the text for your footer. Remember to press **Enter** once or even twice BEFORE typing the text for the footer to create some blank lines. Otherwise, the footer is printed only .16 of an inch below the body text. Press **F7** (Exit) twice to return to the document screen. The footer is not displayed.
4. Press **Shift-F7** (Print) and select **6 View Document** to see what your footer looks like, relative to the rest of the text, when it is printed.

Once more, a simple macro can take care of producing the footer for you.

1. Press **Ctrl-F10** (Macro define). For the name type **FOOTER** and add any description.
2. Press **Shift-F8** (Format). Select **2 Page** and **4 Footers**.
3. Select **1 Footer A** and **2 Every page**.
4. Press **Enter Enter Shift-F6** (Center).
5. Type the copy that is to appear at the bottom of every page.
6. Press **F7** (Exit) **F7** (Exit) to return to the document screen.

Fig. 16-3 is the finished macro, ready to be used.

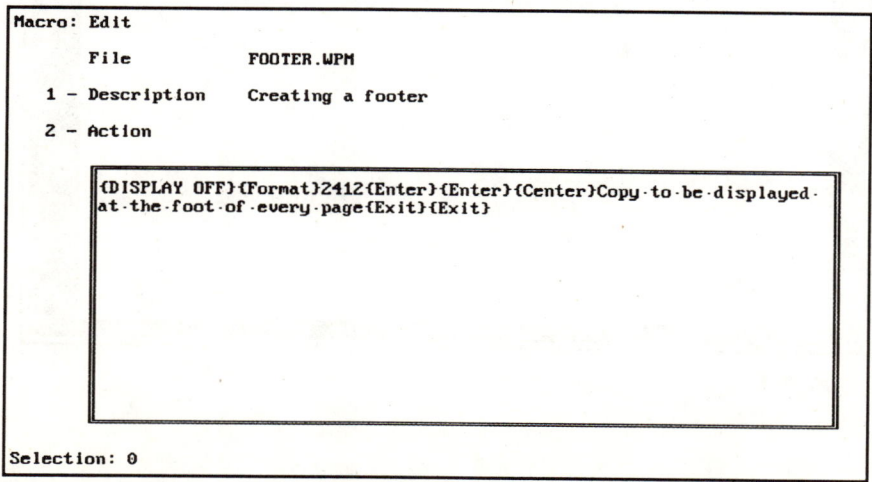

Figure 16-3

Press **Alt-F10**, type **FOOTER**, and press **Enter**. Nothing happens on the screen. Press **Shift-F7** (Print), select **6 View Document**, and press **Down Arrow** to get to the bottom of the page where the footer is displayed as in Fig. 16-4. Press **F7** to return to the document.

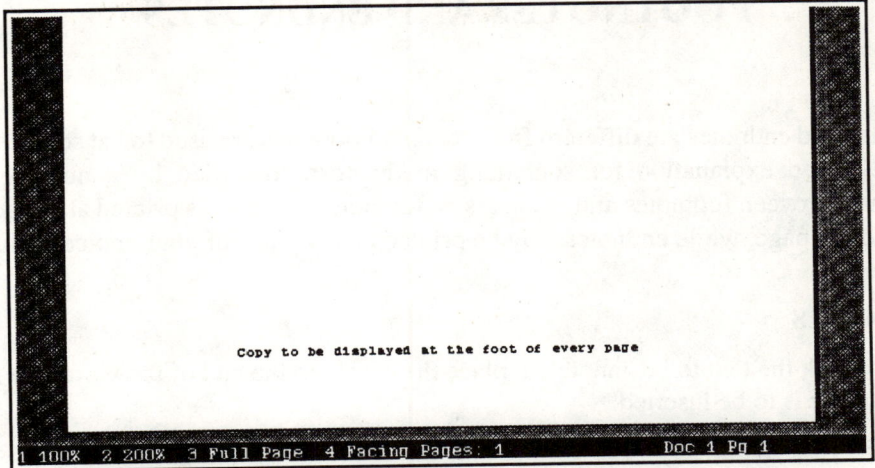

Figure 16-4

## CHAPTER 17
# FOOTNOTES AND ENDNOTES

Footnotes and endnotes are different from footers. Footnotes are used to list sources or to provide added explanation for something in the text, identified by a number. The difference between footnotes and endnotes is: footnotes are always printed at the bottom of the active page, while endnotes may be printed at any place of your choice within the document.

FOOTNOTES

1. To mark the text to be annotated, place the cursor to the end of the word where the number is to be inserted.
2. Press **Ctrl-F7** (Footnote) to display the appropriate menu.
3. Select **1 Footnote** (or 2 Endnote) and select **4 Options**. A list of options along with the default settings is displayed as in Fig. 17-1. You may accept the default settings or you may change them. Press **Enter** to exit the options screen.

```
Footnote Options

    1 - Spacing Within Footnotes              1
             Between Footnotes                0.16"
    2 - Amount of Note to Keep Together       0.5"
    3 - Style for Number in Text              [SUPRSCPT][Note Num][suprscpt]
    4 - Style for Number in Note                      [SUPRSCPT][Note Num][suprscp
    5 - Footnote Numbering Method             Numbers
    6 - Start Footnote Numbers each Page      No
    7 - Line Separating Text and Footnotes    2-inch Line
    8 - Print Continued Message               No
    9 - Footnotes at Bottom of Page           Yes


Selection: 0
```

Figure 17-1

4. Select **1 Create**. You are presented with a blank editing screen with a number displayed at the top left-hand corner. That number is printed along with the footnote

*Footnotes and Endnotes*

and is automatically inserted in the text. The default numbering style is superscript ([1]).

5. Type the text of the footnote. Remember to press **F7** (Exit) when you're finished to return to your document screen where you now see the number inserted at the appropriate position. The footnote itself is not displayed.
6. Press **Shift-F7** (Print) and select **6 View Document** to see what your footnote looks like.

A macro for that purpose first displays the options screen, in case you want to change something. If nothing is to be changed, press **Enter**. The macro then returns, creating the footnote in accordance with the selected options, waiting for you to type the text. After the text is typed, press **Enter**. The macro returns you to the document screen where the footnote number (or other selected symbol) is inserted at the cursor position.

1. Press **Ctrl-F10** (Macro define). For the name type **FOOTNOTE** and enter a description.
2. Press **Ctrl-F7** (Footnote).
3. Select **1 Footnote** and then **4 Options**.
4. Press **Ctrl-PgUp** and select **1 Pause**.
5. Press **Enter**.
6. Press **Ctrl-F7** (Footnote). Select **1 Footnote** and then **1 Create**.
7. Press **Ctrl-PgUp** and select **1 Pause**.
8. Press **Enter**.
9. Press **F7** (Exit).

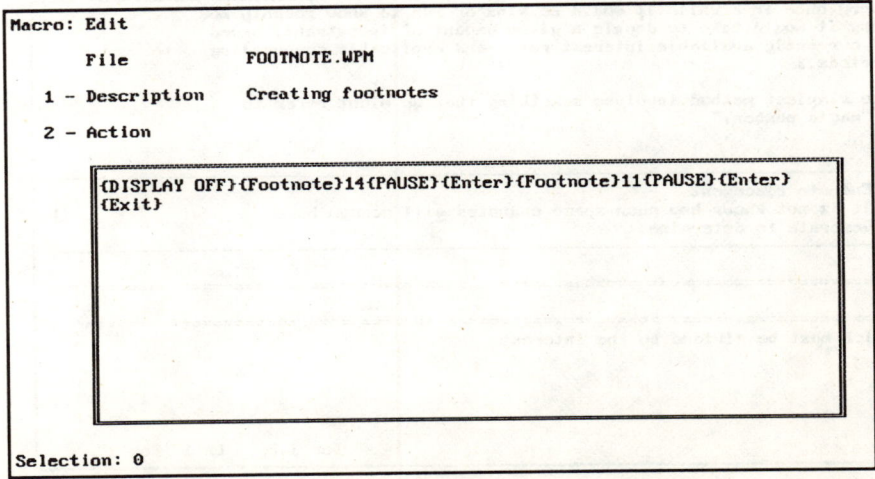

Figure 17-2

10. Press **Ctrl-F10** (Macro define) to end the process.

The completed macro is shown in Fig. 17-2 To test it, place the cursor at the end of any word in some text. Press **Alt-F10** (Macro), type **FOOTNOTE**, and press **Enter**. The option screen is displayed. Either make some changes or press **Enter**. The footnote number, such as [1], is displayed and the cursor is next to it, waiting for you to type the text. Type it and then press **Enter**. You are returned to the document screen where [1] has been inserted at the cursor position.

## ENDNOTES

Endnotes involve a two-step operation. The first step places a number or selected symbol into the text at the cursor position, indicating an endnote is associated with that place in the document. The second part of the operation causes the text to be inserted at the new cursor position.

1. Press **Ctrl-F7** and select **2 Endnote**. Select **1 Create**.

A number appears at the top of a blank document screen, waiting for you to type the text for the endnote. When you're finished, press **F7** (Exit). You're returned to the cursor position in your document where a [1] or similar symbol has been inserted.

Now move the cursor to the place where that text is to appear.

2. Press **Ctrl-F7** (Footnote) and select **3 Endnote Placement**.
3. To the displayed question about numbering reply with either **y** or **n**.
4. A comment box with the message shown in Fig. 17-3 is inserted at the cursor position.

```
Every once in a while it would be kind of fun to know roughly how
long it would take to double a given amount of investment, based
on currently available interest rates and applicable compounding
periods.1

The simplest method involves something that we might refer to as
a "magic number,"

┌─────────────────────────────────────────────────────────────────┐
│ Endnote Placement                                               │
│ It is not known how much space endnotes will occupy here.       │
│ Generate to determine.                                          │
└─────────────────────────────────────────────────────────────────┘

=================================================================
=================================================================
which must be divided by the interest




                                          Doc 1 Pg 2 Ln 1" Pos 1"
```

Figure 17-3

5. Press **Alt-F5** (Mark Text). Select **6 Generate** and **5 Generate Tables, Indexes etc**.
6. To the displayed question reply with **y**.
7. The endnote placement message in Fig. 17-4 is inserted at the cursor position.

```
Every once in a while it would be kind of fun to know roughly how
long it would take to double a given amount of investment, based
on currently available interest rates and applicable compounding
periods.1

The simplest method involves something that we might refer to as
a "magic number,"

  ┌─────────────────────────────────────────────────────────────┐
  │ Endnote Placement                                           │
  └─────────────────────────────────────────────────────────────┘

==================================================================
==================================================================
which must be divided by the interest




                                            Doc 1 Pg 1 Ln 1" Pos 1"
```

Figure 17-4

Press **Shift-F7** (Print) and select **6 View document** and the endnote text is inserted. You may find that its appearance in the text needs to be adjusted. You can do that by using the **Edit** option from the **Footnote** menu.

This routine requires two macros.

1. Press **Ctrl-F10** (Macro define). Name it **ENDNOTE1** and type a description.
2. Press **Ctrl-F7** (Footnote). Select **2 Endnote** and **1 Create**.
3. Press **Ctrl-PgUp** and select **1 Pause**. Press **F7** to return to the document screen.
4. Press **Ctrl-F10** (Macro define) to save that macro.
5. Press **Ctrl-F10** (Macro define). Name it **ENDNOTE2** and type a description.
6. Press **Ctrl-F7** (Footnote). Select **3 Endnote Placement**.
7. To the displayed question type either **y** or **n**.
8. Press **Alt-F5** (Mark Text).
9. Select **6 Generate** and **5 Generate Tables, Indexes etc...**
10. To the displayed question type **y**.
11. Press **Ctrl-F10** (Macro define) to save that macro.

Now place the cursor into position in the text where the reference to the endnote is to appear. Press **Alt-F10** (Macro). Type **ENDNOTE1** and press **Enter**. Type the endnote

*Chapter 17*

text. When finished, press **F7** (Exit). Move the cursor to the position where the endnote text is to be inserted. Press **Alt-F10** (Macro). Type **ENDNOTE2** and press **Enter**. The endnote placement box appears at the designated cursor position in your document. You can repeat using the ENDNOTE2 macro if the text is to appear at several places in the document.

Fig. 17-5 is the ENDNOTE1.WPM macro and Fig. 17-6 is the ENDNOTE2.WPM macro.

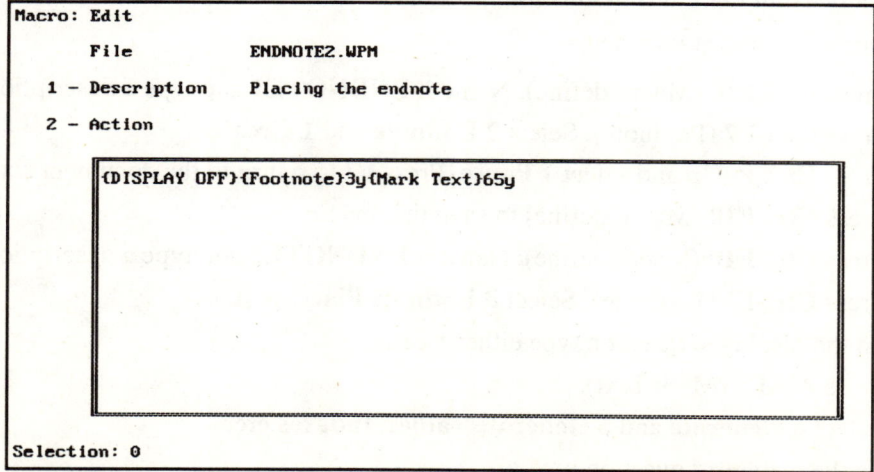

*Figure 17-5*

*Figure 17-6*

## Chapter 18
# AUTOMATIC REFERENCES

Here is a look at another helpful convenience feature that WordPerfect offers. While it is possible to produce documents of most any kind without using these added goodies, they do tend to make life a great deal easier.

The feature discussed here is referred to as **Automatic Reference**. It is used to insert reference numbers, updated automatically when the document is edited and the numbering is affected. For instance, if you are working on a document containing tables of numbers on a given page and text referring to these tables on another page, you want to make sure that the page number that identifies the location of the table remains correct, even if it is changed during subsequent editing.

For the purpose of this example the text file used is a two-page document containing information on one page that must be referenced to some item located on another page. It is shown in Fig. 18-1. You can use any other conveniently available two-page document.

1. Press **Shift-F10** (Retrieve) and retrieve that file. In the two-page document used in this demonstration, reference is made on page 1 to a table on page 2.
2. Move the cursor to the place where the automatic reference is to be inserted. In the demonstration document it is on page 1, the very last line, where reference is made to the table located elsewhere in the document. The reference reads:

**(See Aircraft Performance Table on page  )**

Place the cursor on top of the closing parenthesis.

3. Press **Alt-F5** (Mark Text). Select **1 Automatic Reference** and **3 Mark both, Reference and Target**. In this context, *reference* is the place where the page number is to appear. In this demonstration, it is the place between *page* and the closing parenthesis. *Target*, on the other hand, refers to the item that is to be referenced. In this demonstration it is the AIRCRAFT PERFORMANCE TABLE AT FIVE ALTITUDES.
4. The menu in Fig. 18-2 is now on the document screen. It offers a number of choices. Select **1 Page Number** which returns you to your document.

87

## Chapter 18

```
ALTITUDE SELECTION
Selecting the fastest or the most economic altitude at which to
cruise is one of the most important responsibilities of any
pilot. While aircraft in general tend to be able to develop a
faster cruising speed at higher altitudes, the upper winds often
negate that advantage. The wind component is an important factor
and even winds blowing at a right angle to the aircraft will slow
it down as the pilot is forced to change the heading into the
wind in order to be able to remain on course.

There are a number of computer programs that can be used to
determine the most advantageous altitude, producing printouts
showing the time en route, fuel burn, and ground speed figures
for different altitudes. (See Aircraft Performance Table on page
 .)

Different types of aircraft are affected to a different degree by
the winds aloft. For instance, a 25-knot headwind component will
reduce the ground speed of an aircraft cruising at a true
airspeed of 150 knots by 15% while the same headwind will reduce
the ground speed of a 250-knot aircraft by only 10%.

================================================================
================================================================
AIRCRAFT PERFORMANCE TABLE AT FIVE ALTITUDES

Altitude (feet)    3000      6000      9000      12000     15000
-----------------------------------------------------------------


Time en route      6:34      6:17      6:03      5:52      5:44

Fuel used (gal)    77.4      74.6      72.9      72.0      71.6

Ground speed       113       116       118       120       122

================================================================
================================================================

                                          Doc 1 Pg 5 Ln 1" Pos 1"
```

*Figure 18-1*

```
Tie Reference to:

     1 - Page Number

     2 - Paragraph/Outline Number

     3 - Footnote Number

     4 - Endnote Number

     5 - Graphics Box Number

After selecting a reference type, go to the location of the item you want to
reference in your document and press Enter to mark it as the "target".




Selection: 0
```

*Figure 18-2*

5. Now move the cursor to the first word of the title of the table which in the demonstration document is **AIRCRAFT**. Press **Enter** to identify and mark the target.
6. When asked for the **Target Name** type **aircraft** and then press **Down Arrow**. The cursor automatically returns to the closing parenthesis on the first page, but now the notation reads **(See Aircraft Performance Table on page 2)**.

Create a macro to take care of remembering the sequence of keystrokes.

1. Press **Ctrl-F10** (Macro define). Name it **AUTOREF** and type a description.
2. Press **Alt-F5** (Mark Text) and select **1 Auto Ref**.
3. Select **3 Both Reference and Target** and **1 Page Number**.
4. Press **Ctrl-PgUp** and select **1 Pause**.
5. Press **Ctrl-F10** (Macro define) to end the session. Fig. 18-3 is the finished macro.

```
Macro: Edit
        File            AUTOREF.WPM
    1 - Description     Automatic reference insertion
    2 - Action

        {Mark Text}131{PAUSE}




Selection: 0
```

Figure 18-3

Now place the cursor on the reference position in your document. Press **Alt-F10** (Macro). Type **AUTOREF** and press **Enter**. Macro execution stops while you move the cursor to the target area. Press **Enter Enter**. You're asked to name the target. Type a name. Press **Down Arrow**. The cursor returns to the reference position and the page number is entered at that location.

The page number is automatically adjusted by the reference code if editing changes the relationship between the reference point and the page on which the target is located.

## CHAPTER 19
# INDENTING AND OUTDENTING

There are a number of different ways that WordPerfect lets you format text on a page. Figs. 19-1 and 19-2 show the text document used for this demonstration. It includes several different left margin settings. There are a number of ways to achieve this result, some more convenient than others. If you execute the next sequence of steps, a similar document results.

1. For the first line press **Shift-F6** (Center) and **F6** (Bold). Type the words in uppercase followed by **Enter Enter**. The routine is repeated for the second line.
2. For the third line up to **1990**, start typing at the left margin.
3. Press **Alt-F6** (Flush right) and type **Page 1**. It is aligned with the right margin.
4. Press **Enter Enter** followed by **Alt-F9** (Graphics). Select **5 Line** and **1 Horizontal**. Press **F7** (Exit) to accept the default values. The line does not appear on the screen. To see what it looks like, press **Shift-F7** (Print) and select **6 View Document**.

The next steps involve setting the tab stops to have the various lines start either at the left margin, at Position 2", or Position 3". The following series of keystrokes is used:

1. Press **Shift-F8** (Format) and select **1 Line**. Then select **8 Tab Set**. Press **Home Home Left Arrow Ctrl-End** to delete all tab stops.
2. Move the cursor to Position 2 and type **L**. Move the cursor to position 3 and type **L** (or type **2** and press **Enter** and **3** and press **Enter**). Press **F7** (Exit) twice to return to the document screen.
3. Next type the heading **AVIATION** and press **F4** (→ Indent). The left edge of the entire paragraph moves to the tab stop at Position 2". (Pressing **Tab** would move the cursor to the same position but it would not affect the rest of the paragraph in the same way as **F4** (→ Indent) does.)
4. Type the paragraph of text. Then press **Enter** to add the blank line. Type **Disk #1**. Press **F4** (→ Indent) again to move the cursor to Position 3".
5. Type the block of copy. Since each of the lines in that block of copy ends in a hard return (**Enter**), each of the succeeding lines must be preceded by pressing the indent command twice (**F4 F4**).
6. When the first page is finished, you repeat the heading lines on the second page. Move the cursor to the top of Page 1 (**Home Home Up Arrow**).

```
                              PPG PROGRAMS, INC.

                                Current Software

         Period from August 1 through September 30 1990              Page 1


             AVIATION    A two-disk collection of programs for pilots and FBOs
                         designed to be used with PC DOS or MS DOS computer
                         systems.  The programs are:

                         Disk #1    Business Aircraft Justification
                                    Flight Route File Program
                                    Time Zones Worldwide
                                    Flight Data
                                    Range and Endurance
                                    Weight and Balance
                                    Altitude Selection
                                    Aircraft Expense Records
                                    Air Taxi/Charter Program

                         Disk #2    Perpetual Calendar
                                    Currency Conversion Program
                                    Aircraft for Sale and Prospect File
                                    Cost of Loan Calculation Program
                                    Flight Plan Program
                                    Electronic Logbook
                                    Appointment Calendar
                                    Aircraft, Engine, Avionics Maint.Records

             REAL
             ESTATE      A two-disk collection of programs for real estate
                         brokers designed to be used with PC DOS or MS DOS
                         computer systems.  The Programs are:

                         Disk #1    Mortgage Calculating Program
                                    Residential Properties File
                                    Commercial Properties File
                                    Residential Properties Prospect File
                                    Commercial Properties Prospect File
                                    Rent versus Purchase Analysis
                                    Profit/Loss from Income Property
                                    Empty Acreage Available File
                                    Empty Acreage Prospect File

                         Disk #2    Weights and Measures Conversions
                                    Appointment Calendar
                                    Name/Address List with Print Option
                                    Perpetual Calendar
                                    Annual Income/Expense Records
                                    Advertising Cost versus Returns
                                    Credit Card Register
```

Figure 19-1

*Chapter 19*

```
                         PPG PROGRAMS, INC.

                          Current Software

          Period from August 1 through September 30 1990         Page 2


          MODEL
          RAIL-
          ROADING    A one-disk collection of programs for model railroaders
                     designed to be used with PC DOS or MS DOS computer
                     systems.  The programs are:

                     Disk #1   Converting Linear Measures from/to Scale
                               Converting mph to feet per minute
                               Converting Real Time to Scale Time
                               Digital Stop Watch
                               Prototype Speed by Scale Distance
                               Scale Distance by Prototype Speed
                               Elevation Change versus Distance/Grade
                               Curve Distance Based on Radii
                               Ohm's Law
                               Electrical Wire Resistance
                               Fractions and Decimal Equivalents
                               Gear Speed Ratios
                               Weight and Measures Conversions
```

*Figure 19-2*

## Indenting and Outdenting

7. Press **Alt-F4** (Block). Move the cursor down to just above the A in AVIATION to identify everything above, including the invisible horizontal line, as a block.
8. Press **Ctrl-F4** (Move). Select **1 Block** and then select **2 Copy**. Move the cursor to the very top of the second page and press **Enter**. The entire block is copied to the top of the second page.
9. Press **Home Right Arrow** to place the cursor on the **1** in Page 1. Delete it and replace it with **2**. To make sure that everything is the way it is supposed to be, press **Shift-F7** (Print) and select **6 View Document**.

Examine the two finished pages. Obviously the block of copy following REAL ESTATE should be moved up one line. Also the block of copy on the second page following MODEL RAILROADING should be moved up two lines. WordPerfect can accomplish that easily:

1. Move the cursor to the line on which REAL appears and make a note of the line number appearing in the status line. It is probably **Ln 6.18"**.
2. Now move the cursor to the first letter (**A**) of the paragraph to be moved. Press **Shift-F8** (Format) and select **4 Other**. From it select **1 Advance** and then select **3 Line**. This results in a display at the left bottom corner of the screen of **Adv. to line** and a number.
3. Type the number you jotted down to replace the one displayed. Press **Enter** to secure the new setting. Press **F7** (Exit) to return to the document screen. You notice that nothing has changed. The change does not appear on the screen but it affects the way the document is printed. To make sure, press **Shift-F7** (Print) and select **6 View Document**.
4. Press **Home Down Arrow** to get to the very bottom of the page. You may find that the first line of Page 2 (PPG PROGRAMS, INC.) has suddenly moved to the bottom line of Page 1. Use **Enter** to move it back to its proper position at the top of Page 2 before making the correction for that page.
5. Now repeat the same procedure on the second page. Note the line number for MODEL (probably **Ln 2.35"**) and then place the cursor on the A in the following paragraph, repeating the above steps.
6. Now press **F10** (Save) to save the document and give it a filename.
7. Press **Shift-F7** (Print) and select **1 Full Document** to obtain a hard copy of your efforts.

There are a number of options able to produce a similar result. For one, it is awkward to have to press **Enter F4 F4** after typing each line in those paragraphs describing the files on each disk. A simpler method is:

1. Press **Shift-F8** (Format). Select **1 Line** and **7 Margins, Left/Right**.
2. Type **3**, press **Enter**, and press **F7** (Exit) twice.

All the lines in the block of copy now start three inches from the left edge of the paper. When the block has been typed, use the above steps again, typing either **1** or **2** for the left margin position.

You want to make sure that the beginning of the second page always starts where it is supposed to with no chance of its first line(s) creeping up into the bottom of the preceding page. With the cursor at the end of the last line on Page 1, press **Ctrl-Enter** to produce a hard page break.

When you want blocks of text to be indented left as well as right, press **Shift-F4**. It results in identical indentation on both sides, causing the text to be horizontally centered on the page.

If the text on a given page is too short to fill the page, you might want to have it centered vertically. Place the cursor anywhere on the page to be centered. Press **Shift-F8** (Format). Select **2 Page** and **1 Center Page** (top to bottom). Type **y**. The text now appears evenly centered between the top and the bottom of the page. If a header and/or a footer exists on the page, the text is centered between them.

## CHAPTER 20
# LINE NUMBERING

The line numbering option available with WordPerfect can come in handy under a number of circumstances. One typical example would be a list of hundreds of items, each occupying one line, such as the brief sample in Fig. 20-1. Here 17 software items are listed and the line numbering makes counting the number of items unnecessary. If you use the **Ctrl-F9** (Merge/Sort) option to alphabetize or otherwise resort the list, the line numbering is not affected, as in Fig. 20-2.

```
 1  WordPerfect              1  AutoSketch
 2  dBase IV                 2  dBase IV
 3  Lotus 1-2-3              3  Design CAD 3D
 4  Quattro Pro              4  DrawPerfect
 5  PlanPerfect              5  Energraphics
 6  DrawPerfect              6  Exact
 7  Design CAD 3D            7  Library
 8  Publish It!              8  Lotus 1-2-3
 9  Exact                    9  Pascal
10  Energraphics            10  PC Paintbrush
11  Library                 11  PlanPerfect
12  TurboBASIC              12  Powerbasic
13  Powerbasic              13  Publish It!
14  Pascal                  14  Quattro Pro
15  PC Paintbrush           15  TurboBASIC
16  VP-Expert               16  VP-Expert
17  AutoSketch              17  WordPerfect
```

*Figure 20-1*                *Figure 20-2*

The line numbering option is accessed by pressing **Shift-F8** (Format) and selecting **1 Line** and **5 Line Numbering** and typing **Y** for yes. Fig. 20-3 is the line numbering menu with the available options. In most instances **5 Restart Numbering on Each Page** should be changed to **No** when such lists involve several pages.

Be sure to invoke the line numbering option at the very top of the page. If you don't, it might start numbering farther down, not counting the first few items. To be sure, you can create a macro that performs all necessary steps, as the one in Fig. 20-4. It moves the

Chapter 20

cursor to the very top of the screen, invokes the line numbering option, and makes sure that line numbering continues page after page.

This function is also useful when you're writing for a newspaper or similar periodical where each column occupies a given number of characters and there is only room for a certain number of lines. As you type, it is good to know whether what you are writing is too long or too short.

```
Format: Line Numbering
        1 - Count Blank Lines                          Yes
        2 - Number Every n Lines, where n is           1
        3 - Position of Number from Left Edge          0.6"
        4 - Starting Number                            1
        5 - Restart Numbering on Each Page             Yes




Selection: 0
```

*Figure 20-3*

```
Macro: Edit
        File            LINENUM.WPM
    1 - Description     Line numbering
    2 - Action

        {DISPLAY OFF}{Home}{Home}{Up}{Format}15y5n{Exit}




Selection: 0
```

*Figure 20-4*

To set this up for a column width of 42 characters, take the following steps:

1. Press **Shift-F1** (Setup). Select **8 Units of Measure**.
2. Type **1 p 2 p** to change the units of measure to points all around.
3. Press **F7** (Exit) to return to the document screen.
4. The status line reads Pos 72p because one inch is divided into 72 points. Now type 42 characters in the 10-characters-per-inch (CPI) mode. Typing A through Z and A through P represents 42 characters.
5. Note the Pos number on the status line. Deduct it from 612 (8 ½ inches is 8.5*72 or 612 points) and remember or jot down the result.
6. Press **Shift-F8** (Format). Select **1 Line** and **7 Margins Left/Right**.
7. Both now show 72p. Press **Enter** to accept the default for the left margin. Then type the number that you jotted down in step 5 for the right margin and press **Enter** and **F7** (Exit).

Your page is now set up to accept 42 characters. For the next steps:

8. Press **Shift-F8** (Format). Select **1 Line** and **5 Line Numbering**.
9. Type **Y** to change that line to **Yes**.
10. Press **F7** (Exit) to return to the document screen.

As you now type your column, the number of lines is constantly counted, regardless of whether you are typing in single-space or double-space format. At any time, if you want to see how much you've already written, press **Shift-F7** (Print), select **6 View document**, and select **2** for double size and the numbers are displayed, telling you exactly where you are.

As usual, if this sort of thing is to be used more than just once, a macro eliminates the need for remembering all those keystrokes. Fig. 20-5 is the macro that sets up your page for any specified number of characters per line. It halts execution with the cursor in the Margins Right position. Type the desired number using the chart in Fig. 20-6 to determine the correct number for any number of characters per line. Press **Enter** and macro execution continues.

When you're back at the document screen, use the macro in Fig. 20-4 to activate line numbering. Then start typing. When you're finished, use the macro in Fig. 20-7 to return the units of measure to inches.

Fig. 20-8 is a variation on the original macro. It ends in a command that chains the line numbering macro (LINENUM.WPM) to it. That way you only execute one macro to get ready to start typing.

Finally, you can invoke the line numbering option and use it with previously recorded documents.

## Chapter 20

```
Macro: Edit
        File              42CHAR.WPM
  1 - Description
  2 - Action

    ┌─────────────────────────────────────────┐
    │ {Setup}81p2p{Exit}{Format}17{Enter}     │
    │ {PAUSE}{Enter}                          │
    │ {Exit}                                  │
    │                                         │
    │                                         │
    │                                         │
    │                                         │
    └─────────────────────────────────────────┘

Selection: 0
```

*Figure 20-5*

| Char | points | Char | points | Char | points | Char | points |
|------|--------|------|--------|------|--------|------|--------|
| 1    | 532.8  | 16   | 424.8  | 31   | 316.8  | 46   | 208.8  |
| 2    | 525.6  | 17   | 417.6  | 32   | 309.6  | 47   | 201.6  |
| 3    | 518.4  | 18   | 410.4  | 33   | 303.4  | 48   | 194.4  |
| 4    | 511.2  | 19   | 403.2  | 34   | 295.2  | 49   | 187.2  |
| 5    | 504    | 20   | 396    | 35   | 288    | 50   | 180    |
| 6    | 496.8  | 21   | 388.8  | 36   | 280.8  | 51   | 172.8  |
| 7    | 489.6  | 22   | 381.6  | 37   | 273.6  | 52   | 165.6  |
| 8    | 482.4  | 23   | 374.4  | 38   | 266.4  | 53   | 158.4  |
| 9    | 475.2  | 24   | 367.2  | 39   | 259.2  | 54   | 151.2  |
| 10   | 468    | 25   | 360    | 40   | 252    | 55   | 144    |
| 11   | 460    | 26   | 352.8  | 41   | 244.8  | 56   | 136.8  |
| 12   | 453.6  | 27   | 345.6  | 42   | 237.6  | 57   | 129.6  |
| 13   | 446.4  | 28   | 338.4  | 43   | 230.4  | 58   | 126.4  |
| 14   | 439.2  | 29   | 331.2  | 44   | 223.2  | 60   | 115.2  |
| 15   | 432    | 30   | 324    | 45   | 216    | 61   | 108    |

*Figure 20-6*

# Line Numbering

```
Macro: Edit

        File            CHAR42.WPM
   1 - Description      Restore default condition
   2 - Action

        ┌────────────────────────────────────────┐
        │ {DISPLAY OFF}{Setup}81"2"{Exit}        │
        │                                        │
        │                                        │
        │                                        │
        │                                        │
        └────────────────────────────────────────┘

Selection: 0
```

*Figure 20-7*

```
Macro: Edit

        File            42CHAR.WPM
   1 - Description      42 character per column line
   2 - Action

        ┌────────────────────────────────────────┐
        │ {Setup}81p2p{Exit}{Format}17{Enter}    │
        │ {PAUSE}{Enter}                         │
        │ {Exit}{CHAIN}linenum.wpm~              │
        │                                        │
        │                                        │
        └────────────────────────────────────────┘

Selection: 0
```

*Figure 20-8*

99

CHAPTER 21
# DRAWING LINES

WordPerfect includes a function used for drawing horizontal or vertical lines in different styles. This is a graphic function and requires that your printer can print such lines. To make sure, take these steps:

1. Press **Ctrl-F3** (Screen) and select **2 Line Draw**.
2. Fig. 21-1 is the list of options. Type **1** and use the cursor keys to draw a box.

```
1 |: 2 ||: 3 *: 4 Change; 5 Erase; 6 Move: 1            Ln 1" Pos 1"
```

Figure 21-1

3. Press **Ctrl-F3** (Screen) again. This time you must select **2 Line Draw**. Select a different line style and draw another box.
4. Fig. 21-2 shows boxes in five different line styles. Copy that and send it to your printer (**Shift-F7** (Print) **2 Page**) to see if it prints your work.

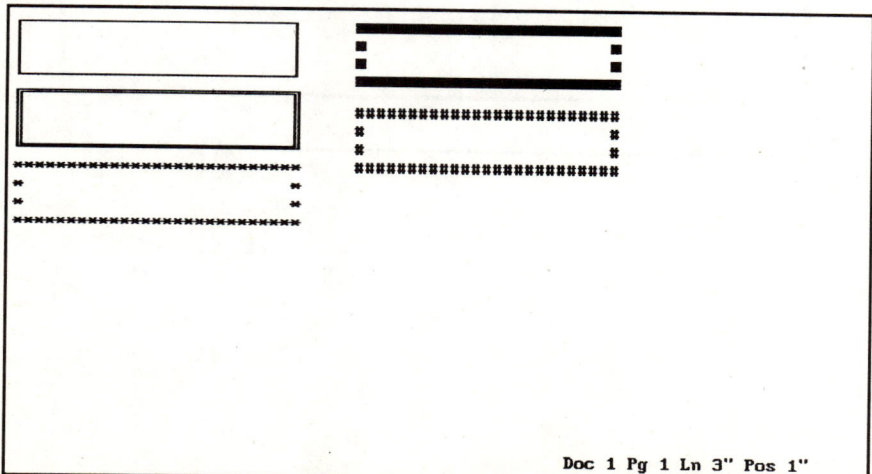

Figure 21-2

100

If it does not print the first two and the fourth box, then it does not print graphics. You can still use the line draw function, but you must use actual keyboard characters such as hyphens (-), underlines (_), vertical lines (|) or any other characters of your choice.

Fig. 21-3 is a macro that stops execution after selecting the single-line option and Fig. 21-4 selects the double-line option. In either case, you can start drawing any rectangular shape you choose, or use these lines to enclose any amount of text to set it off from the rest.

```
Macro: Edit
        File              LINE1.WPM
    1 - Description       Line Draw, single line
    2 - Action
        ┌─────────────────────────────────────────────┐
        │ {DISPLAY OFF}{Screen}21{PAUSE}{Exit}        │
        │                                             │
        │                                             │
        │                                             │
        │                                             │
        └─────────────────────────────────────────────┘
Selection: 0
```

Figure 21-3

```
Macro: Edit
        File              LINE2.WPM
    1 - Description       Line Draw, double line
    2 - Action
        ┌─────────────────────────────────────────────┐
        │ {DISPLAY OFF}{Screen}22{PAUSE}{Exit}        │
        │                                             │
        │                                             │
        │                                             │
        │                                             │
        └─────────────────────────────────────────────┘
Selection: 0
```

Figure 21-4

*Chapter 21*

WordPerfect includes another line-drawing option. This is from inside the graphics function. It can be used to draw horizontal and vertical lines at a predetermined position on the screen and of a predetermined length. Since these are graphic lines, they do not appear on the screen and can only be examined by using the View document option from the print menu.

1. Press **Alt-F9** (Graphics). Fig. 21-5 is the menu line across the bottom of the screen.

```
1 Figure; 2 Table; 3 Text Box; 4 User-defined Box; 5 Line: 0
```

*Figure 21-5*

2. Select **5 Line**. The Line menu is shown in Fig. 21-6.

```
1 Horizontal Line; 2 Vertical Line: 0
```

*Figure 21-6*

3. Select **1 Horizontal**. Fig. 21-7 is the menu. You use these options to determine the horizontal position of the line, the line length, width, and shading. When these determinations are made and **F7** (Exit) is pressed, the line of the selected character appears on the vertical position on the page where the cursor is located.

```
Graphics: Horizontal Line
    1 - Horizontal Position          Left & Right
    2 - Length of Line
    3 - Width of Line                0.01"
    4 - Gray Shading (% of black)    100%
```

*Figure 21-7*

*Drawing Lines*

4. Repeat steps 1 and 2. Select **2 Vertical**. Fig. 21-8 is the menu. It asks that you enter the horizontal and vertical position of the line, the line length, width and shading. Again, press **F7** (Exit) when you're satisfied with your selections.

```
Graphics: Vertical Line

    1 - Horizontal Position           Left Margin
    2 - Vertical Position             Full Page
    3 - Length of Line
    4 - Width of Line                 0.01"
    5 - Gray Shading (% of black)     100%
```

*Figure 21-8*

Fig. 21-9 is a macro used to draw horizontal lines. It stops execution at the menu screen, waiting for you to enter the desired parameters. When that is done, press **Enter**. Macro execution continues, accessing the Print and View document functions, and finally displaying the line on the screen. Fig. 21-10 is an identical macro, except that it displays the menu for vertical lines and eventually displays the vertical line on the screen.

While you can draw very wide lines with controlled shading, it is not possible to print text over such gray areas or to cause a gray area to be placed over text that was typed previously.

```
Macro: Edit
        File            HLINE1.WPM
    1 - Description     Horizontal line
    2 - Action
        ┌─────────────────────────────────────────────────┐
        │ {DISPLAY OFF}{Graphics}5111{PAUSE}{Exit}{Print}61│
        │                                                 │
        │                                                 │
        │                                                 │
        │                                                 │
        └─────────────────────────────────────────────────┘
Selection: 0
```

*Figure 21-9*

## Chapter 21

```
Macro: Edit

      File              VLINE1.WPM
  1 - Description       Vertical line
  2 - Action

      ┌─────────────────────────────────────────────────────────┐
      │ {DISPLAY OFF}{Graphics}5211{PAUSE}{Exit}{Print}61        │
      │                                                         │
      │                                                         │
      │                                                         │
      │                                                         │
      │                                                         │
      └─────────────────────────────────────────────────────────┘

Selection: 0
```

*Figure 21-10*

# CHAPTER 22
# COMMENT BOXES

WordPerfect allows adding comments anywhere in a document. These comments are displayed on the screen enclosed in rectangular boxes. They usually contain instructions as to what to do next. That can be especially useful when WordPerfect is filling out preprinted documents where the printer must be told where to print what. The function can also be used to print letters or documents in a consistently identical format.

Start with a relatively simple example: a letter in which the date, close, and signature are printed flush right while the rest is printed in the normal fashion. Such format would require six comments as in Fig. 22-1.

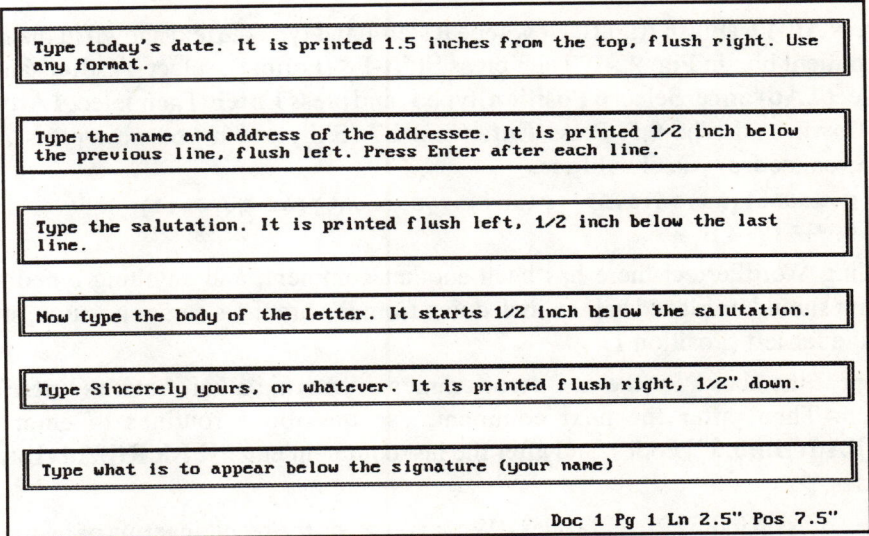

Figure 22-1

## Chapter 22

1. With the document screen blank, press **Ctrl-F5** (Text In/Out) and select **5 Comment**. Then select **1 Create**. The screen displays an empty rectangular box with the cursor in the upper left-hand corner and a reminder in the status line to press Exit when done. Type: **Type today's date. It is printed 1.5 inches from the top, flush right. Use any format.** Do NOT press Enter but rather press **F7** (Exit) and the rectangular box is resized automatically, conforming to the amount of text.

2. If the **Ln** and **Pos** measurements in the status line are displayed as line and column numbers, press **Shift-F1** (Setup) and select **8 Units of Measure**. Select " **inches** (or centimeters if you prefer), then press **Enter F7** (Exit) to return to the document screen. This tells the printer where to print on the page in terms of inches.

3. Press **Shift-F8** (Format), select **4 Other,** and then select **1 Advance**. Select **2 Down,** type **1.5**, and press **Enter F7** (Exit). Now press **Alt-F6** (Flush right) and if you now press **Alt-F3** (Reveal codes), you should see **[Comment][AdvDn:1.5"] [Flsh Rt]**, telling WordPerfect that there has been a comment. Anything typed at this point should be placed one and a half inches from the top of the page (allowing for printed letterheads) and flush right.

4. Press **Alt-F6** (Flush Right). Now repeat step 1 and type the text shown in the second comment box in Fig. 22-1. Then press **Shift-F8** (Format), select **4 Other,** and then select **1 Advance**. Select **6 Position**, type **1**, and press **Enter**. Then select **1 Advance, 2 Down,** and type **0.5**. Press **Enter** and **F7** (Exit) and if you now press **Alt-F3** (Reveal codes) you should see:

   ```
   [Comment][AdvDn:1.5"][Flsh Rt][Comment][AdvToPos:1]
   [AdvDn:0.5"]
   ```

   telling WordPerfect there has been another comment, and anything typed at this point should be placed half an inch down from the previous cursor position, starting at the far left (Position 1).

5. Repeat the above for the next two comments, entering a hard return (**Enter**) after each. Then, after the next comment, use the above routines to enter **[Flsh Rt][AdvDn:0.5"]** codes, and after the last comment enter **[Flsh Rt][AdvDn:1.5"]** codes.

6. Now press **Alt-F3** (Reveal codes). What you see is the result in terms of instructions as to where subsequently typed text is printed as in Fig. 22-2. Press **Alt-F3** (Reveal codes) again to return to the document screen and press **F10** (Save) to save the work using any filename of your choosing.

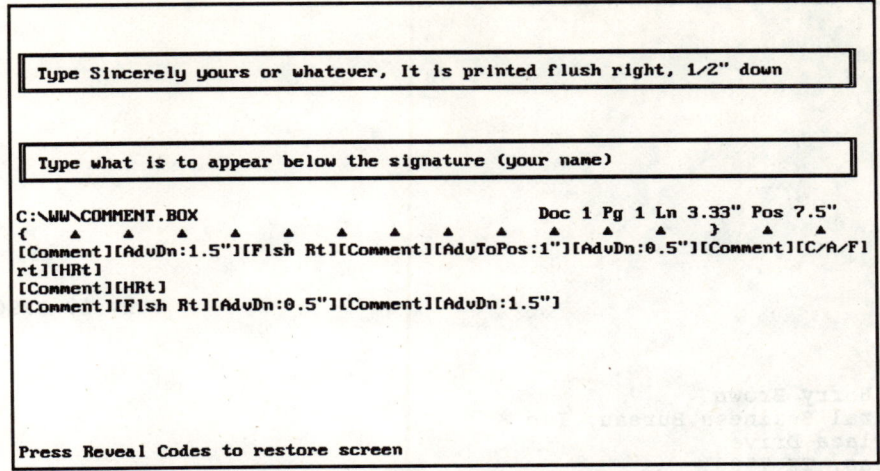

*Figure 22-2*

7. Press **F7** (Exit) and type **n n** to clear the screen. Then press **Shift-F10** (Retrieve) and type the filename that you used to save the letter comment format file. The screen should again look like Fig. 22-1.

8. Now follow the instructions in the first comment box. Type the date, but when finished typing, do NOT press Enter. Rather, press **Right Arrow** and the cursor moves to the top right position under the second comment box. Press **Enter** to move the cursor down one line and flush left. Type the name and address, using **Enter** at the end of each line but press **Right Arrow** after typing the last line.

9. Type the salutation (Dear...), press **Right Arrow**, and then type the body of the letter. When finished, press **Right Arrow**. Then type **Sincerely,** or whatever you like, followed by **Right Arrow**, and finally type your name.

10. Press **Shift-F7** (Print) and select either **1 Full Document** or **2 Page** and when the printer is finished printing your letter, it should look like Fig. 22-3.

Chapter 22

```
                                                           July 1, 1990

Mr. Harry Brown
Central Business Bureau, Inc.
11 Plaza Drive
Dallas, TX 75001

Dear Harry:

This is the body of the letter.  It'll have more than one line
and the automatic wordwrap is in effect.  The letter can be of
any length because the next comment will not appear until you
have finished typing.  When finished, press **RightArrow**.


                                                              Sincerely,




                                                              Paul Garrison
```

Figure 22-3

Comment Boxes

If you want to write a macro that produces the comment boxes, end it with {PAUSE} as in Fig. 22-4.

```
Macro: Edit
        File            COMMENT.WPM
    1 - Description     Adding comment boxes
    2 - Action

            {DISPLAY OFF}{Text In/Out}51{PAUSE}




Selection: 0
```

Figure 22-4

Another way to use this feature is to design a business form into which data can be entered by anyone, even someone unfamiliar with the form. It displays all the necessary prompts in the form of comments.

For the purpose of this demonstration, design an order form similar to the one shown in Fig. 22-5. After that, insert the appropriate comments and enter all codes that cause data being entered to be printed in the appropriate places.

1. Place the cursor several lines below the ORDER FORM line. Make a note of the measure listed in the status line for **Ln**. Press **Shift-F8** (Format) and select **4 Other**. Select **1 Advance** and select **3 Line**. The number that now appears automatically should be the same that you noted down (if not, change it by typing the correct value). Press **Enter Enter** and press **F7** (Exit) to return to the document screen.

2. Press **Alt-F6** (Flush right), press **Ctrl-F5** (Text In/Out), and select **5 Comment** and **1 Create** to create an empty comment box. In it type **Enter today's date** and press **F7** (Exit). The box shrinks to the appropriate size and appears in your document.

3. Place the cursor anywhere on the **Purchase Order #** line and note the value displayed for **Ln**. Press **Shift-F8** (Format), select **4 Other**, then **1 Advance**, and select **3 Line**, and the displayed value should coincide with the one you noted. Press **Enter Enter** and press **F7** (Exit) to return to the document screen.

Chapter 22

**Berger Publications, Inc.**
**2007 Central Expressway**
**Dallas, TX 75011**
**(214) 555 1234**

ORDER FORM

                                        Purchase Order #

Item            Quantity            Price           Total
-----------------------------------------------------------

Totals              +                                   +











Ship to:




Not later than:





                                        Berger Publications, Inc.
                                                              by:

Figure 22-5

# Comment Boxes

4. Press **Alt-F6** (Flush right). Press **Ctrl-F5** (Text In/Out) and select **5 Comment** and **1 Create** to create an empty comment box. In it type **Enter the purchase order number** and press **F7** (Exit). The box shrinks to the appropriate size and appears in your document.

5. Place the cursor just above Item. Press **Alt-F7** (Math/Columns) and select **2 Math Def**. Change the **2** under column **C** to **0**, which displays a **C** after the **Calculation 1** line with the cursor to the right of it. Type **A*B** because you want the quantity to be multiplied by the unit price. Move the cursor to the first **2** in the bottom row and change it to **0** because you want no decimal places to be displayed in the quantity column. Fig. 22-6 is the result. Press **F7** (Exit) twice to return to the document screen.

```
Math Definition           Use arrow keys to position cursor

Columns                   A B C D E F G H I J K L M N O P Q R S T U V W X

Type                      2 2 0 2 2 2 2 2 2 2 2 2 2 2 2 2 2 2 2 2 2 2 2 2

Negative Numbers          ( ( ( ( ( ( ( ( ( ( ( ( ( ( ( ( ( ( ( ( ( ( ( (

Number of Digits to       0 2 2 2 2 2 2 2 2 2 2 2 2 2 2 2 2 2 2 2 2 2 2 2
  the Right (0-4)

Calculation    1     C    A*B
  Formulas     2
               3
               4

Type of Column:
    0 = Calculation    1 = Text      2 = Numeric    3 = Total

Negative Numbers
    ( = Parentheses (50.00)         - = Minus Sign  -50.00


Press Exit when done
```

Figure 22-6

6. Press **Shift-F8** (Format), select **1 Line**, select **8 Tab Set**, and press **Home Home Left Arrow Ctrl-End** to erase all tab settings. Move the cursor to the **3"** position and type **L**. Move the cursor to the **5.1"** position and type **L**. Move the cursor to the **6.5"** position and type **L**. Press **F7** (Exit) twice to return to the document screen.

7. Press **Alt-F7** (Math/Columns) and select **1 Math On**. Press **Ctrl-F5** (Text In/Out) and select **5 Comment** and **1 Create** to create an empty comment box. In it type:

**Type item description,     press Ctrl-F6**
**Type quantity ordered,     press Ctrl-F6**
**Type unit price,           press Tab**
**Press Enter to enter the next item and repeat the above.**

**When finished press Enter and Down Arrow until the cursor is below the "Totals" line. Press Alt-F7 and select 2 Calculate, and then press Down Arrow to get to the next comment.**

111

Chapter 22

Now press **F7** (Exit). The box is resized to the appropriate size and appears in your document.

8. Move the cursor to the line above **Ship to:**, press **Alt-F7** (Math/Columns), and select **1 Math Off**. Place the cursor in a position one line below **Ship to:** and note the value displayed for **Ln**. Press **Shift-F8** (Format), select **4 Other** and then **1 Advance**, and select **3 Line** and the displayed value should coincide with the one you noted. Press **Enter**. Select **1 Advance** and **6 Position**. Then type **1** if it isn't already displayed. Press **Enter Enter** and **F7** (Exit) to return to the document screen.

9. Press **Ctrl-F5** (Text In/Out) and select **5 Comment** and **1 Create**. Into the displayed comment box type **Type the shipping information** and press **F7** (Exit) to return to the document screen with its new comment box.

10. Place the cursor one space to the right of **Not later than:** and note the values displayed for **Ln** and **Pos**. Then press **Shift-F8** (Format) and in succession select **4 Other, 1 Advance, 3 Line,** which should show a value that coincides with the one you noted. Press **Enter** and again in succession select **1 Advance, 6 Position** which should again show a value that coincides with the one you noted. Press **Enter Enter** and press **F7** (Exit) to return to the document screen.

11. Press **Ctrl-F5** (Text In/Out) and select **5 Comment** and **1 Create**. Into the displayed comment box type **Enter date by which merchandise must be shipped** and press **F7** (Exit) to return to the document screen with its new comment box.

12. Place the cursor anywhere on the **by:** line and note the value displayed for **Ln**. Press **Shift-F8** (Format), select **4 Other** and then **1 Advance**, and select **3 Line**. The displayed value should coincide with the one you noted. Press **Enter Enter** and **F7** (Exit) to return to the document screen.

13. Press **Alt-F6** (Flush right). Press **Ctrl-F5** (Text In/Out) and select **5 Comment** and **1 Create**. Into the displayed comment box type **Type your name and title** and press **F7** (Exit) to return to the document screen with its new comment box.

14. Press **F10** (Save) to save your document with all its comment boxes under a filename of your choice.

15. Press **Home Home Up Arrow** to get to the top of the document and use the arrow keys until the cursor is under the first comment box at the right of the screen. Type the date.

16. Use the arrow keys until the cursor is under the second comment box at the right of the screen. Type the purchase order number.

17. Use the arrow keys until the cursor is under the third comment box at the left of the screen. Follow the instructions in the comment box exactly.

18. Use the arrow keys until the cursor is under the fourth comment box at the left of the screen. Type the address to which the merchandise is to be shipped.

19. Use the arrow keys until the cursor is under the fifth comment box at the left middle of the screen. Type the date by which the merchandise must have been shipped.

20. Use the arrow keys until the cursor is under the sixth comment box at the right of the screen. Type your name and title.

21. Save the document (**F10** (Save)) under a filename of your choice. Press **Shift-F7** (Print) and select **1 Full Document**. The printer prints your formatted document. (Depending on your printer, some of these instructions may have to be adjusted.)

To use this function to enter data onto preprinted forms, it is necessary to identify what is to be printed where in terms of measurements. Use a ruler to determine the distances from the top of the form and from the left edge of the form in inches (or centimeters), entering the appropriate codes, using the steps described above. Then enter the appropriate comment boxes and after a certain amount of trial and error, you're in business.

Chapter 22

```
              Berger Publications, Inc.
               2007 Central Expressway
                  Dallas, TX 75011
                   (214) 555 1234

                      ORDER FORM


                                              July 25, 1990


                                     Purchase Order #1794

    Item           Quantity            Price         Total
    ---------------------------------------------------------

    Widgets           17                15.95         271.15
    Gadgets          124               117.50      14,570.00

    Totals:          141                           14,841.15




Ship to:
Berger Printing Corp.
77 Mockingbird Lane
Dallas, TX 75109


Not later than: December 1, 1988


                                     Berger Publications, Inc.
                                     by: Frank Berger, Pres.
```

Figure 22-7

## CHAPTER 23
# USING TWO SCREENS

### ALTERNATING BETWEEN TWO SCREENS

WordPerfect allows working on two entirely separate documents at the same time. This is most useful when working on documents involving tables or charts. While working on the actual document on one screen, you use the other for the table or chart.

1. While active on one document screen (the status line includes **Doc 1**) press **Shift-F3** (Switch) and the screen is instantly replaced by the other, with the note in the status line changing to **Doc 2**.

2. While in the second document screen you can retrieve files, create files, and edit files with all of WordPerfect's commands available to you. To return to the first screen, press **Shift-F3** (Switch) again. WordPerfect retains the work on both document screens as long as the computer remains active or until you intentionally erase any work after it has been saved under a given filename.

### USING SPLIT SCREENS

It is also possible to split your screen into two windows on which different work can simultaneously be displayed. Again, you can work on one window without affecting the other and then switch back.

1. Press **Ctrl-F3** (Screen) and select **1 Window**. The display shows the number of lines in the current window, in other words, the full screen (**Number of lines in this window: 24**). To produce two windows of equal size, change that number to **12** and press **Enter**. Now you have two screens as in Fig. 23-1.

2. You can now switch to the bottom window to work in it or to retrieve a previously saved file. Press **Shift-F3** (Switch) and the cursor moves to the bottom window. Now retrieve any file, just to see what that looks like. Press **Shift-F10** (Retrieve). Enter a filename of your choice and observe the result as in Fig. 23-2.

3. To get rid of the second window, press **Ctrl-F3** (Screen) again. Once more select **1 Window**, change the number to **0**, and press **Enter**. The second window disappears, but whatever work was active on it is not lost.

4. Press **Shift-F3** (Switch) and the full second document screen replaces the current one with the previously retrieved file still in display. (The **Switch** function works in toggle fashion, switching document screens back and forth each time it is used.)

## Chapter 23

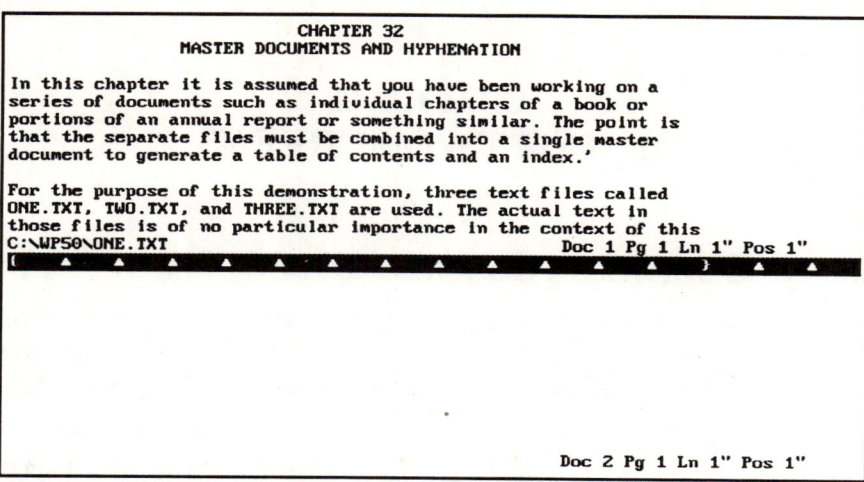

*Figure 23-1*

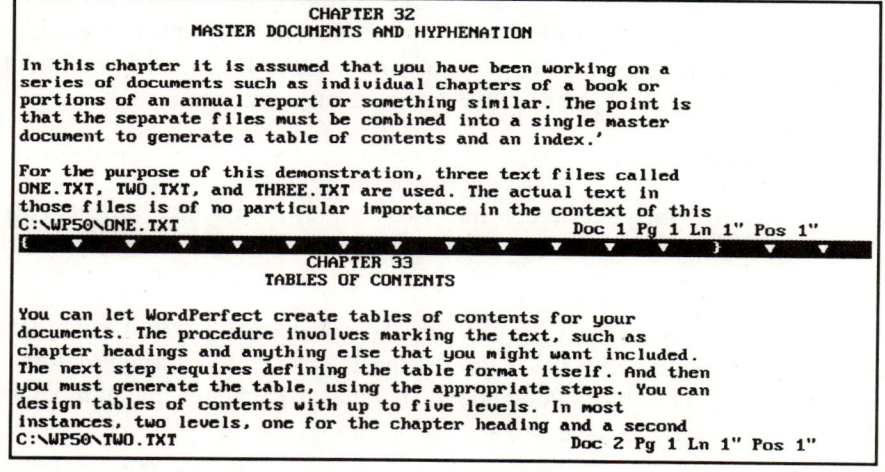

*Figure 23-2*

There are many uses for the two-document option. While writing your main document on the **Doc 1** screen, create a list of illustrations complete with captions on the **Doc 2** screen. Or use the alternate screen to enter key words or phases to be used in an index. They can be alphabetized later. As long as you remember that the second screen is available, you're sure to find uses for it.

## Chapter 24
# LIST FILES OPTIONS

Businesses and professional persons tend to accumulate an enormous amount of documents of every conceivable kind. After a while it tends to be difficult to figure out which filename stands for what. WordPerfect offers ways that make it relatively easy to identify what one or the other document is all about without actually having to retrieve it in toto.

One way is to use the **6 Look** option from the **F5** (List Files) command:

1. Press **F5** (List Files) and use the arrow keys to highlight any specific file you may be interested in.
2. The default selection that is active when **List Files** has been used is **6 Look**. Press **Enter** and you are confronted by a rectangular box containing the date on which the file was created and the top of the file itself, usually just one line, as in Fig. 24-1.

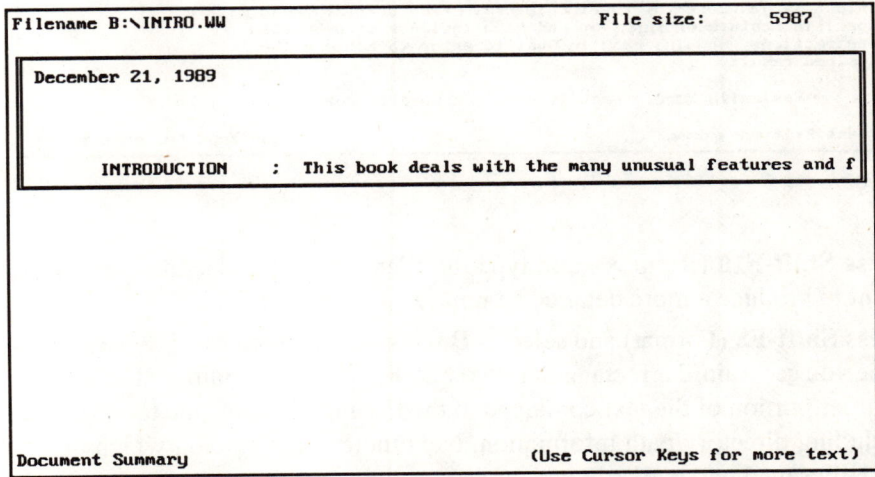

Figure 24-1

3. If that one line is insufficient, press **Down Arrow** and an entire screen representing the top portion of the file is displayed.

Chapter 24

4. You can now decide if this is a file you want to use or edit (use **1 Retrieve**), print as is (**4 Print**), or if you want to keep it at all, move it to a different directory or disk (**3 Move/Rename**), or simply delete it (**2 Delete**).

The Document Summary, shown in Fig. 24-2, is generated automatically by WordPerfect the first time a document or a portion of a document is saved. WordPerfect also includes a means of adding a considerable amount of information to such a document summary, information that tends to come in handy, especially in organizations where more than one person is involved in the task of writing letters, reports, and other documents.

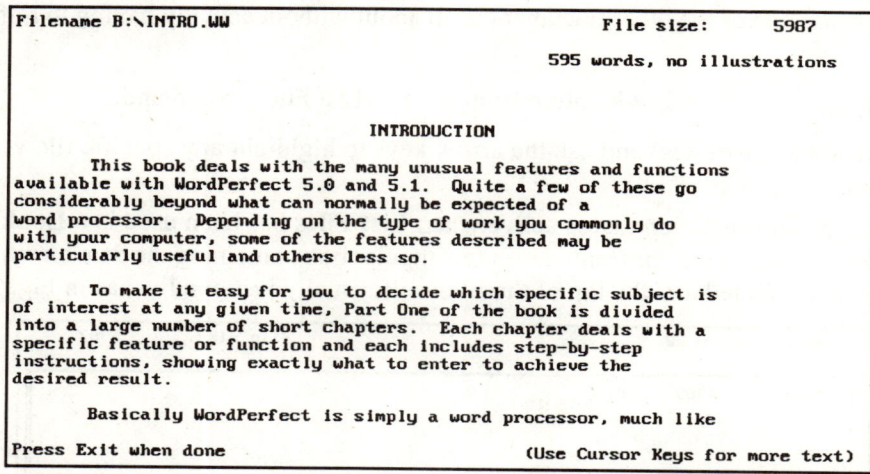

Figure 24-2

1. Press **Shift-F10** (Retrieve) and type the filename of the document for which you want to produce a more detailed summary.
2. Press **Shift-F8** (Format) and select **3 Document** and then select **5 Summary**. This time you see a similar rectangular box, but there is some additional information and a larger portion of the text contained in the file Fig. 24-3. At the top is the filename including directory/path information. Next there is the date on which this file was initially saved under WordPerfect.

```
Document Summary
        System Filename            C:\WP50\ONE.TXT
        Date of Creation           November 9, 1990
    1 - Descriptive Filename
    2 - Subject/Account
    3 - Author
    4 - Typist
    5 - Comments
    ┌─────────────────────────────────────────────────────────────┐
    │ CHAPTER 32 ;  MASTER DOCUMENTS AND HYPHENATION ; In this chapter it is │
    │ assumed that you have been working on a series of documents such as   │
    │ individual chapters of a book or portions of an annual report or something │
    │ similar. The point is that the separate files must be combined into a │
    │ single master document to generate a table of contents and an index. │
    └─────────────────────────────────────────────────────────────┘
```

*Figure 24-3*

3. Select **1 Descriptive Filename** and type a description of your file. Press **Enter**.
4. Select **2 Subject/Account** and enter whatever data you deem appropriate here. Press **Enter**.
5. Select **3 Author** and enter your name. Press **Enter**.
6. Select **4 Typist** if you want to identify the person who actually typed the document. Press **Enter**.
7. Select **5 Comments** and the cursor is moved to the beginning of the text in the box and you may now enter whatever explanatory text may seem appropriate. As you type, the original text in the box moves to the right as long as you're not in the **Typeover** mode. Fig. 24-4 shows a possible result.

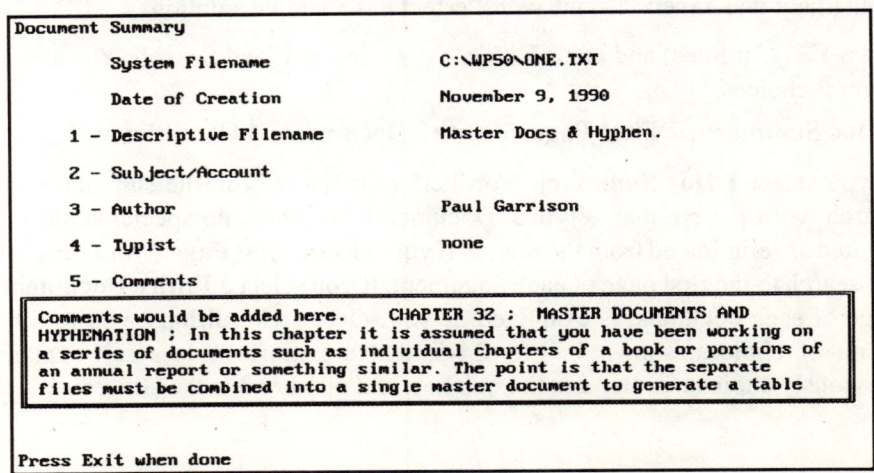

*Figure 24-4*

8. Press **F10** (Save) and you're returned to the actual document. Now press **F10** (Save) again and at any time in the future, you can invoke the document summary by retrieving the file and using **Shift-F8, 3 Document, 5 Summary**.

9. Alternately, if you press **F5** (List Files), move the highlighting to the file for which you've created the expanded summary, and select **6 Look**, WordPerfect displays all of the information in that summary in a greatly expanded rectangular box, as in Fig. 24-5.

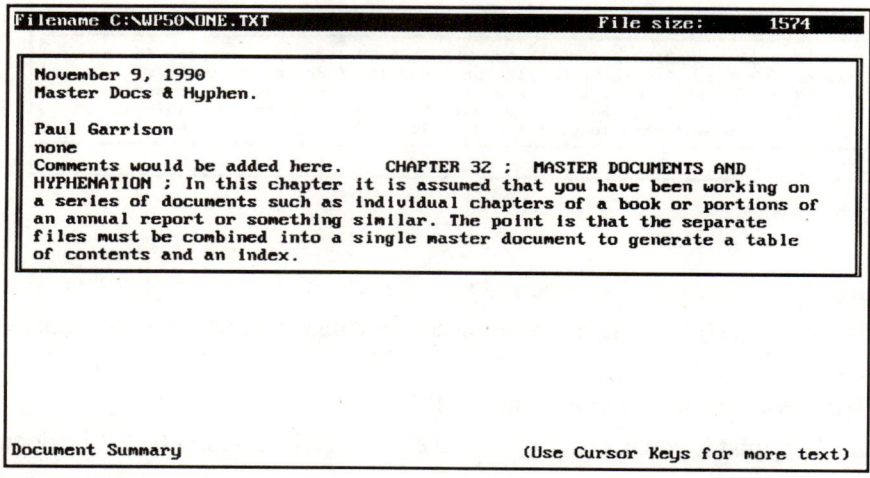

Figure 24-5

There are times, especially after you've created and saved hundreds of documents, when you may want to find a given document but you can't for the life of you remember under what filename it was saved. Again, WordPerfect has a simple solution.

1. Press **F5** (List Files) and press **Enter**. Now select **9 Word Search**. You are offered several choices:

   **1 Doc Summary; 2 First Page; 3 Entire Document; 4 Conditions: 1**

2. If you select **1 Doc Summary** WordPerfect looks only in the summaries for the search word pattern that is typed. Documents for which no special summary was created are eliminated from the search. If you select **2 First Page**, WordPerfect limits the search to the first page of each document. If you select **3 Entire Document** each page of each document is examined. If you select **4 Conditions**, you're offered a menu of choices, shown in Fig. 24-6, that are more or less self-explanatory. Obviously choice number **1** is the quickest and number **3** is the slowest.

```
Word Search

1 - Perform Search on            All 104 File(s)

2 - Undo Last Search

3 - Reset Search Conditions

4 - File Date                    No
      From (MM/DD/YY):           (All)
      To   (MM/DD/YY):           (All)

              Word Pattern(s)

5 - First Page
6 - Entire Doc
7 - Document Summary
      Creation Date (e.g. Nov)
      Descriptive Name
      Subject/Account
      Author
      Typist
      Comments

Selection: 1
```

*Figure 24-6*

3. Once a selection has been made from the above choices, it's time to enter a word pattern. A "word pattern" is either an entire word such as *desktop* or a portion of a word such as *desk*. Alternately it can include so-called wildcards. For instance, *d?sk* would stand for *desk, disk* and *dusk*. And *d\*sk* would stand for *damask, desk, disk* and *dusk*.

4. When either **2 First Page** or **3 Entire Document** is selected, WordPerfect searches through all files on the currently logged disk or directory. It places an asterisk (\*) next to every filename that includes the word pattern. In addition, the number of marked files is displayed at the right top corner of the screen, as in Fig. 24-7.

```
11/09/90  16:26            Directory C:\WP50\*.*
Document size:        0    Free: 34719744   Used:    13802    Marked: 5

. <CURRENT>    <DIR>                      .. <PARENT>   <DIR>
LEARN    .     <DIR>     11/05/90 16:26   8514A    .WPD    3466  04/27/88 14:24
A        .WPM      83    11/06/90 10:15   ADDRESS  .LST     749  11/06/90 14:39
AIRPLANE .WPG    8484    04/27/88 14:24   ALTI     .WPM      74  11/06/90 10:10
ALTY     .WPM     328    11/09/90 11:57   AND      .WPG    1978  04/27/88 14:24
ANNOUNCE .WPG    5388    04/27/88 14:24   APPLAUSE .WPG    1522  04/27/88 14:24
ARROW1   .WPG     366    04/27/88 14:24   ARROW2   .WPG     738  04/27/88 14:24
AWARD    .WPG    1746    04/27/88 14:24   BADNEWS  .WPG    3750  04/27/88 14:24
BASIC    .WPM     117    11/09/90 12:39   BOOK     .WPG    1800  04/27/88 14:24
BORDER   .WPG   13518    04/27/88 14:24   CH26     .TXT    1412* 11/09/90 15:07
CH28     .TXT    1650*   11/09/90 15:13   CH44     .TXT    1995* 11/09/90 15:58
CHECK    .WPG    1074    04/27/88 14:24   CLOCK    .WPG    6234  04/27/88 14:24
CODER    .WPM     127    11/06/90 16:40   CODES    .WPM     151  11/06/90 16:39
CONFIDEN .WPG    3226    04/27/88 14:24   DB1      .PF      321  11/06/90 10:56
DB1      .WPM     101    11/06/90 11:05   DB2      .PF      321  11/06/90 10:57
DB2      .WPM     101    11/06/90 11:09   DB3      .PF      321  11/06/90 10:57
DB3      .WPM     101    11/06/90 11:09   DB4      .PF      321  11/06/90 11:01
DB4      .WPM     101    11/06/90 11:07   DB5      .PF      572  11/06/90 12:24
EGA512   .FRS    3584    04/27/88 14:24 ▼ EGAITAL  .FRS    3584  04/27/88 14:24

1 Retrieve; 2 Delete; 3 Move/Rename; 4 Print; 5 Text In;
6 Look; 7 Other Directory; 8 Copy; 9 Word Search; N Name Search: 6
```

*Figure 24-7*

5. When **1 Doc Summary** is selected, WordPerfect searches only through those files for which complete document summaries were produced, using the above described method which speeds up the search considerably.
6. When **4 Condition** is selected, you might enter two dates in the **4 File Date** option representing the time frame during which you know that the document you're looking for was created. Press **Enter** and a moment later all files created during that time frame are marked with an asterisk (*). Alternately, you might enter a name in the **7 Author** place if you remember the name of the person who authored the document in question and so on.

WordPerfect can be programmed to automatically save the document that you're working on at specific intervals. **Shift-F1** (Setup) is used for that purpose and the **Timed Backup** question should be answered with **y**. Select **15 minutes** or less for the time interval because thunderstorms and other unforeseen circumstances can cause momentary power failures.

The timed backup files are stored under the filename **WP{WP}BK1** for documents created on the number 1 document screen and **WP{WP}BK2** for documents created on the number 2 document screen. They are included in the files displayed using **F5** (**List Files**) and can be retrieved using **1 Retrieve** which produces the question **Retrieve into current document? (Y/N) No**. If you accept **No** and press **Enter**, nothing happens. If you type **y** to change the **No** to **Yes**, the document appears on the currently active document screen AHEAD of any document that you're currently working on.

A word of caution: In creating these timed backup files, WordPerfect looks only at the primary filename and not at the extension. Thus **FILE.XXX** and **FILE.YYY** create the same backup file if both are being worked on from the same document screen.

These **.BK1** or **.BK2** files remain intact even if a power failure or some other mishap causes the computer to be shut down. They can then be retrieved and very little if anything is lost. They are erased when WordPerfect is exited in the accepted manner using **F7** (Exit) and typing **n y** because the program assumes that you have saved your file(s) before typing that command.

If WordPerfect was shut down by any means other than the accepted exit manner then, once reactivated, the computer beeps at the first timed saving, displaying **Old Backup File Exists. 1 Rename 2 Delete:**. This gives you the option of saving it under a different name or of deleting it, assuming it is no longer needed.

By the way, no matter whether you're using a hard disk or floppy disks, both can develop problems or be damaged in some way. It should be an automatic habit to copy all new files onto a separate floppy disk before shutting down the computer at the conclusion of each work session. These backup diskettes should be stored in a safe place and should never be used as work disks.

By now, if you have a fairly large number of files, it might be a good idea to do a little house cleaning. For instance, you might create a separate disk or directory to hold all files with a given extension, like all **.WPM** files representing all of your library of macros. Remember, you can have different macro files with the identical filenames on different disks or directories, so don't copy them from more than one disk or directory to the same disk, or you'll lose some in the process.

CHAPTER 25
# MULTIPLE FONTS

Depending on the printer that is installed with your system, the variety of available base fonts varies considerably, as was discussed in Chapter 5. In addition to these base fonts, WordPerfect offers a considerable number of possible modifications in terms of size and appearance. If you plan to use distinctive font styles and sizes in your documents, you should find out how your printer handles these choices.

For that purpose prepare a test document:

1. If you have more than one printer installed with your system, press **Shift-F7** (Print) and check the displayed printer. If it is not the one you're going to use, select **S Select Printer** and choose the appropriate option. Press **F7** (Exit) when finished.
2. Press **Ctrl-F8** (Font). Select the font style and size you want to use as your base font. Select **1 Select** to return to the document screen.
3. Type a sentence that includes the selected font identification. Press **Enter** to go to the next line.
4. Press **Ctrl-F8** (Font) and select **1 Size**. The menu across the bottom of the screen is shown in Fig. 25-1.

```
1 Suprscpt; 2 Subscpt; 3 Fine; 4 Small; 5 Large; 6 Ury Large; 7 Ext Large: 0
```

Figure 25-1

5. Select **3 Fine**. Type a very short sentence including the word **Fine**.
6. Repeat the procedure for **4 Small, 5 Large, 6 Very Large,** and **7 Extra Large**.
7. Press **Ctrl-F8** (Font) and select **2 Appearance** to display the menu in Fig. 25-2. Repeat the procedure for **5 Outline, 6 Shadow, 7 Small Caps,** and **8 Redline**.

```
1 Bold 2 Undrln 3 Dbl Und 4 Italc 5 Outln 6 Shadw 7 Sm Cap 8 Redln 9 Stkout: 0
```

*Figure 25-2*

8. Place the cursor on the first letter of the line containing the word **Fine** and press **Alt-F4** (Block).
9. Move the cursor to the bottom to identify all those nine lines as a block. Press **F10** (Save) and give it a name. Your block should resemble the one in Fig. 25-3.

```
The same, Fine
The same, Small
The same, Large
The same, Very Large
The same, Extra Large
The same, Outline
The same, Shadow
The same, Small Caps
The same, Redline
```

*Figure 25-3*

10. Now select the next available base font. Type a line including the name of the base font. Press **Enter** to go to the next line. Press **Shift-F10** (Retrieve) and retrieve the block you just saved.
11. Repeat this for all base fonts available or the ones you're interested in. When you're finished, press **Shift-F7** (Print) and let your printer print the document.

This procedure demonstrates how the different font styles and sizes are treated by your printer. Depending upon the printer, many of the style and size commands have only limited effect. If you have more than one printer available, try this test document on each printer, noting the print differences.

There are times when using different font styles and sizes is useful, and there are situations when it's a waste of time.

## Chapter 25

When you prepare documents in the final form to be used either as they are, or as camera-ready mechanicals to be reproduced via offset, Xerox, or similar methods, then making use of different fonts can improve the effectiveness of your document.

When, on the other hand, what you are producing is going to be typeset, then using fancy fonts serves little if any purpose. In addition, if the typesetting is accomplished directly from the disk(s) on which you saved your document, then most font and formatting codes are ignored and may actually have to be removed before the typesetting system can handle your files.

To remove the formatting and other codes entered during the preparation of your document, WordPerfect offers two options. One uses the **Text In/Out** option and the other uses the **CONVERT.EXE** program that is included with WordPerfect.

To use the first, you again have two options. For the first one:

> Press **Ctrl-F5** (Text In/Out) and from the menu in Fig. 25-4 select **1 DOS Text**. A new menu, Fig. 25-5, is displayed. Select **1 Save** and type a new filename. Formatting codes are converted to ASCII text.

```
1 DOS Text; 2 Password; 3 Save Generic; 4 Save WP 4.2; 5 Comment: 0
```

Figure 25-4

```
1 Save; 2 Retrieve (CR/LF to [HRt]); 3 Retrieve (CR/LF to [SRt] in HZone): 0
```

Figure 25-5

To use the other option:

> Press **Ctrl-F5** (Text In/Out) and select **3 Save Generic**. Type a new filename and press **Enter**. The new file is in a generic word processing format without WordPerfect-specific codes.

To use the CONVERT program:

1. At the DOS prompt, type **PATH\CONVERT**, where PATH is the disk/directory information regarding the location of the CONVERT.EXE file.
2. You are asked to enter the input file data. Type **PATH\FILENAME.EXT**.
3. You are asked to enter the output file data. Type **PATH\FILENAME.EXT**.
4. A menu, shown in Fig. 25-6, is displayed, offering a collection of file formats from which files can be converted to or from WordPerfect. Select **1 WordPerfect to another format**.

```
Name of Input File? c:\ww\m
Name of Output File? c:\ww\mm

0 EXIT
1 WordPerfect to another format
2 Revisable-Form-Text (IBM DCA Format) to WordPerfect
3 Final-Form-Text (IBM DCA Format) to WordPerfect
4 Navy DIF Standard to WordPerfect
5 WordStar 3.3 to WordPerfect
6 MultiMate Advantage II to WordPerfect
7 Seven-Bit Transfer Format to WordPerfect
8 WordPerfect 4.2 to WordPerfect 5.0
9 Mail Merge to WordPerfect Secondary Merge
A Spreadsheet DIF to WordPerfect Secondary Merge
B Word 4.0 to WordPerfect

Enter number of Conversion desired
```

Figure 25-6

5. A new menu, shown in Fig. 25-7, is displayed. This one identifies file formats to which WordPerfect files can be converted. Select **7 ASCII text file**. The program produces a new file in the ASCII format.

Chapter 25

```
Name of Input File? c:\ww\m
Name of Output File? c:\ww\mm


0 EXIT
1 Revisable-Form-Text (IBM DCA Format)
2 Final-Form-Text (IBM DCA Format)
3 Navy DIF Standard
4 WordStar 3.3
5 MultiMate Advantage II
6 Seven-Bit Transfer Format
7 ASCII text file
8 WordPerfect Secondary Merge to Spreadsheet DIF

Enter number of output file format desired
```

Figure 25-7

## CHAPTER 26
# EDITING PARALLEL COLUMNS

It is not at all unusual for large lists of data to be recorded in the form of parallel columns. Fig. 26-1 is a single page representing only a small part of a file that contains in excess of 1,000 lines. (For those who are interested, the list consists of data relative to aviation navigation aids, where *STATION* is the location, *ID* is the state ID, *FIX* is the three-letter station ID, *FRQ* is the VHF frequency, *LAT* is the latitude, *LONG* is the longitude, *VAR* is the magnetic variation and *ELEV* is the station elevation in feet above sea level.)

The problem discussed in this chapter arises when, for one reason or another, one or several of the columns must be deleted. The normal Backspace or Del keys are of no use, and since the columns were created using Tab stops rather than the Column define option available with WordPerfect, it is not possible to turn a single column into a block that could then be deleted.

There is a fairly simple means by which to accomplish the task quite expeditiously. Figs. 26-2 and 26-3 are two macros, saved as ALTU.WPM and ALTV.WPM, that take care of the problem beautifully.

For argument's sake, you may want to delete the LAT and LONG columns because your airplane doesn't have the kind of instruments that need that kind of information. Here is what you would do:

1. Place the cursor on the 3 of 34-22.N in the LAT column.
2. Press **Alt-V**. You can watch the column being erased, one line at a time, without any effort on your part. When the process finally arrives at the very bottom of the list, press **F1** (Cancel) to stop the macro from going on and on.
3. Place the cursor on the 1 of 100-17.3W in the LONG column.
4. Press **Alt-V** and watch that column disappear. Fig. 26-4 is a printout of the sample page with the two columns removed in this manner.
5. Now use **Del** or **Backspace** to delete the portion of the double line, the LAT, and LONG.
6. Press **Shift-F8** (Format) and select **1 Line** and **8 Tab Set**. Adjust the tabs by eliminating the two no longer needed and moving the remaining ones over.

## Chapter 26

| STATION | ID | FIX | FRQ | LAT | LONG | VAR | ELEV |
|---|---|---|---|---|---|---|---|
| CHILDRESS | TX | CDS | 117.6 | 34-22.1N | 100-17.3W | 10E | 1920 |
| CIMARRON | NM | CIM | 116.4 | 36-29.5N | 104-52.3W | 13E | 6550 |
| CINCINNATI | OH | CVG | 117.3 | 39-01.0N | 084-42.2W | 00 | 880 |
| CLARION | PA | CIP | 112.9 | 41-08.8N | 079-27.5W | 06W | 1530 |
| CLARKSBURG | WV | CKB | 115.1 | 39-15.2N | 080-16.1W | 04W | 1430 |
| CLARKSVILLE | IN | CKV | 110.6 | 36-37.3N | 087-24.8W | 01E | 540 |
| CLAYTON | GA | LYN | 113.6 | 33-38.1N | 084-26.8W | 01E | 1010 |
| COALDALE | NV | OAL | 117.7 | 38-00.2N | 117-46.2W | 17E | 4800 |
| COCHISE | AZ | CIE | 115.8 | 32-02.0N | 109-45.5W | 13E | 4230 |
| CODY | WY | COD | 111.8 | 44-37.2N | 108-57.9W | 17E | 4790 |
| COEUR D'ALENE | ID | COE | 108.8 | 47-46.4N | 116-49.2W | 20E | 2290 |
| COFIELD | NC | CVI | 114.4 | 36-22.4N | 076-52.3W | 06W | 70 |
| COLLEGE STATION | TX | CLL | 113.3 | 30-36.3N | 096-25.2W | 08E | 370 |
| COLLIER COUNTY | FL | CCE | 108.6 | 26-09.2N | 081-46.7W | 00 | 9 |
| COLORADO SPRINGS | CO | COS | 112.5 | 38-56.7N | 104-38.0W | 13E | 6930 |
| COLTS NECK | NJ | COL | 115.4 | 40-18.7N | 074-09.6W | 11W | 120 |
| COLUMBIA | SC | CAE | 114.7 | 33-51.4N | 081-03.3W | 02W | 410 |
| COLUMBUS | NM | CUS | 111.2 | 31-49.1N | 107-34.4W | 12E | 4008 |
| COLUMBUS | NE | OLU | 112.2 | 41-27.0N | 097-20.4W | 08E | 1443 |
| COLUMBUS | GA | CSG | 117.1 | 32-36.9N | 085-01.1W | 01E | 630 |
| CONCORD | NH | CON | 112.9 | 43-13.2N | 071-34.6W | 15W | 710 |
| CONCORD | CA | CCR | 117.0 | 38-02.7N | 122-02.7W | 17E | 10 |
| CORONA | NM | CNX | 115.5 | 34-22.0N | 105-40.7W | 13E | 6411 |
| CORPUS CHRISTI | TX | CRP | 115.5 | 27-54.2N | 097-26.7W | 09E | 54 |
| CORTEZ | CO | CEZ | 108.4 | 37-23.4N | 108-33.7W | 14E | 6220 |
| CORVALLIS | OR | CVO | 108.4 | 44-30.0N | 123-17.6W | 21E | 250 |
| COTULLA | TX | COT | 115.8 | 28-27.7N | 099-07.1W | 09E | 520 |
| COYLE | NJ | CYN | 113.4 | 39-49.0N | 074-25.9W | 10W | 210 |
| CRAZY WOMAN | WY | CZI | 117.3 | 44-00.0N | 106-26.1W | 15E | 4798 |
| CRESCENT CITY | CA | CEC | 109.0 | 41-46.8N | 124-14.4W | 19E | 50 |
| CRESTVIEW | FL | CEW | 115.9 | 30-49.6N | 086-40.8W | 03E | 254 |
| CROSS CITY | FL | CTY | 112.0 | 29-35.9N | 083-02.9W | 01E | 30 |
| CUNNINGHAM | KY | CNG | 113.6 | 37-00.5N | 088-50.2W | 03E | 480 |
| CUSTER COUNTY | NE | CUZ | 108.2 | 41-29.0N | 099-41.4W | 09E | 2850 |
| CUT BANK | MT | CTB | 114.4 | 48-33.9N | 112-20.6W | 20E | 3780 |
| DAGGETT | CA | DAG | 113.2 | 34-57.8N | 116-34.6W | 15E | 1760 |
| DAISETTA | TX | DAS | 116.9 | 30-11.4N | 094-38.7W | 08E | 74 |
| DALHART | TX | DHT | 112.0 | 36-05.5N | 102-32.7W | 12E | 4020 |
| DALLAS-FORT WORTH | TX | DFW | 117.0 | 32-52.0N | 097-01.7W | 08E | 560 |
| DANVILLE | VA | DAN | 113.1 | 36-34.1N | 079-20.2W | 06W | 570 |
| DANVILLE | IL | DNV | 111.0 | 40-17.6N | 087-33.4W | 02E | 700 |
| DARWIN | MN | DWN | 109.0 | 45-05.3N | 094-27.2W | 07E | 1130 |
| DAVENPORT | IA | CVA | 113.8 | 41-42.5N | 090-29.0W | 04E | 760 |
| DAVIS | OK | MEE | 108.4 | 35-39.8N | 095-22.1W | 08E | 610 |
| DAYTON | OH | DAY | 114.5 | 40-01.0N | 084-23.8W | 01W | 990 |
| DE LANCEY | NY | DNY | 112.1 | 42-10.7N | 074-57.4W | 11W | 2560 |
| DECATUR | AL | DCU | 112.8 | 34-38.9N | 086-56.4W | 03E | 590 |
| DECATUR | IL | DEC | 117.2 | 39-44.3N | 088-51.4W | 03E | 700 |
| DEER PARK | NY | DPK | 111.2 | 40-47.5N | 073-18.3W | 12W | 120 |
| DELLS | WI | DLL | 110.4 | 43-33.1N | 089-45.8W | 03E | 1020 |
| DELTA | UT | DTA | 116.1 | 39-18.2N | 112-30.3W | 16E | 4600 |
| DEMING | NM | DMN | 108.6 | 32-16.6N | 107-36.3W | 12E | 4205 |
| DENVER | CO | DEN | 117.0 | 39-48.0N | 104-53.2W | 12E | 5233 |
| DES MOINES | IA | DSM | 114.1 | 41-26.3N | 093-38.9W | 07E | 940 |
| DETROIT LAKES | MN | DTL | 111.2 | 46-49.5N | 095-52.9W | 08E | 1388 |
| DEVILS LAKE | ND | DVL | 111.0 | 48-06.8N | 098-54.5W | 11E | 1450 |
| DICKINSON | ND | DIK | 112.9 | 46-51.6N | 102-46.4W | 14E | 2523 |
| DILLON | MT | DLN | 113.0 | 45-14.9N | 112-32.8W | 18E | 5260 |
| DODGE CITY | KS | DDC | 108.2 | 37-51.0N | 100-00.3W | 11E | 2565 |
| DOGWOOD | MO | DGD | 109.4 | 37-01.4N | 092-52.6W | 06E | 1600 |
| DOUGLAS | WY | DGW | 108.6 | 42-40.6N | 105-13.5W | 14E | 4903 |
| DOUGLAS | AZ | DUG | 108.8 | 31-28.4N | 109-36.1W | 13E | 4160 |
| DOVE CREEK | CO | DVC | 114.6 | 37-48.5N | 108-55.8W | 14E | 6990 |
| DOWNTOWN | LA | DTN | 108.6 | 32-32.4N | 093-44.5W | 07E | 180 |
| DRAKE | AR | DAK | 108.8 | 36-02.6N | 094-11.9W | 07E | 1530 |
| DRUMMOND | MT | DRU | 117.1 | 46-38.2N | 113-11.2W | 19E | 4160 |
| DRYER | OH | DJB | 113.6 | 41-21.5N | 082-09.7W | 05W | 780 |
| DUBLIN | GA | DBN | 113.1 | 32-33.6N | 082-50.0W | 01W | 300 |
| DUBOIS | ID | DBS | 116.9 | 44-05.3N | 112-12.5W | 18E | 4915 |
| DUBUQUE | IA | DBQ | 115.8 | 42-24.1N | 090-42.5W | 04E | 1060 |
| DULUTH | MN | DLH | 112.6 | 46-48.1N | 092-12.2W | 05E | 1430 |
| DUNKIRK | NY | DKK | 116.2 | 42-29.4N | 079-16.5W | 07W | 680 |
| DUNOIR | WY | DNW | 113.4 | 43-49.7N | 110-20.1W | 17E | 7720 |
| DUPAGE | IL | DPA | 108.4 | 41-53.4N | 088-21.0W | 02E | 800 |
| DUPREE | SD | DPR | 116.8 | 45-04.7N | 101-42.9W | 13E | 2530 |
| DURANGO | CO | DRO | 108.2 | 37-09.2N | 107-44.9W | 14E | 6660 |
| DYERSBURG | IN | DYR | 116.8 | 36-01.1N | 089-19.1W | 03E | 380 |
| EAGLE LAKE | TX | ELA | 108.6 | 29-39.8N | 096-19.0W | 08E | 190 |

Figure 26-1

```
Macro: Edit
       File           ALTU.WPM
  1 - Description     Delete word, down, next
  2 - Action

       {DISPLAY OFF}{Del to EOL}{Down}{CHAIN}ALTU.WPM




Selection: 0
```

*Figure 26-2*

```
Macro: Edit
       File           ALTU.WPM
  1 - Description     Delete word, down, next
  2 - Action

       {DISPLAY OFF}{Del Word}{Down}{CHAIN}ALTU.WPM



```

*Figure 26-3*

# Chapter 26

| STATION | ID | FIX | FRQ | LAT | LONG | VAR | ELEV |
|---|---|---|---|---|---|---|---|
| CHILDRESS | TX | CDS | 117.6 | | | 10E | 1920 |
| CIMARRON | NM | CIM | 116.4 | | | 13E | 6550 |
| CINCINNATI | OH | CVG | 117.3 | | | 00 | 880 |
| CLARION | PA | CIP | 112.9 | | | 06W | 1530 |
| CLARKSBURG | WV | CKB | 115.1 | | | 04W | 1430 |
| CLARKSVILLE | IN | CKV | 110.6 | | | 01E | 540 |
| CLAYTON | GA | LYN | 113.6 | | | 00 | 1010 |
| COALDALE | NV | OAL | 117.7 | | | 17E | 4800 |
| COCHISE | AZ | CIE | 115.8 | | | 13E | 4230 |
| CODY | WY | COD | 111.8 | | | 17E | 4790 |
| COEUR D'ALENE | ID | COE | 108.8 | | | 20E | 2290 |
| COFIELD | NC | CVI | 114.4 | | | 06W | 70 |
| COLLEGE STATION | TX | CLL | 113.3 | | | 08E | 370 |
| COLLIER COUNTY | FL | CCE | 108.6 | | | 00 | 9 |
| COLORADO SPRINGS | CO | COS | 112.5 | | | 13E | 6930 |
| COLTS NECK | NJ | COL | 115.4 | | | 11W | 120 |
| COLUMBIA | SC | CAE | 114.7 | | | 02W | 410 |
| COLUMBUS | NM | CUS | 111.2 | | | 12E | 4008 |
| COLUMBUS | NE | OLU | 112.2 | | | 08E | 1443 |
| COLUMBUS | GA | CSG | 117.1 | | | 01E | 630 |
| CONCORD | NH | CON | 112.9 | | | 15W | 710 |
| CONCORD | CA | CCR | 117.0 | | | 17E | 10 |
| CORONA | NM | CNX | 115.5 | | | 13E | 6411 |
| CORPUS CHRISTI | TX | CRP | 115.5 | | | 09E | 54 |
| CORTEZ | CO | CEZ | 108.4 | | | 14E | 6220 |
| CORVALLIS | OR | CVO | 108.4 | | | 21E | 250 |
| COTULLA | TX | COT | 115.8 | | | 09E | 520 |
| COYLE | NJ | CYN | 113.4 | | | 10W | 210 |
| CRAZY WOMAN | WY | CZI | 117.3 | | | 15E | 4798 |
| CRESCENT CITY | CA | CEC | 109.0 | | | 19E | 50 |
| CRESTVIEW | FL | CEW | 115.9 | | | 03E | 254 |
| CROSS CITY | FL | CTY | 112.0 | | | 01E | 30 |
| CUNNINGHAM | KY | CNG | 113.6 | | | 03E | 480 |
| CUSTER COUNTY | NE | CUZ | 108.2 | | | 09E | 2850 |
| CUT BANK | MT | CTB | 114.4 | | | 20E | 3780 |
| DAGGETT | CA | DAG | 113.2 | | | 15E | 1760 |
| DAISETTA | TX | DAS | 116.9 | | | 08E | 74 |
| DALHART | TX | DHT | 112.0 | | | 12E | 4020 |
| DALLAS-FORT WORTH | TX | DFW | 117.0 | | | 08E | 560 |
| DANVILLE | VA | DAN | 113.1 | | | 06W | 570 |
| DANVILLE | IL | DNV | 111.0 | | | 02E | 700 |
| DARWIN | MN | DWN | 109.0 | | | 07E | 1130 |
| DAVENPORT | IA | CVA | 113.8 | | | 04E | 760 |
| DAVIS | OK | MEE | 108.6 | | | 08E | 610 |
| DAYTON | OH | DAY | 114.5 | | | 01W | 990 |
| DE LANCEY | NY | DNY | 112.1 | | | 11W | 2560 |
| DECATUR | AL | DCU | 112.8 | | | 03E | 590 |
| DECATUR | IL | DEC | 117.2 | | | 03E | 700 |
| DEER PARK | NY | DPK | 111.2 | | | 12W | 120 |
| DELLS | WI | DLL | 110.4 | | | 03E | 1020 |
| DELTA | UT | DTA | 116.1 | | | 16E | 4600 |
| DEMING | NM | DMN | 108.6 | | | 12E | 4205 |
| DENVER | CO | DEN | 117.0 | | | 12E | 5233 |
| DES MOINES | IA | DSM | 114.1 | | | 07E | 940 |
| DETROIT LAKES | MN | DTL | 111.2 | | | 08E | 1388 |
| DEVILS LAKE | ND | DVL | 111.0 | | | 11E | 1450 |
| DICKINSON | ND | DIK | 112.9 | | | 14E | 2523 |
| DILLON | MT | DLN | 113.0 | | | 18E | 5260 |
| DODGE CITY | KS | DDC | 108.2 | | | 11E | 2565 |
| DOGWOOD | MO | DGD | 109.4 | | | 06E | 1600 |
| DOUGLAS | WY | DGW | 108.6 | | | 14E | 4903 |
| DOUGLAS | AZ | DUG | 108.8 | | | 13E | 4160 |
| DOVE CREEK | CO | DVC | 114.6 | | | 14E | 6990 |
| DOWNTOWN | LA | DTN | 108.6 | | | 07E | 180 |
| DRAKE | AR | DAK | 108.8 | | | 07E | 1530 |
| DRUMMOND | MT | DRU | 117.1 | | | 19E | 4160 |
| DRYER | OH | DJB | 113.6 | | | 05W | 780 |
| DUBLIN | GA | DBN | 113.1 | | | 01W | 300 |
| DUBOIS | ID | DBS | 116.9 | | | 18E | 4915 |
| DUBUQUE | IA | DBQ | 115.8 | | | 04E | 1060 |
| DULUTH | MN | DLH | 112.6 | | | 05E | 1430 |
| DUNKIRK | NY | DKK | 116.2 | | | 07W | 680 |
| DUNOIR | WY | DNW | 113.4 | | | 17E | 7720 |
| DUPAGE | IL | DPA | 108.4 | | | 02E | 800 |
| DUPREE | SD | DPR | 116.8 | | | 13E | 2530 |
| DURANGO | CO | DRO | 108.2 | | | 14E | 6660 |
| DYERSBURG | IN | DYR | 116.8 | | | 03E | 380 |
| EAGLE LAKE | TX | ELA | 108.6 | | | 08E | 190 |

Figure 26-4

*Editing Parallel Columns*

At other times you might want to delete several columns at a time all the way to the far right of the page, such as personnel files that should not be available to everyone. If that kind of information is stored in right-hand columns, then the other macro is the one to use. To demonstrate, the previous list file is used once more. This time, all columns to the right of **FRQ** are to be deleted.

1. Place the cursor on the **3** of **34-22.1N** in the **LAT** column.
2. Press **Alt-U** and, like some kind of hungry PACMAN, the macro gets rid of the four right-hand columns.
3. When the end of the file has been reached, press **F1** (Cancel) to stop macro execution. Print the file or preview it to see the results.

The action of both macros is achieved by chaining them to themselves. They execute the **Delete Word** or **Delete to End of Line** function and then start all over again. The chain reaction can be stopped at any time by pressing **F1** (Cancel).

When you are dealing with parallel columns created using the **Column Define** option from **Math/Columns** (press **Alt-F7** (Math/Columns) and select **4 Column Def**), then you can block items in the individual columns and use **Del** to delete the information, one block at a time.

## CHAPTER 27
# SLIDE SHOWS

You may at one time or another wish you could find a simple way to produce a slide show for a class of students, or one to run automatically at a display in an exhibition or at a convention, or maybe just for your kids for the fun of it. If this sort of thing is something that might interest you, you're in luck. WordPerfect can be used to create very effective slide shows, either using the monitor screen direct, or by projection, placing the monitor face up beneath a Viewgraph to display the image on a large screen.

The first thing you need are the pictures you want to use and possibly some explanatory text. As far as the pictures are concerned, you can use existing art that is contained in any of the many clip-art libraries. Or you can use the graphic images included with DrawPerfect, the new graphics program from WordPerfect.

Another option is to use one of the drawing programs available with Microsoft Windows, PC Paintbrush, PaintShow, and others to create your own freehand illustrations. This isn't as easy as it sounds. A fair amount of practice, not to mention talent, is needed.

Yet another avenue opens up if you have access to a scanner. Scanners are those miraculous machines that turn any kind of printed image, including halftones and photographs, into graphic files that can be treated like any other computer graphic.

No matter the source of your pictures, the files must be of a format WordPerfect can deal with. Those formats include .PCX files produced by PC Paintbrush and some other programs, .CGM files produced by the Publisher's PicturePak clip-art libraries, .IMG used by GEM Paint and others, .TIF files produced by scanners and by PaintShow, and, of course, .WPG files, the ones contained in the clip-art libraries included with WordPerfect 5.0, 5.1, and DrawPerfect.

If the pictures you want to use are not available in a file format WordPerfect can deal with directly, then there are reasonably priced file-conversion programs, such as HiJaak from InSet Systems, Inc., discussed in detail in Chapter 30. Those programs can convert most any file format to most any other format.

As far as explanatory text is concerned, you have two options. One calls for typing the text into the upper left-hand corner of the screen and then using the view double size option available with the print function (press **Shift-F7** select **6** and **2**). That places that portion of the page onto the screen during the slide presentation.

# Slide Shows

The other option involves the use of a conversion program like HiJaak. It is capable of converting ASCII text files into graphic files in a format that WordPerfect can deal with. Produce the text you want to use, using a text editor that produces ASCII files, or use WordPerfect and then use the CONVERT.EXE program included with WordPerfect, to convert the WordPerfect file to an ASCII file. This method saves the original WordPerfect file in addition to the ASCII file. Or you can press **Ctrl-F5** from WordPerfect and select **1 DOS** and then **1 Save** which saves your work in an ASCII format. This method saves only the ASCII file.

Save your picture and text files on a separate floppy disk or on a unique directory on your hard disk. The file directory might look something like:

    PIC1.WPG
    PIC2.PCX
    PIC3.TIF
    TXT1.IMG
    TXT2.IMG
    TXT3.IMG

where the PIC?.??? files are the picture files and the TXT?.IMG files are ASCII files converted to the .IMG graphics file format.

Once you have the pictures and text as individual files saved on a floppy or the hard disk, you're ready for the next step. It involves writing a macro that, once activated, takes over and runs the slide show for you. (You can run the show without a macro, but that involves a lot of keystrokes and, in turn, many opportunities to hit the wrong keys.)

Fig. 27-1 is the macro you want to produce to run your slide show with text files written using WordPerfect and NOT converted to graphics files. Fig. 27-2 is the macro you want to write if you have converted your text files to graphics files.

To run the slide show, activate WordPerfect and access the directory containing the macro file. Press **Alt-F10** and type **SHOW** (if SHOW.WPM is the name of the macro file) and press **Enter**. The first screen display is either Fig. 27-3 or Fig. 27-4, depending on whether you converted the ASCII text to a graphic file. Fig. 27-3 uses the **View document double size** option from within WordPerfect. Fig. 27-4 shows the text converted to a graphic file. Execution is halted until you press **Enter**. Then the first graphic slide, such as the demonstration image in Fig. 27-5, appears on the screen.

Depending on the way in which some of the commands are used in the macro, you can cause the slide to remain on the screen for a predetermined period of time. Alternately, you can hold it on the screen until **Enter** is pressed. This latter option is useful if you want to include spoken comments and possibly questions and answers. The automatic version is most useful if you want to accompany the slide show with recorded commentary. In that case the timing can be synchronized with the recording.

Chapter 27

The macro shown here assumes six slides and six text screens. You can use as many or as few slides as you like and, if you prefer, the text screens can be eliminated altogether or can also be automated to remain on the screen for a predetermined period of time.

For this process to work, you must be using WordPerfect 5.0 or 5.1, and your system must include some type of graphic adapter. A CGA or Hercules card produces only monochrome images. An EGA or VGA card combined with a color monitor can produce images in color. Either way, assembling such slide shows can be a lot of fun in addition to being potentially useful. And once the basic macro has been written, adjusting it to fit different conditions or requirements is a simple matter.

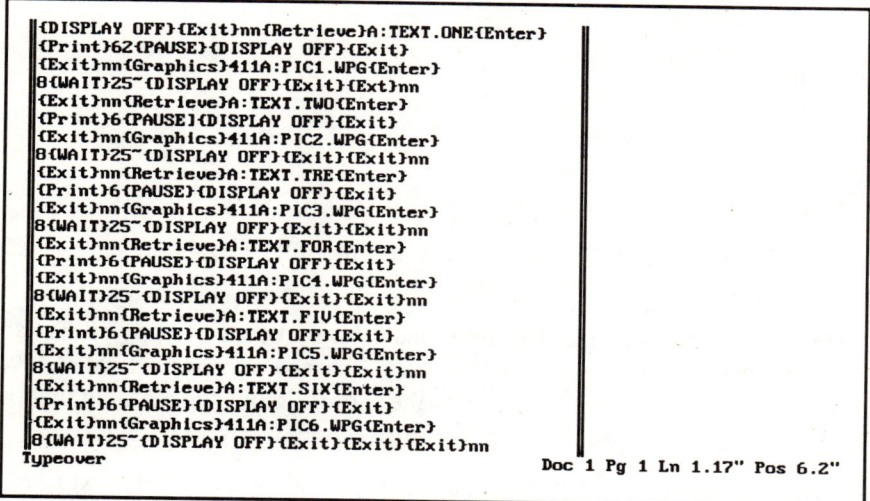

Figure 27-1

*Slide Shows*

```
{DISPLAY OFF}{Exit}nn{Graphics}411A:TXT1.IMG{Enter}
8{PAUSE}{DISPLAY OFF}{Exit}
{Exit}nn{Graphics}411A:PIC1.WPG{Enter}
8{WAIT}25~{DISPLAY OFF}{Exit}{Exit}nn
{Exit}nn{Graphics}411A:TXT2.IMG{Enter}
8{PAUSE}{DISPLAY OFF}{Exit}
{Exit}nn{Graphics}411A:PIC2.WPG{Enter}
{WAIT}25~{DISPLAY OFF}{Exit}{Exit}nn
{Exit}nn{Graphics}411A:TXT3.IMG{Enter}
8{PAUSE}{DISPLAY OFF}{Exit}
{Exit}nn{Graphics}411A:PIC3 .WPG{Enter}
8{WAIT}25~{DISPLAY OFF}{Exit}{Exit}nn
{Exit}nn{Graphics}411A:TXT4.IMG{Enter}
8{PAUSE}{DISPLAY OFF}{Exit}
{Exit}nn{Graphics}411A:PIC4.WPG{Enter}
8{WAIT}25~{DISPLAY OFF}{Exit}{Exit}nn
{Exit}nn{Graphics}411A:TXT5.IMG{Enter}
8{PAUSE}{DISPLAY OFF}{Exit}
{Exit}nn{Graphics}411A:PIC5.WPG{Enter}
8{WAIT}25~{DISPLAY OFF}{Exit}{Exit}nn
{Exit}nn{Graphics}411A:TXT6.IMG{Enter}
8{PAUSE}{DISPLAY OFF}{Exit}
{Exit}nn{Graphics}411A:PIC6.WPG{Enter}
8{WAIT}25~{DISPLAY OFF}{Exit}{Exit}{Exit}nn
C:\WW\SHOW2.BOX                        Doc 1 Pg 1 Ln 4.83" Pos 5.9"
```

*Figure 27-2*

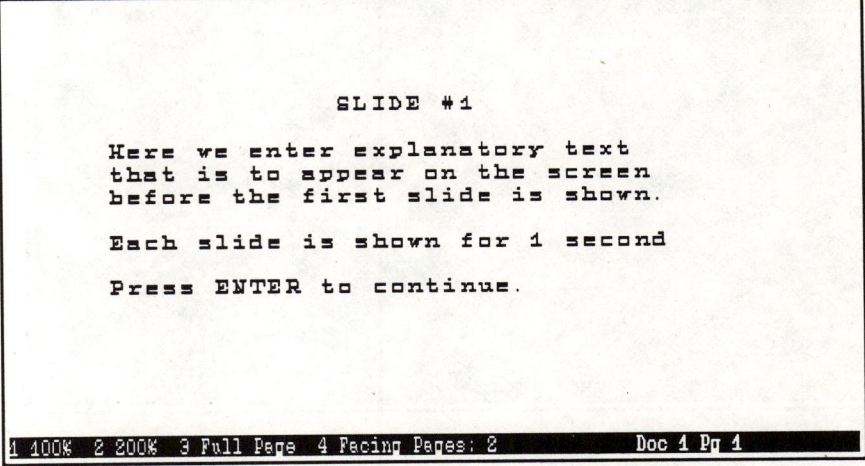

*Figure 27-3*

Chapter 27

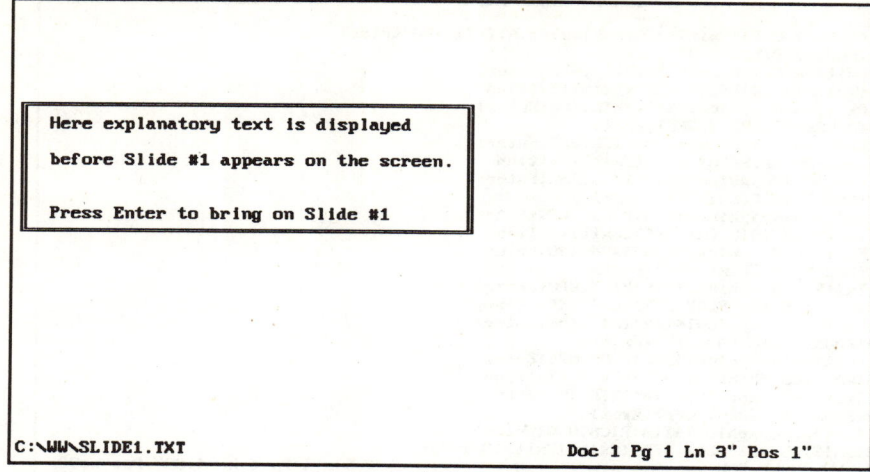

Figure 27-4

Figure 27-5

The following is an explanation of the commands and keystrokes making up the two macros.

*Fig 27-1, Line 1:*
1. {DISPLAY OFF} is provided automatically by the MACRO DEFINE (**Ctrl-F10**) option. To be able to enter the commands that follow, press **Ctrl-F10** to activate the **Macro edit** mode.
2. Press **F7** and type **n n** to produce {Exit}nn to clear the screen.

3. Press **Shift-F10**, type **A:TEXT.ONE**, and press **Enter** to place {Retrieve}A:TEXT.ONE{Enter} onto the line. (A: is used if the graphics and text files are on the disk in the A: drive. **TEXT.ONE** is an ASCII text file.)

*Line 2:*
1. Press **Shift-F7** and type **6 2** to place {Print}62 onto the line. (This displays the ASCII text in double size on the screen.) Exit the macro edit mode (**Ctrl-F10**).
2. Press **Ctrl-PgUp** to display macro commands. Use **Down Arrow** to scroll down until {PAUSE} is highlighted. Press **Enter**.
3. Use **Down Arrow** to scroll down until {DISPLAY OFF} is highlighted. Press **Enter**. Press **F7**. This places {PAUSE}{DISPLAY OFF}{Exit} onto line 2. (The {PAUSE} command causes macro execution to halt until a key is pressed.)

*Line 3:*
1. Press **F7** and type **n n**.
2. Press **Alt-F9**, type **4 1 1 A:PIC1.WPG**, and press **Enter** which places {Exit}nn{Graphics}411A:PIC1.WPG{Enter} on the line. ({Graphics}411 activates the graphics mode and calls for a filename to be entered. **PIC1.WPG** stands for any arbitrary graphics file.)

*Line 4:*
1. Type **8**. Press **Ctrl-PgUp**, use **Down Arrow** to highlight {WAIT}nn~, and press **Enter**.
2. Type **25~**. Press **Ctrl-PgUp**, use **Down Arrow** to highlight {DISPLAY OFF}, and press **Enter**. Press **F7 F7** and type **n n** to place 8{WAIT}25~{DISPLAY OFF}{Exit}{Exit}nn on line 4. (The **8** is the *Edit* command in the graphics mode. {WAIT} followed by a number and a tilde (~) causes execution to pause for a time period determined by the number.)

The remaining lines are repeats of the above and are therefore self-explanatory.

Fig. 27-2 is identical to Fig. 27-1, except that the text files are now graphics files (TXT1.IMG, TXT2.IMG, etc.). Also the Fig. 27-1 command sequence:{Retrieve}A:TEXT.ONE{Enter}{Print}62{PAUSE} is replaced by the command sequence: {Graphics}411A:TXT1.IMG{Enter}8{PAUSE} throughout the entire macro.

# CHAPTER 28
# GRAPHICS

This chapter examines the various aspects of WordPerfect's graphics capabilities. WordPerfect is not actually a full-fledged desktop publishing program. Still, it does include a sufficient number of functions and features to make it not only possible but relatively easy to produce simple documents such as letterheads, newsletters, pamphlets, announcements and the like.

Your computer must be equipped with some type of graphics adapter (CGA, EGA, Hercules, etc.) to be able to use the graphics functions, and your printer must be able to print graphics if you want to be able to print your work. But even if your printer is incapable of printing graphics (many dot-matrix and all daisy-wheel printers cannot print graphics), as long as a graphics adapter is installed, you can always use the View Document feature to see what your printed page would look like.

First place an empty box onto a page with text and have WordPerfect wrap the text around the box:

1. Press **Shift-F10** (Retrieve) and type the name of any text file. WordPerfect fills the screen with text.
2. Press **Alt-F9** (Graphics).
3. Select **1 Figure** and then select **1 Create**. This produces a menu with eight choices as in Fig. 28-1.

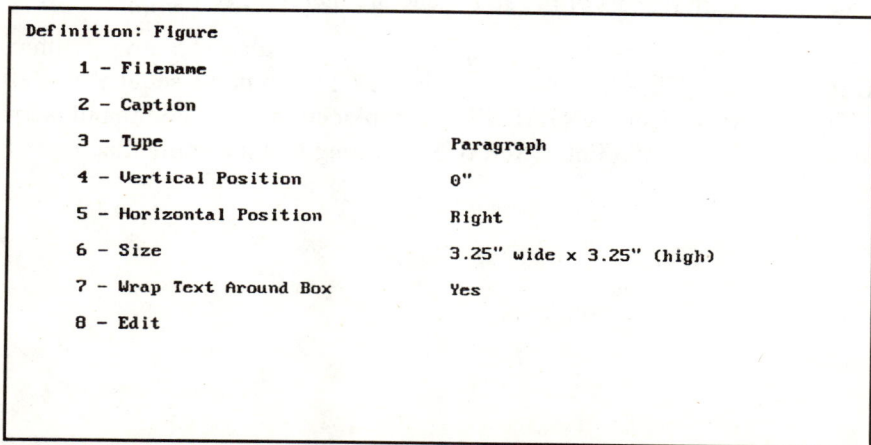

Figure 28-1

# Graphics

4. For the moment, ignore Filename and Caption and accept the defaults for everything except the Vertical position. Select **4 Vertical Position,** type **2,** and press **Enter**. The measurement is changed to 2".

5. Press **F7** (Exit) to return to the document screen. The text has remained unchanged and there is no sign of the box that is supposed to have been created.

6. Use **Down Arrow** to scroll the cursor down across the document and suddenly the box does appear, as in Fig. 28-2.

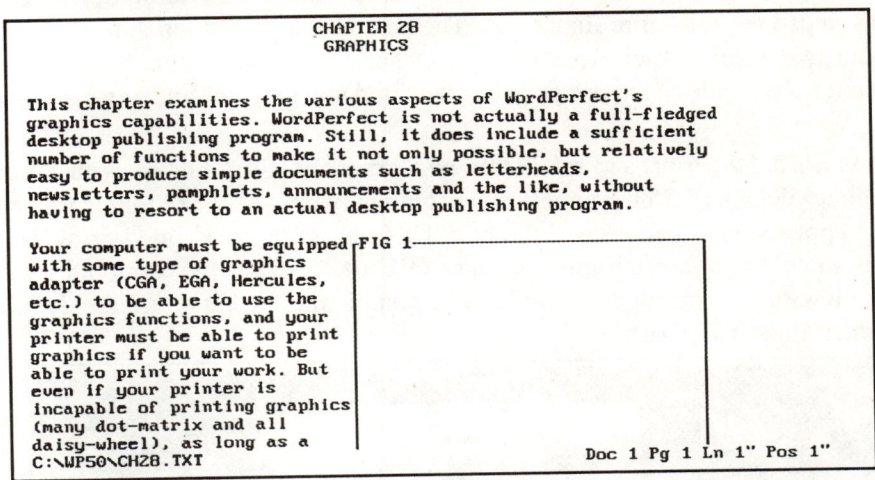

Figure 28-2

7. Press **Shift-F7** (Print) and select **6 View Document** and you see your full page with the box positioned two inches down the page flush with the right margin.

## INSERT GRAPHIC IMAGE AND ADD A CAPTION

Next create a similar box, but this time put a picture into it and write a caption to go with it.

1. Press **F7** (Exit) and type **n n** to clear the screen without saving the file with the empty graphics box.

2. Press **Shift-F10** (Retrieve) and type the name of the text file.

3. Press **Alt-F9** (Graphics).

4. Select **1 Figure** and then select **1 Create**.

5. Select **1 Filename** and type **B:\CLOCK.WPG** if the graphic files (.WPG) are on that disk. If not, use the appropriate information (If you are working in the disk or directory that holds the .WPG files, then the disk/directory/path information is not necessary.) and press **F7** (Exit).

*Chapter 28*

6. Select **2 Caption** (3 in version 5.1) which places **Figure 1** at the top of an empty document screen. Press the **Spacebar** twice and type **Three O'Clock High** as the caption. Press **F7** (Exit).
7. Select **4 Vertical Position** (5 in version 5.1), type **2**, and press **Enter**.
8. Select **5 Horizontal Position** (6 in version 5.1) and from the options displayed on the status line select **1 Left**.
9. Press **F7** (Exit) to return to the document screen full of text. Scroll down in the file so you can see the entire figure box. The box appears at the left side of the screen, some two inches down from the top. Depending on your monitor and graphics adapter, the inside of the box may be blank and you may not find any caption under it.
10. Press **Shift-F7** (Print) and select **6 View Document**. First the box with a clock set at three o'clock (8:25 in version 5.1) is gradually drawn. When that is finished the text appears, wrapped around the box. Underneath the box, lined up with its left bottom corner, appears **Figure 1 Three O'Clock High** as the caption. Fig. 28-3 is the view of the entire page. To view the graphic more clearly, use the double-size format. Press **F7** (Exit).

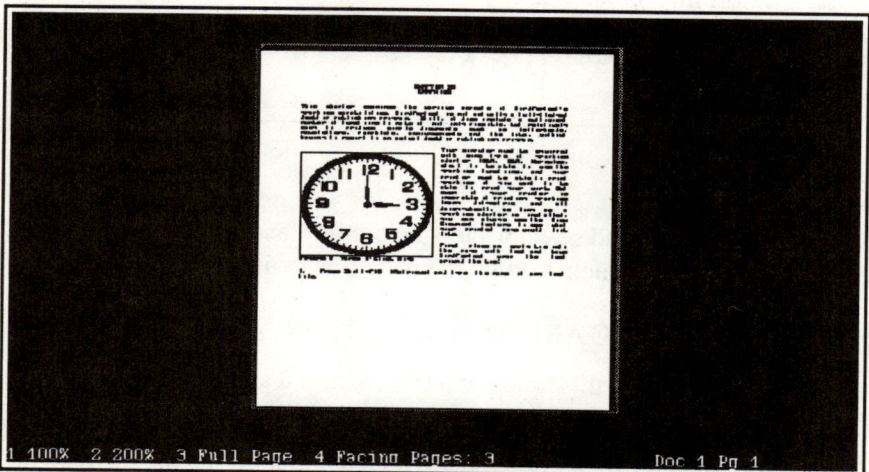

Figure 28-3

11. If your printer is capable of printing graphics, press **Shift-F7** (Print) and select **2 Page** to print the page with the graphic image added to the text.
12. Press **F7** (Exit) and type **y** because you want to use this later on, enter a filename of your choice (GRAPH.ONE), and then type **n** to clear the document screen.

*Graphics*

## INSERT A TABLE

This time use one of the other options. Select the Table option and then place any arbitrary graphic picture into it.

1. Press **Shift-F10** (Retrieve) and type the name of your text file once more.
2. Press **Alt-F9** (Graphics).
3. Select **2 Table** and then select **1 Create**.
4. Select **1 Filename**, type **USAMAP.WPG** plus the disk/directory/path information if necessary, and press **F7** (Exit).
5. Select **2 Caption**, and **Table I** is displayed at the top of the document screen. Press **Spacebar** twice, type **United States of America**, and press **F7** (Exit).
6. Select **4 Vertical Position**, type **1** and press **Enter**. Select **5 Horizontal Position**, **1 Left**, and press **F7** (Exit).
7. The document screen full of text is displayed. Press **Home Down Arrow**. A box, very similar to the preceding one, appears with the text wrapped around it as in Fig. 28-4. Press **Shift-F7** and select **6 View Document** and you see a different type of box with a map of the United States inside and the caption **Table I United States of America** this time at the top. Fig. 28-5 is the double-size view. If you wish, you may now print it, assuming your printer can handle it.
8. Press **F7** (Exit) and type **n n** to clear the document screen.

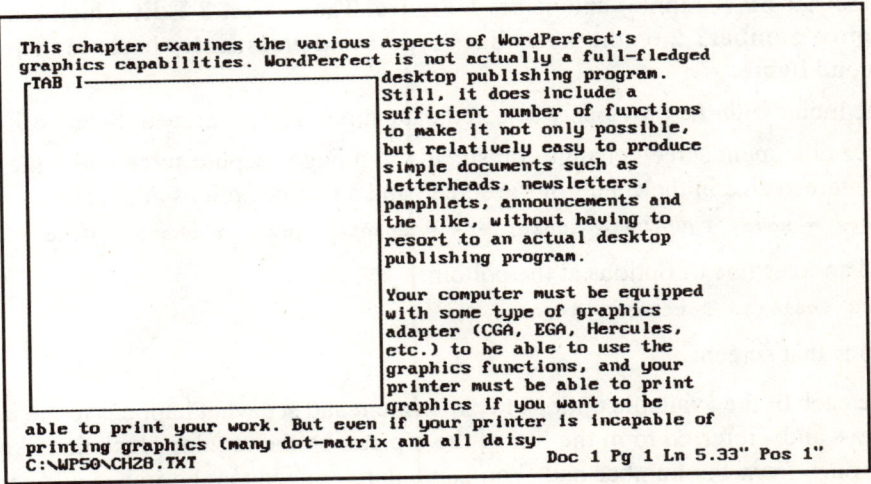

Figure 28-4

143

Chapter 28

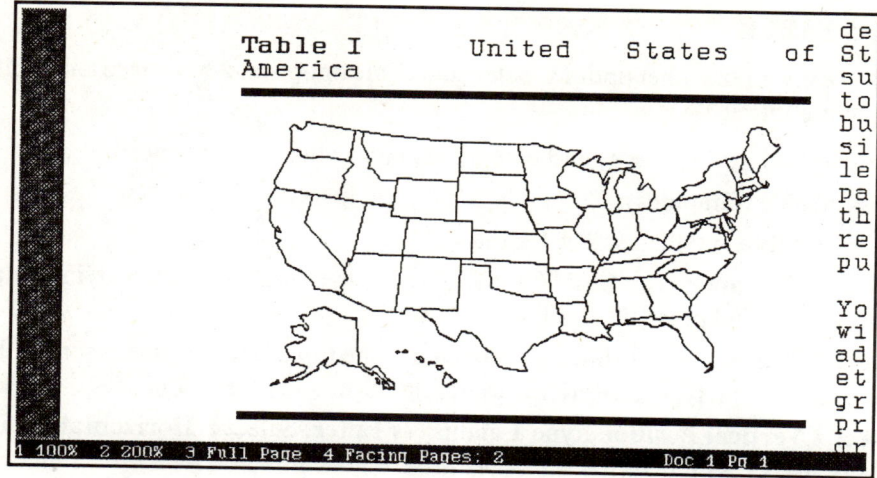

Figure 28-5

## EDIT A GRAPHIC IMAGE

Next explore some of the ways to manipulate the image in one of those graphic boxes.

1. Press **Shift-F10** (Retrieve) and type **GRAPH.ONE** or whatever filename you used when you saved the page with the clock graphic.

2. Press **Alt-F9** (Graphic) and select **1 Figure**. Then select **2 Edit** which results in **Figure number? 2** on the status line. Type **1** and press **Enter** because there is no second figure.

3. The menu with the previously selected data appears in the screen. Select **8 Edit**.

4. Your document screen changes drastically to a huge graphic screen with the clock full screen size in the center of the screen and a line of options at the top:

```
Arrow keys = Move; PgUp/Dn = Scale; +/- = Rotate; Ins = % change; Goto = Reset
```

and another line of options at the bottom:

```
1 Move; 2 Scale; 3 Rotate; 4 Invert: 0.
```

Fig. 28-6 is that screen.

5. Use each of the available options to experiment and see what happens to the image. The **+** and **-** referred to in the line at the top can be the regular plus/minus keys or the ones from the number pad. You can enlarge or reduce the image and move it horizontally and vertically; you can rotate it, invert it, and, at any time, you can press **Ctrl-Home** (Goto) and the original image is returned to you. Fig. 28-7 results from using 50 percent of the vertical scale.

6. With that edited version of the image, press **F7** (Exit) **F7** (Exit) **Shift-F7** (Print) and select **6 View Document**. The image is now shown in the edited version.

*Graphics*

*Figure 28-6*

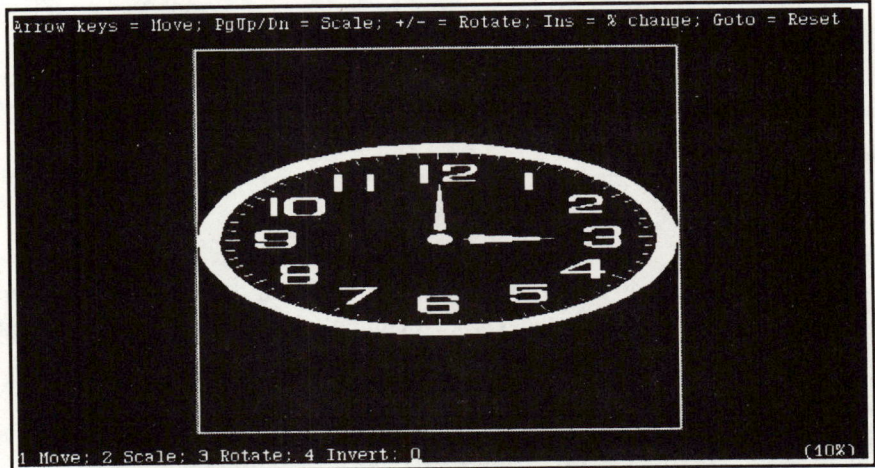

*Figure 28-7*

## EDIT THE GRAPHICS BOX

Now try something else, using the **Options** option.

1. Press **F7** (Exit) and type **n n** to clear the document screen and then once more retrieve GRAPH.ONE.
2. Press **Alt-F9** (Graphics), select **1 Figure**, and select **4 Options**, which displays a new menu as in Fig. 28-8.

```
Options:     Figure

       1 - Border Style
               Left                              Single
               Right                             Single
               Top                               Single
               Bottom                            Single
       2 - Outside Border Space
               Left                              0.16"
               Right                             0.16"
               Top                               0.16"
               Bottom                            0.16"
       3 - Inside Border Space
               Left                              0"
               Right                             0"
               Top                               0"
               Bottom                            0"
       4 - First Level Numbering Method          Numbers
       5 - Second Level Numbering Method         Off
       6 - Caption Number Style                  [BOLD]Figure 1[bold]
       7 - Position of Caption                   Below box, Outside borders
       8 - Minimum Offset from Paragraph         0"
       9 - Gray Shading (% of black)             0%

Selection: 0
```

*Figure 28-8*

3. You can use this menu to change any of the attributes of the box itself. Experiment with making changes and use the View Document option to see what they actually look like.

## INSERT A TEXT BOX

Sometimes it is important to be able to have a box of text inserted into a page of regular text:

1. With the document screen blank, retrieve your text file again.
2. Press **Alt-F9** (Graphics), select **3 Text Box**, and then select **1 Create**.
3. Ignore the Filename option. Select **2 Caption** and a **1** appears top center. Press **Spacebar** twice, type **This is a sample text box**, and press **F7** (Exit).
4. Select **4 Vertical position**, type **1**, and press **Enter**.
5. Press **F7** (Exit) and press **Alt-F9** (Graphics) again. Select **3 Text Box** and select **2 Edit**.
6. Change the **Figure number? 2** to **1** and press **Enter**.

7. If you want to enter text into the box, select **8 Edit**, type the text to be entered, and press **F7** (Exit) twice to return to the document screen.
8. Press **Home Down Arrow** and the text box is there, but most probably it is empty.
9. Press **Shift-F7** (Print), select **6 View Document** and this time the text is in the text box and the caption is below it, as in Fig. 28-9. Press **F7** (Exit) to return to the document screen.

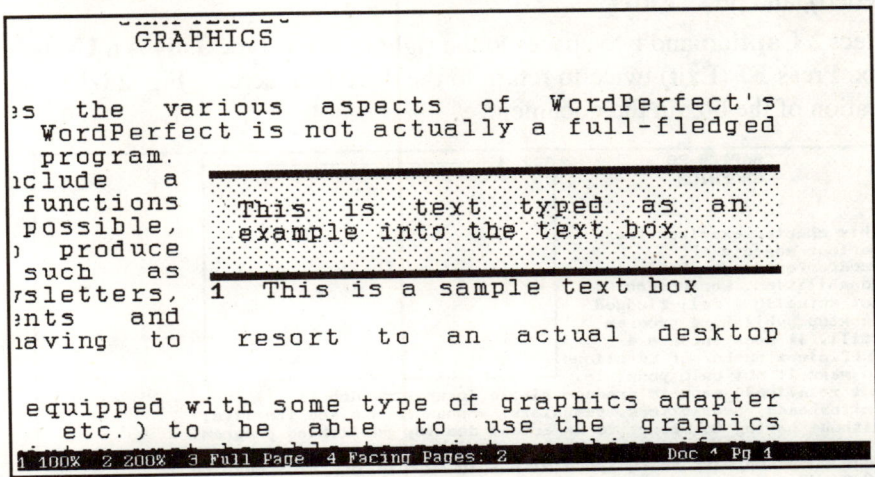

Figure 28-9

10. Press **Alt-F9** (Graphics), again select **3 Text Box**, and then select **4 Options**, and the screen offers a wide variety of conditions, all of which can be changed.
11. Select **9 Gray Shading** (% of black), type **30**, and press **Enter** to enter a darker gray shading.
12. Press **F7** (Exit) and return to the document screen. Press **Shift-F7** (Print), select **6 View Document** and this time the box is more heavily shaded.

About the **Type** option, you have three possible options: **Paragraph**, **Page**, and **Character** type. **Paragraph** type remains in the same text area. Editing tends to change its position on the page and can even move it to another page. **Page** type remains fixed in its original position, even if the text around it is moved. **Character** type treats the box, regardless of its size, as a single character. The latter is the only type box that can be used inside footnotes and endnotes.

Chapter 28

## INSERT A USER-DEFINED BOX

Next create a box that does not conform to the categories that you have examined so far.

1. With a blank document screen, retrieve your text file as before.
2. Press **Alt-F9** (Graphics), select **4 User defined**, and then select **1 Create**.
3. Select **1 Filename**, type **KEY.WPG** (include disk/directory/path information if needed), and press **Enter**.
4. Select **2 Caption** and two spaces to the right of the **1**, type **This is a User-defined Box**. Press **F7** (Exit) twice to return to the document screen. Fig. 28-10 shows the location of the box in the document.

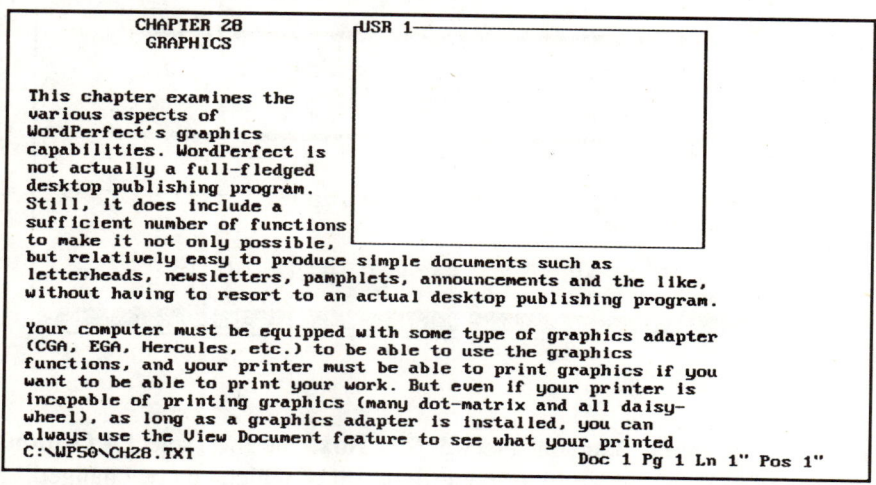

Figure 28-10

5. Press **Shift-F7** (Print), select **6 View Document**, and type **1**, and you see a key and the caption but no border of any kind. Also, that key is really too large, as in Fig. 28-11 (on the following page). Press **F7** (Exit).
6. Press **Alt-F9** (Graphics), select **4 User defined**, and then select **4 Options**. Change the Border Style from NONE to any one of the choices displayed on the status line when **1 Border Style** is selected. Press **F7** (Exit).
7. Press **Alt-F9** (Graphics), select **4 User defined, 2 Edit**, type **1**, and press **Enter**, and from the displayed menu, select **8 Edit**.
8. Select **Scale** and change it to **50%** (X and Y) and press the plus key (**+**) or type a number to rotate the image. Press **F7** (Exit) twice.
9. Press **Shift-F7** (Print), select **6 View Document**, and you see that the key is now reduced in size, that it is displayed vertically, and the caption is now located outside a double-line border. Press **F7** (Exit).

*Graphics*

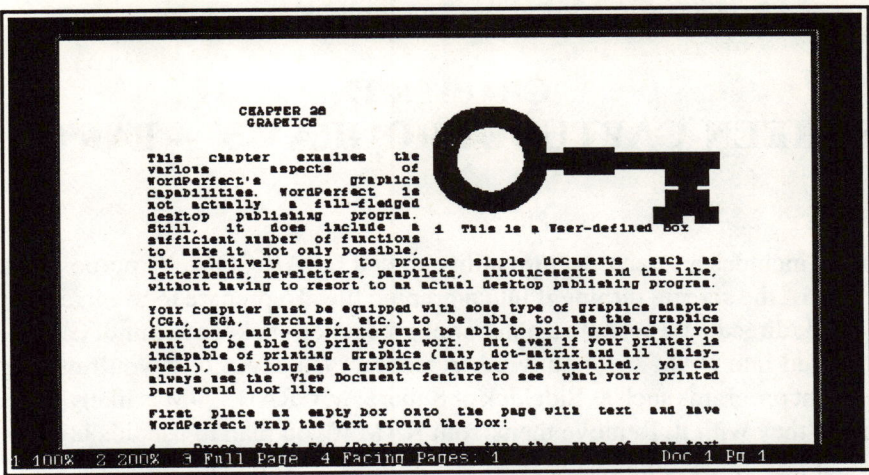

**Figure 28-11**

By experimenting with the options available in the graphics mode, you can arrive at many effective variations.

## Chapter 29
# SCREEN-CAPTURE PROGRAMS — PART I

WordPerfect includes a screen-capture utility, called GRAB.COM. Its purpose is to take a "snapshot" of the screen, turning it into a graphic file. To prepare to use it, copy it onto the active disk/directory. There are a number of precautions to keep in mind. GRAB.COM must be loaded into RAM *before* any other program is activated. If you're using other RAM-resident programs such as Sidekick or SuperKey, GRAB.COM is likely to interfere with them or they with it. Remove them from RAM if you plan to use this utility.

If RAM resident programs are called automatically from your AUTOEXEC.BAT file, prepare another disk containing COMMAND.COM. Then write a new AUTOEXEC.BAT file that might looks similar to this: **C:**

### GET CLOCK

If you're using a mouse requiring a program (like the Logitech mice using MOUSE.COM, CLICK.COM, or MENU.COM), then this command should be included in the new version of the AUTOEXEC.BAT file. After that the routine is:

1. Turn the computer off.
2. Place the new disk containing COMMAND.COM and the new AUTOEXEC.BAT file into drive A:.
3. Turn the computer on in the usual manner.
4. Change directories (**cd\\**) to the one on which GRAB.COM is located and press **Enter**.
5. Type **GRAB** and press **Enter**. The screen displays a box saying that the GRAB utility has been successfully installed.
6. Activate the graphics program that contains the image you want to capture. Run that program until the desired image is on the screen.
7. Press **Alt-Shift-F9**. The computer responds with a two-tone chime, and a dashed-line rectangular box appears superimposed over the image to be captured. (If a low buzzing sound is heard instead, the screen is not in the graphics mode and screen capture is not possible with GRAB.COM.)
8. Use the **arrow keys** to move the box. Use **Shift-arrow** to resize the box and enclose the portion of the image that you want to capture. A bit of experimentation helps to familiarize yourself with how this works. Use the **Ins** key to toggle between large and small increments when moving or resizing the box.

## Screen-Capture Programs — Part I

9. When the portion of the image that you want to capture is safely within the confines of the box, press **Enter**. Again a two-tone chime is heard. A new file called GRAB.WPG is saved on the logged disk/directory. If you capture more than one image, the filenames are GRAB1.WPG, GRAB2.WPG all the way up to GRAB9999.WPG.
10. Copy the GRAB file(s) to your WordPerfect work disk. You can now use them just like any other graphics files, using **Alt-F9** (Graphics) and the appropriate commands from the graphics menu.

Now for a practical example. For the purpose of this demonstration a desktop publishing program called Publish It! is used to produce an image to be incorporated in a WordPerfect document.

1. Turn the computer off. Insert the disk containing COMMAND.COM and AUTOEXEC.BAT into drive A: and turn the computer back on.
2. Move to the disk/directory that contains the copy of GRAB.COM, type **GRAB**, and press **Enter**. This places GRAB.COM into RAM. The screen returns to the DOS prompt.
3. Move to the disk/directory that contains Publish It! (or the graphics program that you want to use).
4. Activate Publish It! or your selected graphics program.
5. Select clip-art or another graphics file and retrieve it into display. Fig. 29-1 is an example, displayed on the Publish It! work area.

Figure 29-1

Chapter 29

6. With the desired image on the screen, press **Alt-Shift-F9**. Wait for the chime and the appearance of the rectangle.
7. Resize and move the rectangle to enclose the image, as in Fig. 29-2.

Figure 29-2

8. Press **Enter**.
9. Select **Exit** from the File menu and click the mouse button or whatever is appropriate to return to the DOS prompt.
10. Copy GRAB.WPG to your WordPerfect work disk/directory and delete it from the disk/directory containing the graphics program you used.
11. Activate WordPerfect in the usual manner.
12. Press **Alt-F9** (Graphics), select **1 Figure**, and select **1 Create**.
13. From the graphics menu select **1 Filename** and type **GRAB.WPG**.
14. Select **5 Horizontal** and select **3 Center**.
15. Press **F7** (Exit) to return to the document screen. The indication of a graphics box is displayed.
16. Press **Shift-F7** (Print) and select **6 View Document**. Your captured image now appears at the top of the page, centered, as in Fig. 29-3.

*Screen-Capture Programs — Part I*

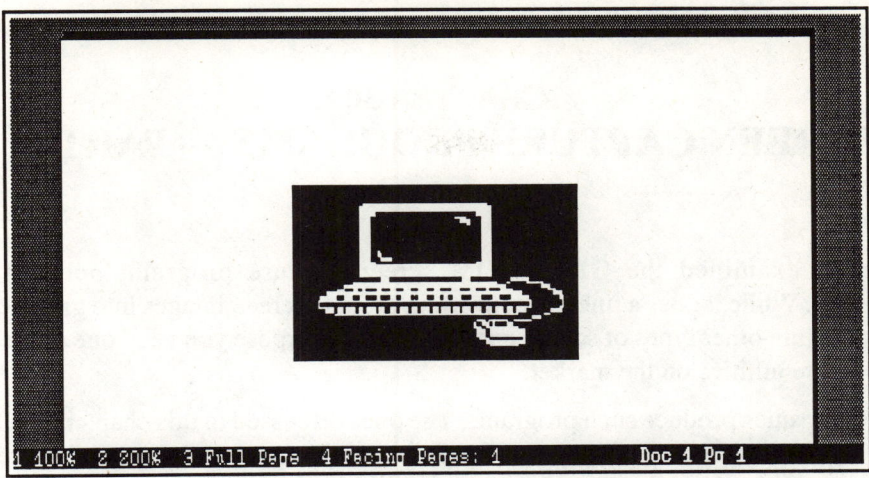

**Figure 29-3**

17. If you like, you can now return to the graphics menu and select **8 Edit**. The image appears on the editing screen where you can manipulate it like any other WordPerfect graphics image.

This utility increases the versatility of WordPerfect by making it possible to incorporate various graphic images available from other application programs.

# Chapter 30
# SCREEN CAPTURE PROGRAMS — PART II

Chapter 29 examined the GRAB.COM screen capture program included with WordPerfect. While it does a fine job converting graphic screen images into graphic files, it cannot capture other types of screen images. For that purpose you need one of the other screen capture utilities on the market.

Several companies produce such programs. The ones discussed in this chapter are HiJaak and InSet, both from Inset Systems, Inc. Both programs include many features not necessarily pertinent here. The features applicable for use with WordPerfect are CONVERT and CAPTURE, available with both systems, but functioning somewhat differently with each.

## HIJAAK

HiJaak includes CAPTURE.EXE and CONVERT.EXE. CAPTURE.EXE is installed as a RAM-resident program, always available to capture either graphics or text screens. The resulting files are saved in the FILENAME.PIX format, which cannot be imported into WordPerfect. To be used, they must be converted to one of the file formats that WordPerfect can deal with. The CONVERT.EXE program takes care of that. It converts .PIX files into a wide variety of file formats. Included are .WPG, .IMG, and .PCX, all of which can be imported into WordPerfect files without difficulty.

The HiJaak capture utility always captures the full screen. If any cropping is needed, you have to resort to one of the many graphics or desktop publishing programs designed specifically for manipulating graphics.

One of the unique capabilities of HiJaak has to do with text screens and text files. The capture option can be used to capture any text screen, just like any graphics screen. Fig. 30-1 is the current text screen captured and then converted to a graphics file.

The other feature uses the CONVERT.EXE program to convert ASCII text files directly into graphics files. The file is converted into a .WPG file that can be used and manipulated by WordPerfect.

## Screen-Capture Programs —Part II

```
                    CHAPTER 30
            SCREEN CAPTURE PROGRAMS - PART II

   Chapter 29 examined the GRAB.COM screen capture program included
   with WordPerfect. While it does a fine job converting graphic
   screen into graphic files, it cannot capture other types of
   screen images. For that purpose you need one of the other screen
   capture utilities on the market.

   Several companies produce such programs. The ones discussed in
   this chapter are Hijaak and InSet, both from Inset Systems, Inc.
   Both programs include many features not necessarily pertinent
   here. The features applicable for use with WordPerfect are
   CONVERT and CAPTURE, available with both systems, but functioning
   somewhat differently with each.

   HIJAAK
   Hijaak includes CAPTURE.EXE and CONVERT.EXE. CAPTURE.EXE is
   installed as a RAM-resident program, always available to capture
   either graphics or text screens. The resulting files are saved in
   the FILENAME.PIX format, which cannot be imported into
   WordPerfect. To be used, they must be converted to one of the
   file formats that WordPerfect can deal with. The CONVERT.EXE
                              Doc 1 Pg 1 Ln 4.83" Pos 7"
```

Figure 30-1

### INSET

The screen capture program in InSet includes a cropping feature. You can determine exactly what portion of the screen to capture. The resulting files are also in the FILENAME.PIX format. They must be converted to a WordPerfect-compatible format, just like the ones produced by HiJaak.

The CONVERT option is different from the one described for Hijaak. It captures any 80-character text screen and converts it into a graphics screen that can be edited or annotated using the InSet EDIT option. The details of how this works in practice are beyond the scope of this book. InSet owners should consult the InSet manual for the needed information.

Other screen-capture utilities are The Graphics Link and HotShot. They function similarly to those described here.

# CHAPTER 31
# COMPARING DOCUMENTS

WordPerfect includes a feature that compares a document on disk with the one currently displayed. Text included in the on-screen document but missing in the file on disk is redlined. Any discrepancies detected are indicated in the on-screen document. Conversely, text included in the file on disk but not found in the on-screen version is added to the on-screen text enclosed in strikeout codes. To demonstrate, this paragraph was saved on disk. Then several sentences were deleted. Fig. 31-1 is a printout of this paragraph with the redlined and strikeout modes indicating differences between the two versions. On the screen, the redline/strikeout copy is displayed in contrasting colors on color monitors or in different shadings on monochrome monitors.

```
        WordPerfect includes a feature that compares a document on
disk with the one currently displayed and in RAM.....Text.that.is
included.in.the.on-screen.document.but...is.missing.in.the.file.on
disk.is.redlined.  Any discrepancies that are detected are
indicated in the on-screen document.  Text that is included in
the on-screen document but is missing in the file on disk is
redlined.  Conversely, text that is included in the file on disk
but is not found in the on-screen version is added to the on-
screen text enclosed in strikeout codes...To.demonstrate,.this
paragraph.was.saved.on.disk...Then.several.sentences.were
deleted.
```

Figure 31-1

To demonstrate:

1. Retrieve any text document of your choice and make a few changes.
2. Press **Alt-F5** (Mark Text) and select **6 Generate**.
3. Select **2 Compare Screen and Disk Documents and Add Redline and Strikeout**.
4. If the displayed filename is not the one of the file on disk, enter the correct filename.
5. Press **Enter**.

In a moment the cursor appears at the top of the screen. Use the cursor keys to move down across the document. The differences between the two versions are clearly indicated.

If WordPerfect finds that a block of text has been moved from one location in the document to another, the legend "The Following Text was Moved" appears before the block of text in question, and "The Preceding Text was Moved" appears at the end of that block.

When you're ready to return to your screen document and want to get rid of the redline and strikeout codes, the steps are:

1. Press **Alt-F5** (Mark Text).
2. Select **6 Generate**.
3. Select **1 Remove Redline Markings and Strikeout Text from Document**.
4. Type **y** to remove the codes or **n** if you have changed your mind and want to retain them.

This removes not only the redline and strikeout codes, but also the text that was found in the document on disk but was missing in the on-screen document. If you want to remove the codes but retain the text in the on-screen version of the document, move the cursor to the top of the document and use these steps:

1. Press **Alt-F2** (Find and Replace). Press **Enter** to accept the default.
2. Press **Ctrl-F8** (Font) and select **2 Appearance**.
3. Select **8 Redln**.
4. Press **F2** (Find).
5. Press **F2**. All redline codes are deleted.

Repeat the above (except in step 3 select **9 Stkout**) to get rid of the strikeout codes. If you have to do this with any degree of frequency, create the macros shown in Fig. 31-2 and Fig. 31-3. CODES.WPM is chained to CODER.WPM. When you press **Alt-F10** (Macro), type **CODER**, and press **Enter**, all redline and strikeout codes in the on-screen document are deleted.

## Chapter 31

```
Macro: Edit
      File           CODER.WPM
   1 - Description   Remove redline codes
   2 - Action

   ┌─────────────────────────────────────────────────────────┐
   │ {DISPLAY OFF}{Home}{Home}{Up}{Replace}{Enter}           │
   │ {Font}28{Search}{Search}{CHAIN}CODES.WPM~               │
   │                                                         │
   │                                                         │
   │                                                         │
   │                                                         │
   └─────────────────────────────────────────────────────────┘

Selection: 0
```

*Figure 31-2*

```
Macro: Edit
      File           CODES.WPM
   1 - Description   Remove strikeout codes
   2 - Action

   ┌─────────────────────────────────────────────────────────┐
   │ {DISPLAY OFF}{Home}{Home}{Up}{Up}{Replace}{Enter}       │
   │ {Font}29{Search}{Search}                                │
   │                                                         │
   │                                                         │
   │                                                         │
   │                                                         │
   └─────────────────────────────────────────────────────────┘

Selection: 0
```

*Figure 31-3*

## CHAPTER 32
# MASTER DOCUMENTS AND HYPHENATION

In this chapter it is assumed that you have been working on a series of documents such as individual chapters of a book or portions of an annual report or something similar. The point is that the separate files must be combined into a single master document to generate a table of contents and an index.

For the purpose of this demonstration, three text files called ONE.TXT, TWO.TXT, and THREE.TXT are used. The actual text in those files is of no particular importance in the context of this demonstration.

### HYPHENATION

1. Press **Shift-F10** (Retrieve) and type the name of any text file that you can use to play with.
2. To improve the physical appearance of the text, tell WordPerfect to hyphenate the words that fall at the end of lines when right justification is turned on.
3. Press **Home Home Up Arrow** to get to the top of the document.
4. Press **Shift-F8** (Format). Select **1 Line, 1 Hyphenation,** and **3 Auto**.
5. Select **3 Justification** and type **y**. Press **Enter** and **F7** (Exit) to return to the document screen.
6. Press **Home Home Down Arrow** to scroll through the entire document. Observe how WordPerfect automatically hyphenates certain words, each time asking if the hyphenation is OK, though right justification is not being displayed.
7. Press **Shift-F7** (Print) and select **6 View Document** to see that it is now right justified. Press **F7** (Exit) and **F10** (Save) to return to the document screen and save the new version.
8. Press **F7** (Exit) and type **n n** to clear the screen.

You're now ready to retrieve and reformat a second and third text document in the same manner.

*Chapter 32*

## CREATING A MASTER DOCUMENT

Next you must create the Master Document as a special file used to combine several files in a specific order.

1. Press **F7** (Exit) and type **n n** to clear the screen.
2. Press **Shift-F6** (Center) **F6** (Bold), type **MASTER DOCUMENT** or any other name that appeals to you, and press **F6** (Bold) again.
3. Press **Enter** a few time to add blank lines.
4. Press **Ctrl-Enter** to enter a hard page break.
5. Press **Alt-F5** (Mark Text) and select **2 Subdocument**. When asked for a filename, type the name of the first of the text files and press **Enter**.
6. Press **Ctrl-Enter** to place a hard page break after the box that was automatically created, as in Fig. 32-1.

```
                          MASTER DOCUMENT


    ================================================================
    | Subdoc: ONE.TXT                                              |
    ================================================================




                                              Doc 1 Pg 3 Ln 1" POS 1"
```

Figure 32-1

7. Press **Alt-F5** (Mark Text) and select **2 Subdocument**. When asked for a filename, type the name of the second of the text files and press **Enter**.
8. Press **Ctrl-Enter** to place a hard page break after the box.
9. Press **Alt-F5** (Mark Text) and select **2 Subdocument**. When asked for a filename, type the name of the third of the text files and press **Enter**.
10. Press **Ctrl-Enter** to place a hard page break after the box. The screen now looks like Fig. 32-2.
11. Press **F10** (Save) and enter a filename.

```
                    MASTER DOCUMENT


================================================================

  Subdoc: ONE.TXT


================================================================

  Subdoc: TWO.TXT


================================================================

  Subdoc: THREE.TXT


================================================================
                                         Doc 1 Pg 5 Ln 1" POS 1"
```

*Figure 32-2*

Now you are ready to use your Master Document to place the three text files into one combined file:

1. Move the cursor to the top of the file. Press **Alt-F5** (Mark Text) and select **6 Generate**. Then select **3 Expand Master Document**. WordPerfect enters all three text documents. Each one is preceded by a box reading **Subdoc Start:** *FILENAME* and followed by another box reading **Subdoc End:** *FILENAME*, as in Fig. 32-3.

```
                    MASTER DOCUMENT

================================================================

  Subdoc Start: ONE.TXT
                        CHAPTER 32
              MASTER DOCUMENTS AND HYPHENATION

  In this chapter it is assumed that you have been working on a
  series of documents such as individual chapters of a book or
  portions of an annual report or something similar. The point is
  that the separate files must be combined into a single master
  document to generate a table of contents and an index.'

  For the purpose of this demonstration, three text files called
  ONE.TXT, TWO.TXT, and THREE.TXT are used. The actual text in
  those files is of no particular importance in the context of this
  demonstration.

  Subdoc End: ONE.TXT
  C:\WP50\MASTER.WW                     Doc 1 Pg 1 Ln 1.16" POS 1"
```

*Figure 32-3*

2. When it's all done, press **F10** (Save) to save the new Master Document that now includes the three files.

In this manner you can combine any number of documents. But keep in mind that the floppy disks on which you will eventually want to save and store these files have a limited amount of space. Don't create a master document that occupies 400,000 bytes and try to save it on a 360K floppy. It won't work. (WordPerfect includes a **Condense Master Document** feature as one of the **Alt-F5** (Mark Text) options. It removes the subdocument boxes but is not likely to have a major effect on the total number of bytes occupied by the document.)

## Chapter 33
# TABLES OF CONTENTS

You can let WordPerfect create tables of contents for your documents. The procedure involves marking the text, such as chapter headings and anything else that you might want included. The next step requires defining the table format itself. And then you must generate the table, using the appropriate steps. You can design tables of contents with up to five levels. In most instances, two levels, one for the chapter heading and a second for some explanatory text, are sufficient.

**MARK THE TEXT**

1. Press **Alt-F4** (Block) and block the text, word, or phrase that is to be included in the table.
2. Press **Alt-F5** (Mark Text).
3. Select **1 ToC**.
4. Type a number from **1** to **5** to indicate the level in which you want the text to be included.

**DEFINE THE TABLE**

1. Press **Home Home Up Arrow** to move the cursor to the head of the document.
2. Press **Ctrl-Enter** to create a hard page break.
3. Press **Up Arrow** to move the cursor into the page preceding the hard page break.
4. Type **TABLE OF CONTENTS** or any other heading.
5. Press **Enter** twice to add some blank lines.
6. Press **Alt-F5** (Mark Text).
7. Select **5 Define**. This displays the menu in Fig. 33-1.

Chapter 33

```
Mark Text: Define
     1 - Define Table of Contents
     2 - Define List
     3 - Define Index
     4 - Define Table of Authorities
     5 - Edit Table of Authorities Full Form




Selection: 0
```

*Figure 33-1*

8. Select **1 Define Table of Contents**. This displays a menu with three choices.
9. Type **1** to select **Number of Levels**.
10. Type a number from **1** to **5** to define the number of levels to be included.
11. From the menu in Fig. 33-2 make the appropriate choices for the format used in your table of contents.

```
Table of Contents Definition
     1 - Number of Levels                    1
     2 - Display Last Level in               No
         Wrapped Format
     3 - Page Numbering - Level 1     Flush right with leader
                          Level 2
                          Level 3
                          Level 4
                          Level 5




Selection: 1
```

*Figure 33-2*

## GENERATE

1. Press **Alt-F5** (Mark Text).
2. Select **6 Generate** to display the menu in Fig. 33-3.

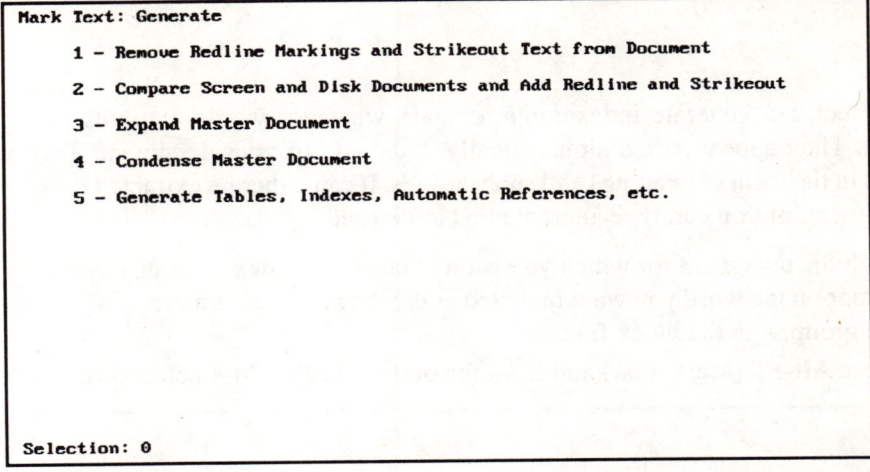

Figure 33-3

3. Select **5 Generate Tables, Indexes, Automatic References, etc.**
4. Type **y** to begin the process of generating the table.

During the generating process, a counter at the bottom of the screen keeps track of what is going on inside the computer.

Using this function may, in some instances, be more trouble than it's worth. If the document is a book made up of many chapters, even if all are combined into a master document, it could be simpler to create a table of contents as a regular text document, formatted to your liking.

# CHAPTER 34
# INDEXES

WordPerfect can generate indexes that contain whatever words or phrases you want included. They appear sorted alphabetically at the end of your document. Text may be included in the form of headings and subheadings. It can either be extracted directly from the document, or you can type alternate text to be used instead.

1. With the document for which you want to create an index on your screen, place the cursor on the word you want included in the index, or, if it's a group of words, mark the group with the block function.
2. Press **Alt-F5** (Mark Text) and from the options in Fig. 34-1 select **3 Index**.

```
1 Auto Ref; 2 Subdoc; 3 Index; 4 ToA Short Form; 5 Define; 6 Generate: 0
```

Figure 34-1

3. Press **Enter** to use the displayed text or type your own text for the index heading and press **Enter**. The status line asks for the subheading.
4. Simply press **Enter** for no subheading or enter whatever text you might want to use and press **Enter**.
5. Repeat the above four steps for the entire document.
6. When finished place the cursor at the very end of your document (**Home Home Down Arrow**) and press **Ctrl-Enter** to enter a hard page break.
7. Type a heading for the index, such as **Shift-F6** (Center) and **INDEX** or whatever appeals to you. Press **Enter Enter** to insert some blank lines.
8. Press **Alt-F5** (Mark Text) and select **5 Define**.
9. From the menu, displayed in Fig. 34-2, select **3 Define Index**. If you want to create a concordance file which is used only when one and the same word or phase appears frequently in the same document, then enter a filename of your choice. If not, simply press **Enter**.

```
Mark Text: Define

     1 - Define Table of Contents

     2 - Define List

     3 - Define Index

     4 - Define Table of Authorities

     5 - Edit Table of Authorities Full Form




Selection: 0
```

*Figure 34-2*

10. From the five options contained in the next menu in Fig. 34-3, select a style in which you want the page numbers to appear in the index.

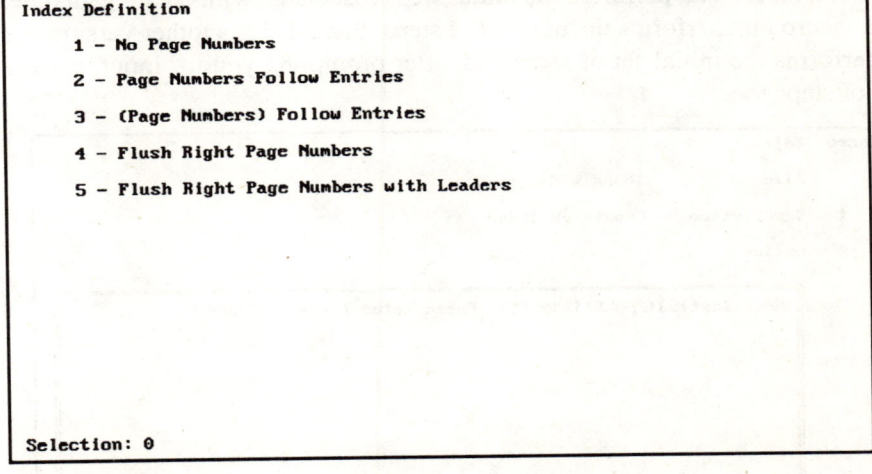

*Figure 34-3*

11. Now you're ready to generate the actual index. Press **Alt-F5** (Mark Text) and select **6 Generate**.
12. From the displayed menu, shown in Fig. 34-4, select **5 Generate Tables, Indexes, Automatic References, etc.**

## Chapter 34

```
Mark Text: Generate

     1 - Remove Redline Markings and Strikeout Text from Document
     2 - Compare Screen and Disk Documents and Add Redline and Strikeout
     3 - Expand Master Document
     4 - Condense Master Document
     5 - Generate Tables, Indexes, Automatic References, etc.




     Existing tables, lists, and indexes will be replaced.  Continue? (Y/N) Yes
```

*Figure 34-4*

13. Type **y** or any other key except **n** to start the process of generating the index. A counter at the bottom of the page keeps track of the progress.

Fig. 34-5 is a macro that performs the initial steps associated with creating an index. Fig. 34-6 is a macro that performs the next set of steps. Fig. 34-7 is another version. Here the macro performs the initial set of steps and, after prompting you for input, performs the next set of steps too.

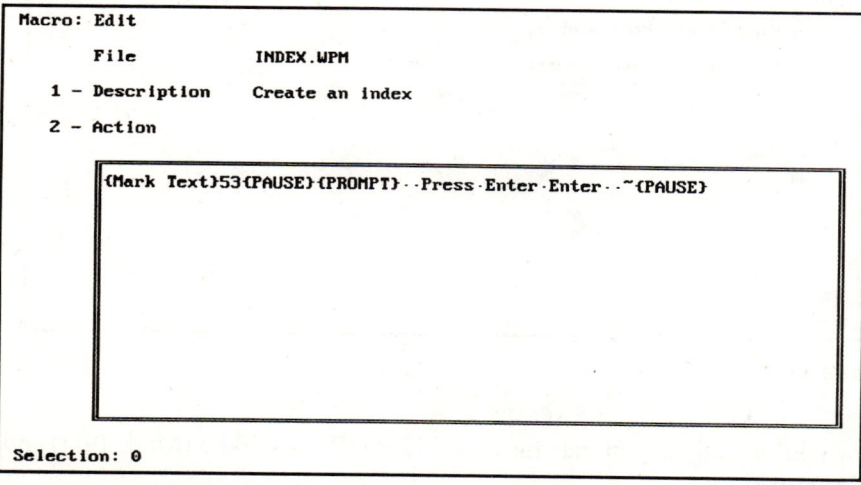

*Figure 34-5*

```
Macro: Edit
        File            INDEX2.WPM
   1 - Description      generate index
   2 - Action
        ┌─────────────────────────────────────────────┐
        │ {DISPLAY OFF}{Mark Text}65y                 │
        │                                             │
        └─────────────────────────────────────────────┘

Selection: 0
```

*Figure 34-6*

```
Macro: Edit
        File            INDEX.WPM
   1 - Description      Create an index
   2 - Action
        ┌─────────────────────────────────────────────────────────┐
        │ {Mark Text}53{PAUSE}{Enter}{PROMPT}Select style, then press Enter
        │ Enter..~{PAUSE}{CHAIN}index2.wpm                        │
        └─────────────────────────────────────────────────────────┘

Selection: 0
```

*Figure 34-7*

If an index is to be created for an entire book, consisting of a number of individual chapters, each saved under a different filename, then a number of steps have to be taken to generate a single index for the entire book:

1. Start at the very beginning of the manuscript (Preface, Introduction, or whatever) and note the page number of the last page. Go to the next chapter and press **Shift-F8** (Format), select **2 Page**, and select **6 New Page Number**. Type the next page number based on the last page of the preceding chapter. Continue this process all the way to the very end of the book manuscript.
2. Use the above described routine to generate indexes for each chapter. In each case they are appended to the end of each chapter.
3. Create a new empty file to contain the index. For each chapter press **Alt-F4** and block the entire index portion.
4. Then press **Ctrl-F4** (Move) and select **1 Block**.
5. Select **4 Append** and enter the name of the file that you just created. (If you forgot to create a file, one is automatically created.)
6. Repeat the above for each chapter in the book. Then, with the Index file retrieved, press **Ctrl-F9** (Merge/Sort) and use the **Sort** function to place everything into alphabetical order.

There is another and in some respects simpler way to accomplish this. It uses the **Master Document** function discussed in Chapter 32. That function combines all your chapters into one giant document with continuous page numbers. You can then simply treat the entire document as one, while generating your index that is then appended to the end of the whole thing.

## Chapter 35
# CONCORDANCE FILES

If the document for which you want to produce an index includes words or phrases that occur frequently, you can create a concordance file. Such a file is a regular WordPerfect document used internally during the index generating process. Whenever WordPerfect encounters any words or phrases contained in the concordance file, it enters the appropriate page number into the index.

To create a concordance file:

1. Type a list of words or phrases that occur frequently in the documents that make up the master document. After each entry press **Enter**. Entries can be of any length.
2. When all entries have been made, press **F10** (Save). For a filename give it CONCORD.FIL (any other will do).

To use the file during the process of generating an index, the initial steps are the same as described in Chapter 34. During the process of defining the index, the steps are:

1. Move the cursor to the end of your document.
2. Press **Ctrl-Enter** to insert a hard page break.
3. Type a heading and press **Enter** twice.
4. Press **Alt-F5** (Mark Text).
5. Select **5 Define**, which displays a group of choices.
6. Select **3 Define Index**. The display asks that you enter the name of your concordance file, as in Fig. 35-1. This tells WordPerfect to include the words contained in the concordance file in the index. Type a name and press **Enter**.
7. From the displayed choices shown in the menu in Fig. 35-2, select the numbering style you want to use.

From then on the steps used to actually generate the index are the same as described in Chapter 34.

## Chapter 35

A word of warning about using concordance files. In some cases certain words or phrases occur so often that it would be wrong to include each and every one in the index. For instance, in generating an index for this book, if the word WordPerfect would be included in the concordance file, it would appear in the index with an enormous number of page numbers. Limit the entries in concordance files to words and phrases that occur in several places where the reader would find information worth looking for. Just because a given word appears somewhere on a page does not mean that it should, necessarily, be included in the index.

```
Mark Text: Define
    1 - Define Table of Contents
    2 - Define List
    3 - Define Index
    4 - Define Table of Authorities
    5 - Edit Table of Authorities Full Form




















Concordance Filename (Enter=none):
```

*Figure 35-1*

```
Index Definition
    1 - No Page Numbers
    2 - Page Numbers Follow Entries
    3 - (Page Numbers) Follow Entries
    4 - Flush Right Page Numbers
    5 - Flush Right Page Numbers with Leaders














Selection: 0
```

*Figure 35-2*

## CHAPTER 36
# WIDOWS, ORPHANS, AND CONDITIONAL END-OF-PAGE FEATURES

Widows are short lines, usually the first line that is left behind when a paragraph continues to the following page. Orphans are short lines, usually the last line in a paragraph, that fall at the top of the next column or page. Both are esthetically unattractive and can be avoided by using the **Widow/Orphan Protection** feature.

1. Press **Shift-F8** (Format).
2. Select **1 Line**.
3. From the menu in Fig. 36-1 select **9 Widow/Orphan Protection**.

```
Format: Line
          1 - Hyphenation                        Off
          2 - Hyphenation Zone - Left            10%
                                 Right           4%
          3 - Justification                      Yes
          4 - Line Height                        Auto
          5 - Line Numbering                     No
          6 - Line Spacing                       1
          7 - Margins - Left                     1"
                        Right                    1"
          8 - Tab Set                            0", every 0.5"
          9 - Widow/Orphan Protection            No

Selection: 0
```

Figure 36-1

4. Type **y**.
5. Press **F7** (Exit) to return to the document screen.

When this feature is active, there is never a single line at the top or bottom of a column or page, unless that single line is a stand-alone line, such as a chapter heading. Whenever WordPerfect finds a paragraph encountering a page break between the second to last and the last line, it moves the page break up one line. The result makes for an overall attractive document.

Sometimes it is desirable to keep a group of lines together, even if it falls across the normal page break. For instance, with a list of some kind included in your document you want to make sure that the lines don't end up split apart at the end of a page.

WordPerfect includes a **conditional end-of-page** feature used for that purpose.

1. Move the cursor to the line above the lines that are to be kept together.
2. Press **Shift-F8** (Format).
3. Select **4 Other**. The menu in Fig. 36-2 is displayed.

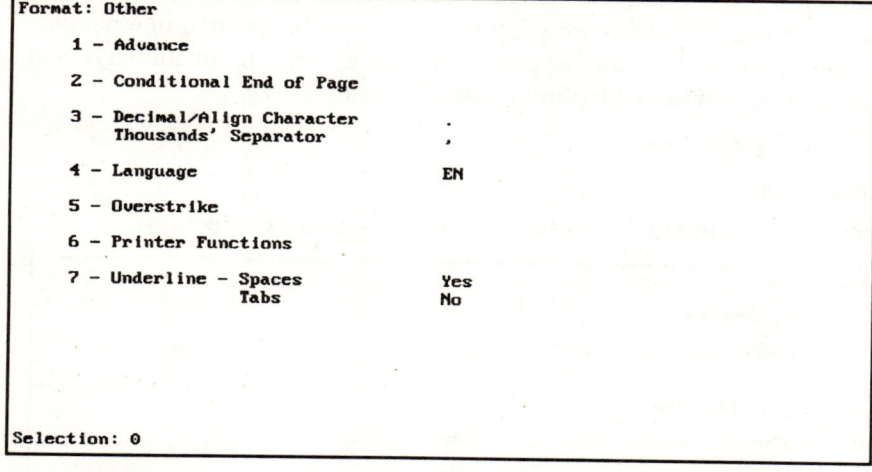

Figure 36-2

4. Select **2 Conditional End of Page**. At the bottom of the screen appears the prompt: **Number of Lines to Keep Together:**.
5. Type the number of lines that you want kept together.
6. Press **F7** (Exit) twice to return to the document screen.

Subsequently, even if editing causes the group of lines to be moved across the end of a page, they are retained as an unbroken block of text.

Another method serving a similar purpose is the **block protect** feature. It is used to keep a block of text together, even if subsequent editing changes the number of lines making up the block.

1. Press **Alt-F4** (Block) and block the text that is to be kept together.
2. Press **Shift-F8** (Format). A prompt appears at the bottom of the screen: **Protect Block? (Y/N) No**.
3. Type **y** and **[BlockPro:On] [BlockPro:Off]** codes are inserted in the document.

The block is always printed unbroken, even if a soft page break is encountered.

If you want to print a block of text contained in your document without leaving the editing session, it is easy.

1. Press **Alt-F4** (Block) and block the text that you want to print.
2. Press **Shift-F8** (Format). At the bottom of the page a prompt reads: **Print Block? (Y/N) No.**
3. Type **y**. The block is printed without interrupting the editing session.

When the printing is done, the previously blocked text is unblocked.

## CHAPTER 37
# RUNNING DOS PROGRAMS

A limited number of DOS programs can be run without exiting WordPerfect. This comes in handy when looking for data included in another program.

1. Press **Ctrl-F1** (Shell).
2. The prompt reads **1 Go to DOS: 0**. Type **1**. The screen changes to one similar to Fig. 37-1.

```
Microsoft(R) MS-DOS(R) Version 4.01
          (C)Copyright Microsoft Corp 1981-1988

Enter 'EXIT' to return to WordPerfect
C:\WP50>
```

Figure 37-1

You can now change directories and activate any program located anywhere on your hard disk or on a floppy disk in one of the floppy drives.

But there are limits. WordPerfect occupies quite a bit of RAM and if you attempt to run a big program, the message on the screen tells you **Program too big to fit in memory**, as in Fig. 37-2 where an attempt was made to run another version of WordPerfect from inside WordPerfect.

```
Microsoft(R) MS-DOS(R) Version 4.01
          (C)Copyright Microsoft Corp 1981-1988

Enter 'EXIT' to return to WordPerfect
C:\WP50>cd\wp51

Enter 'EXIT' to return to WordPerfect
C:\WP51>wp
Program too big to fit in memory

Enter 'EXIT' to return to WordPerfect
C:\WP51>
```

Figure 37-2

A bit of experimenting can show you which programs work and which do not. It depends on the amount of RAM in your system and the size of the program you want to run. For instance, with 640K RAM, programs like dBASE or Lotus 1-2-3 don't work, but you could run Turbo Pascal 3.0. The later versions of that program or of Turbo BASIC won't work.

You can run the WordPerfect CONVERT.EXE program in this manner. This is helpful when importing text previously created in some other format. Use the program to convert it to WordPerfect and then retrieve it into the current document.

Alternately, you can convert the on-screen document (or just a block of text) to ASCII or another format in this same manner. To convert just a block, press **Alt-F4** (Block). Block the text and press **Shift-F10** (Save) and give it a name. The block is saved as a separate file that can then be converted.

# CHAPTER 38
# MATHEMATICAL AND SCIENTIFIC SYMBOLS IN WORDPERFECT 5.0

If you want to include the special characters used in mathematical equations and scientific formulas, you may need to employ one of the external programs designed to deal with that. In this area the 5.0 and 5.1 versions of WordPerfect differ greatly. This chapter deals only with WordPerfect 5.0. Chapter 39 covers the functions available with WordPerfect 5.1.

With the 5.0 version you can use the **Compose** (Ctrl-V) function to create the characters contained in the 11 character sets. To find out which of these your printer can print, load the CHARMAP.TST file from the Conversion disk and print it. It includes all available special characters, but most printers can print only a limited number of them.

If you only need a few specific characters and don't want to print the entire CHARMAP.TST file, you can see if your printer can deal with them by performing the following steps:

1. Check pages 471 through 474 in the WordPerfect Reference Manual. Note the map number and the number within the map that correspond to the needed character.
2. Press **Ctrl-V**. A Key = prompt appears on the screen.
3. Type the map number followed by a comma.
4. Type the character number within the map.
5. Press **Enter**.

Repeat the above for each special character you need. Not all characters that you select are actually displayed on the monitor. Some end up looking like small solid rectangles even though they can be handled by the printer. Then print the characters and check which ones your printer printed and which, if any, were ignored.

If that method is unsatisfactory, you have no choice but to resort to a program like Exact or MathEdit to produce the characters needed. In this chapter Exact is examined. It is a RAM-resident program. That means that you must load Exact before you activate WordPerfect. The program is then called up while you work on your document.

Here is a demonstration of the way you can produce math and scientific characters and insert them into the documents produced using WordPerfect 5.0. First you must tell Exact that you're ready to type the formula. You do this by enclosing the steps making up the formula itself with the reserved words HEAD and FOOT enclosed in slashes and preceded by a dollar sign ($/HEAD/ and $/FOOT/).

$/HEAD/
$*?2F(x) = $/FR/1$,$/RA/2$p$.$. $=
$*?2$J$*%-$I$**$+$#x $=
$*?2e$*#-$/FR/1$,2$.y$#2$** dy
$/FOOT/

These Exact commands control the type of characters to be printed.

To see the characters while you type, you can use the Exact editing screen by pressing **Right Shift-F7**. This produces the split screen shown in Fig. 38-1. In that mode, as you type the math formula, it appears in the upper enclosed portion of the screen, as in Fig. 38-2. When you're finished, press **Esc**. Then, with the cursor in an empty line below the $/HEAD/ command and above the $/FOOT/ command, press **Right Shift-F10**. The formula you typed in the editing window is imported into your WordPerfect document. Pressing **Right Shift-F4** activates "Publication Quality Printing." Then print your document in the usual manner. The result, using the formula shown above, appears in Fig. 38-3.

Exact includes means of controlling printed character size and offers many other special and useful features. They all can be used in conjunction with WordPerfect, expanding its versatility considerably.

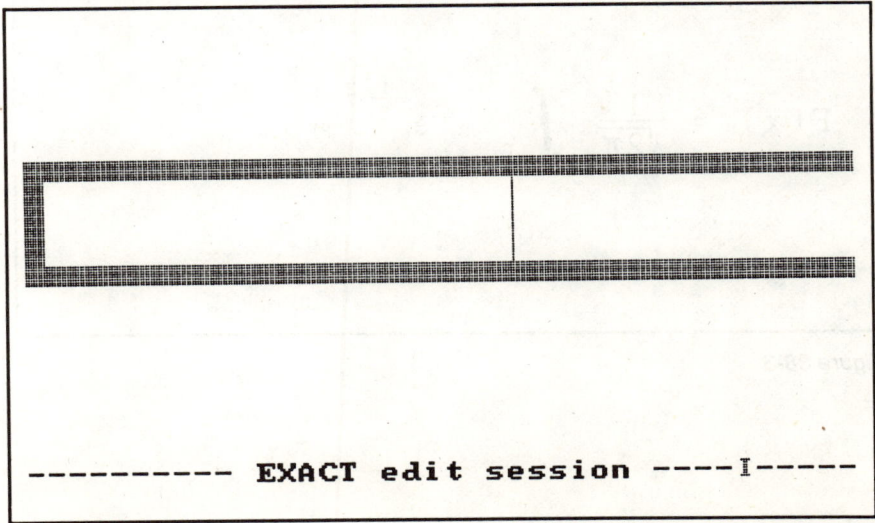

Figure 38-1

# Chapter 38

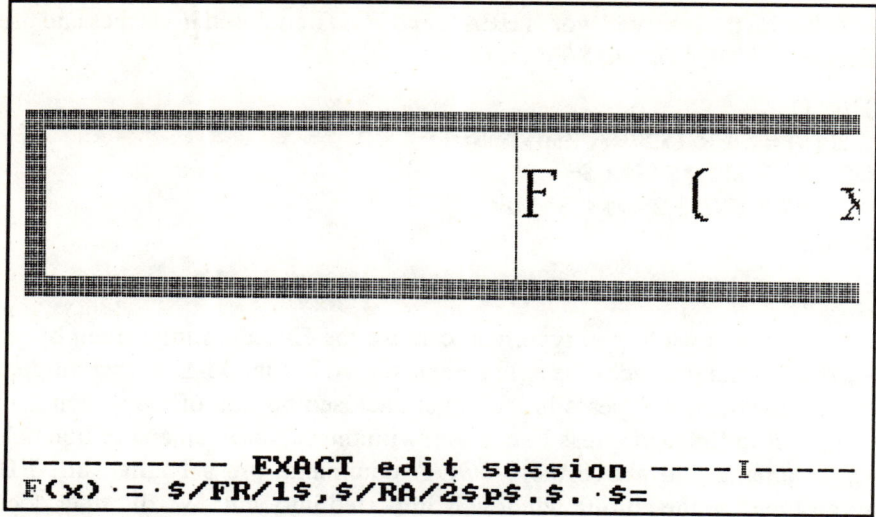

Figure 38-2

Figure 38-3

180

# CHAPTER 39
# MATHEMATICAL AND SCIENTIFIC SYMBOLS IN WORDPERFECT 5.1

Chapter 38 dealt with using an external program in conjunction with WordPerfect 5.0 to produce math and scientific symbols not readily available. WordPerfect 5.1 has added a graphics function called **Equation**, greatly simplifying the task of creating all manner of such symbols. To see the entire array of math and science symbols available with the program, load the PRINTER.TST file and print it. If your printer can handle graphics, all symbols are printed. (If your printer cannot handle graphics, or if your system is not equipped with a graphics adapter, skip this chapter.)

To find out how this new feature works, perform the following steps:

1. Press **Alt-F9** (Graphics) and select **6 Equation**.
2. Select **1 Create**. The usual graphics menu is displayed. The word **Equation** is displayed.
3. Select **9 Edit**. The screen changes to the **Equation** editing screen shown in Fig. 39-1.

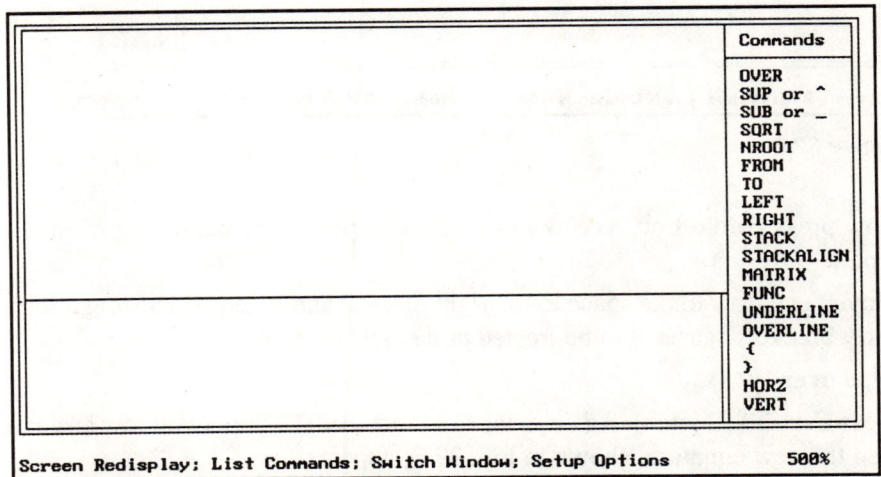

Figure 39-1

Chapter 39

WordPerfect 5.1 now lets you enter math equations by typing them more or less the way they are spoken. It then uses that input to display the actual equation in the upper portion of the screen. To demonstrate, continue with the next steps.

4. With the cursor in the edit window (bottom), type **x =**.
5. Press **F5** (List) to move the cursor into the equation palette (right). Use the arrow keys to move the cursor to **SQRT** and press **Enter**. SQRT appears in the editing window. Alternately, you could type **root** or **SQRT** in the edit window, and the result would be the same.
6. Type **2** in the edit window.
7. Press **Ctrl-F3** (Switch). After a moment the equation appears in the upper window, as in Fig. 39-2.

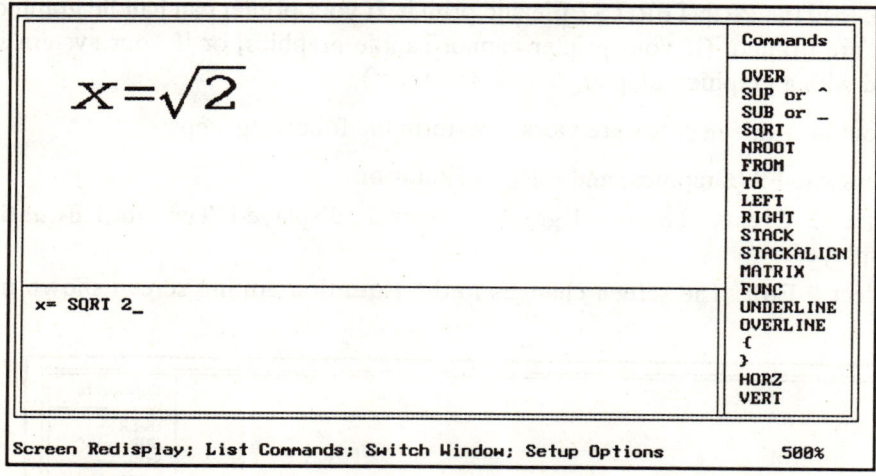

Figure 39-2

8. Now press **Home Left Arrow** to move the cursor to the beginning of the line and type **{**.
9. Move the cursor to the space to the right of the **2** and type **}**. Enclosing a formula in curly brackets causes it to be treated as a single character.
10. Type **over {y*5}**.
11. Press **Ctrl-F3** (Switch). Again, it takes a moment. The upper window is cleared and then the new equation, shown in Fig. 39-3, appears.

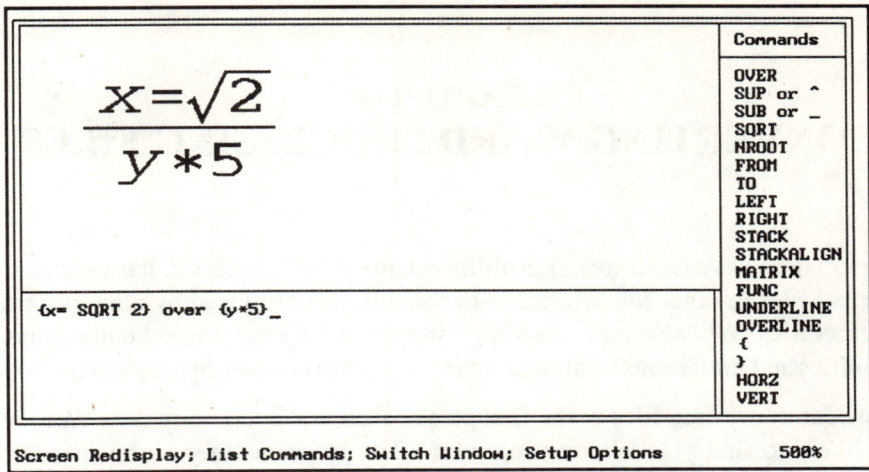

Figure 39-3

12. Press **F7** (Exit) twice to return to the document screen.
13. Press **Shift-F7** (Print) and select **6 View document**.
14. Select **2 Double size**. The equation now appears as shown in Fig. 39-4.

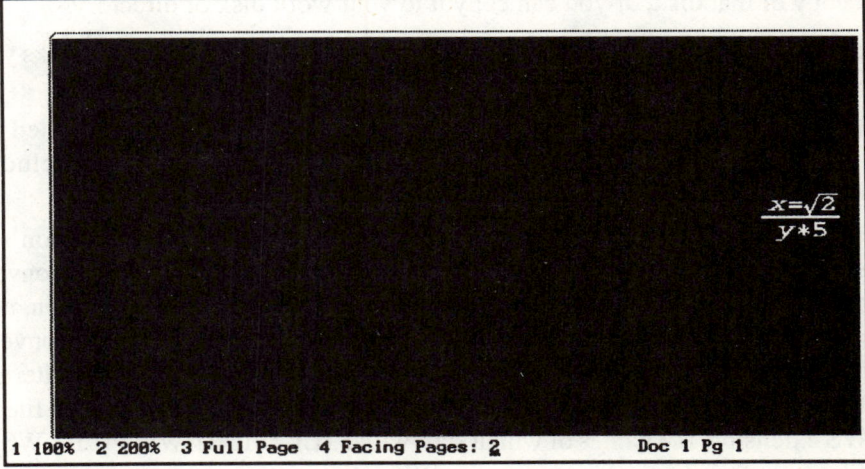

Figure 39-4

Equations like this are treated just like any graphic image. Use the graphics editing screen to determine the position on the page and the size of the area to be occupied by the equation. You can have text preceding and following it, or you can cause text to be wrapped around the equation.

A bit of experimenting in the equation editing screen can turn you into an expert in no time.

# Chapter 40
# CONVERTING WORD PROCESSING FILES

WordPerfect includes a file conversion utility called CONVERT.EXE. It is used to convert WordPerfect files to other file formats or to convert files produced by other programs to WordPerfect files. While using CONVERT appears to be easy, a good understanding of its capabilities and limitations minimizes the chance of encountering unpleasant surprises.

Why consider converting files in the first place? Well, not everybody uses WordPerfect. You are likely to find yourself working with other programs in your business that are designed specifically to produce databases, spreadsheets, or other specialized documents. Further, you might want someone else to edit your work, and that person may be using WordStar, Microsoft Word, or some other word processor.

The CONVERT.EXE program is a stand-alone program and not actually a part of the WordPerfect program itself. It is located on the CONVERSION disk. You can either use it from a copy of that disk, or you can copy it to your work disk or directory.

1. From the DOS prompt, type **CONVERT** and press **Enter**. Your screen asks you for the name of the file to be converted.

2. Type the name of the input file including its extension and if it is not located on the same disk/directory as the CONVERT.EXE file, be sure to include the disk/directory/path information.

3. Next you're asked for the output filename. That name or path information should differ from the input file because the input file remains intact during the conversion process. If you want to convert more than one file with the same extension, use the \* or ? option. For instance, **\*.EXT** as input file and **\*.WP** as output file converts all files on the designated disk/directory with the **.EXT** extension. Alternately, **FILE????.WS** as input file and **FILE????.WP** as output file converts all files with a **.WS** extension, the names of which start with **FILE** (FILE1.WS, FILE2.WS, etc.) to files with the identical names and a **.WP** extension.

4. You're now presented with the options shown in Fig. 40-1. (The options vary slightly between versions 5.0 and 5.1.) If you want to convert from a WordPerfect file to another format, select **1 WordPerfect to another format**. If you want to convert a file in another format to WordPerfect, select one of the other displayed options.

```
Name of Input File? one.txt
Name of Output File? one.ws


0 EXIT
1 WordPerfect to another format
2 Revisable-Form-Text (IBM DCA Format) to WordPerfect
3 Final-Form-Text (IBM DCA Format) to WordPerfect
4 Navy DIF Standard to WordPerfect
5 WordStar 3.3 to WordPerfect
6 MultiMate Advantage II to WordPerfect
7 Seven-Bit Transfer Format to WordPerfect
8 WordPerfect 4.2 to WordPerfect 5.1
9 Mail Merge to WordPerfect Secondary Merge
A Spreadsheet DIF to WordPerfect Secondary Merge
B Word 4.0 to WordPerfect
C DisplayWrite to WordPerfect

Enter number of Conversion desired
```

*Figure 40-1*

What follows is an explanation of the different formats and conversion options that WordPerfect can handle.

**Revisable-Form-Text (IBM DCA Format)**

The DCA format is a format that is used by IBM minicomputers and mainframes to facilitate moving documents between applications.

**Final-Form-Text (IBM DCA Format)**

This converts WordPerfect files to the DCA format used by IBM minicomputers and mainframes in a format that does not permit editing and revisions.

**Navy DIF Standard**

This is a format used exclusively by the Navy. There is little likelihood that you'll be exposed to it.

**WordStar 3.3**

This is the format used by WordStar, and even though it specifies version 3.3, it works perfectly well with version 4.0.

**MultiMate Advantage II**

This is the format produced by the MultiMate word processor from Ashton-Tate.

**Seven-Bit Transfer Format**

Under normal circumstances, each data "word" consists of eight bits. But several of the communication networks, such as Telenet, Tymnet, and others reserve one of those eight bits for their own use. Files received via one of those networks need to be converted to the WordPerfect format.

### WordPerfect 4.2

This is the version of WordPerfect that preceded versions 5.0 and 5.1. Since there are considerable differences between these versions, files must be converted from one to the other to be usable. When converting from 4.2 files, use the STANDARD.CRS file included with WordPerfect 5.0 to convert as many of the codes as possible.

### Mail Merge

This option is used when dBASE or WordStar Mail Merge files are to be converted. The resulting file is in WordPerfect secondary merge format where ^R separates fields and ^E separates records. When using this option you're asked for field delimiters, record delimiters, and any characters to be deleted from the files. Carriage returns and line feeds following delimiters must be specified as part of the delimiter by typing {13}{10}. Decimal values must be entered between curly braces {}.

### Spreadsheet DIF to WordPerfect Secondary Merge

This option converts spreadsheet .DIF files to WordPerfect secondary merge files. Rows become records and cells become fields. (Lotus 1-2-3 files with the .WKS or .WK1 extension can be converted to .DIF files by using the TRANSLATE utility included with Lotus 1-2-3.)

If you select the **1 WordPerfect to another format** option, you're presented with a new menu of eight possible selections as in Fig. 40-2.

```
Name of Input File? one.txt
Name of Output File? one.ws

0 EXIT
1 Revisable-Form-Text (IBM DCA Format)
2 Final-Form-Text (IBM DCA Format)
3 Navy DIF Standard
4 WordStar 3.3
5 MultiMate Advantage II
6 Seven-Bit Transfer Format
7 ASCII Text File
8 WordPerfect Secondary Merge to Spreadsheet DIF

Enter number of output file format desired
```

Figure 40-2

### Revisable-Form-Text (IBM DCA Format)

This converts WordPerfect files to the DCA format used by IBM minicomputers and mainframes in a format that permits editing and revisions.

### Seven-Bit Transfer Format

This converts WordPerfect files to a format that can be used by the communications networks that specify seven-bit file formats.

### ASCII text file

This converts WordPerfect files to ASCII text which is important if files are to be used by certain external desktop publishing programs or typesetting systems. (You can convert WordPerfect files to ASCII files by using **Ctrl-F5 Text In/Out** and selecting **1 DOS Text** and then selecting **1 Save**. This facility can also be used to retrieve ASCII files for editing in WordPerfect.)

### WordPerfect Secondary Merge to Spreadsheet DIF

This option converts WordPerfect secondary merge files to spreadsheet .DIF files, converting records to rows and fields to cells.

Converting from one format to another is not necessarily a straightforward process. WordPerfect offers certain options, such as **Flush Right, Indent,** and different font sizes and styles, that are not recognized by other word processors. This means that such commands are simply lost and the converted document should always be examined carefully to make whatever changes or improvements may be needed.

To test the effectiveness of conversions, it is a good idea to prepare several test programs. One such program should be written using WordPerfect, and another in the format from which you may want to convert. In each case, as many of the editing commands as possible should be included. For convenience sake, keep the document short.

## CHAPTER 41
# USING ASTERISKS (*) IN LIST FILES

As every hard-disk user should know and remember, it is always a good idea to periodically copy all important files onto floppy disks. Not only does it restore usable space on the hard disk, it also avoids disaster if something goes wrong with the hard disk.

A problem arises when an attempt is made to copy more files to the floppy disk than it has room for. Granted, when lists of files are displayed under DOS, the number of bytes for each is included, but trying to add them all up is a major nuisance.

Here WordPerfect comes to the rescue once again.

1. Press **F5** (List Files) and press **Enter**.
2. Move the highlighting to each of the files you intend to move to a floppy disk.
3. Press **Shift-*** to place an asterisk next to each of the filenames. Fig. 41-1 shows a **List Files** screen on which 19 macro files are marked, occupying a total of 2775 bytes.

```
11/09/90  11:49              Directory C:\WP50\*.*
Document size:          0  Free: 34732032   Used:      2775     Marked: 19

.  <CURRENT>   <DIR>                  ..  <PARENT>   <DIR>
LEARN    .       <DIR>     11/05/90 16:26    8514A    .WPD     3466  04/27/88 14:24
A        .WPM        83*  11/06/90 10:15    ADDRESS  .LST      749  11/06/90 14:39
AIRPLANE .WPG      8484   04/27/88 14:24    ALTI     .WPM       74* 11/06/90 10:10
AND      .WPG      1978   04/27/88 14:24    ANNOUNCE .WPG     5388  04/27/88 14:24
APPLAUSE .WPG      1522   04/27/88 14:24    ARROW1   .WPG      366  04/27/88 14:24
ARROW2   .WPG       738   04/27/88 14:24    AWARD    .WPG     1746  04/27/88 14:24
BADNEWS  .WPG      3750   04/27/88 14:24    BOOK     .WPG     1800  04/27/88 14:24
BORDER   .WPG     13518   04/27/88 14:24    CHECK    .WPG     1074  04/27/88 14:24
CLOCK    .WPG      6234   04/27/88 14:24    CODER    .WPM      127* 11/06/90 16:40
CODES    .WPM       151*  11/06/90 16:39    CONFIDEN .WPG     3226  04/27/88 14:24
DB1      .PF        321   11/06/90 10:56    DB1      .WPM      101* 11/06/90 11:05
DB2      .PF        321   11/06/90 10:57    DB2      .WPM      101* 11/06/90 11:09
DB3      .PF        321   11/06/90 10:57    DB3      .WPM      101* 11/06/90 11:09
DB4      .PF        321   11/06/90 11:01    DB4      .WPM      101* 11/06/90 11:07
DB5      .PF        572   11/06/90 12:24    EGA512   .FRS     3584  04/27/88 14:24
EGAITAL  .FRS      3584   04/27/88 14:24    EGASMC   .FRS     3584  04/27/88 14:24
EGAUND   .FRS      3584   04/27/88 14:24    ENVELOPE .WPM      289* 11/06/90 10:34
FLAG     .WPG       730   04/27/88 14:24 ▼  GAVEL    .WPG      856  04/27/88 14:24

1 Retrieve; 2 Delete; 3 Move/Rename; 4 Print; 5 Text In;
6 Look; 7 Other Directory; 8 Copy; 9 Word Search; N Name Search: 6
```

*Figure 41-1*

4. Either select **3 Move/Rename** and type **y** in answer to the first prompt. Then type **B:** in answer to the second prompt, assuming that a formatted floppy disk is ready

## Using Asterisks (*) in List Files

in the B: drive. In that case the marked files are moved to the disk in drive B: and removed from the hard disk.

Or select **8 Copy** and type **y** in answer to the first prompt and **B:** in answer to the second prompt. In that case the files are copied to the disk in drive B: but also remain available on the hard disk.

Every hard-disk user knows that saving files to floppy disks for safekeeping is really a good idea. But too many of us ignore the practice. One way to make sure that anything worked on each day is saved is to create a macro that you use automatically each day before shutting down the computer.

Fig. 41-2 is such a macro.

1. Place a new formatted floppy disk into drive B:.
2. Press **Alt-Y** (or whatever macro filename was used).
3. You watch different screens go by until the **Word Search** screen is displayed. You are prompted to enter today's date.
4. You are then prompted to enter today's date again.
5. After that the macro takes over and all files saved with the day's date are copied to the disk in drive B: but also retained on the hard disk.

With such a macro always ready for use, it is easy to get into the habit of copying the day's work before shutting down.

```
Macro: Edit

        File           ALTY.WPM

    1 - Description    Copy today's files to floppy disk

    2 - Action

        {DISPLAY OFF}{List Files}{Enter}
        944{Enter}{PROMPT}Enter today's date. Then press Enter ~{PAUSE}
        {Enter}
        {PROMPT}Again, enter today's date. Then press Enter ~{PAUSE}
        {Enter}
        6y{Enter}
        {Enter}
        8yb:{Enter}
        {Exit}



Selection: 0
```

Figure 41-2

# CHAPTER 42
# MOUSE OPERATION WITH WORDPERFECT 5.0

The 5.0 version of WordPerfect is not designed to be used with a mouse. But, several types of mice can be programmed for use in conjunction with applications programs not intended for mouse operation. This chapter demonstrates and lists programs written for the C7 Mouse from Logitech.

The C7 Mouse is a three-button mouse that makes it easy to display three different menus by pressing one of the three buttons. Fig. 42-1 is a main menu activated when the computer is first turned on. The commands needed to copy the mouse menu files to RAM are included in the AUTOEXEC.BAT file. This menu displays a selection of applications programs, including WordPerfect 5.0 and WordPerfect 5.1, to be called up by highlighting the appropriate choice and pressing the left mouse button.

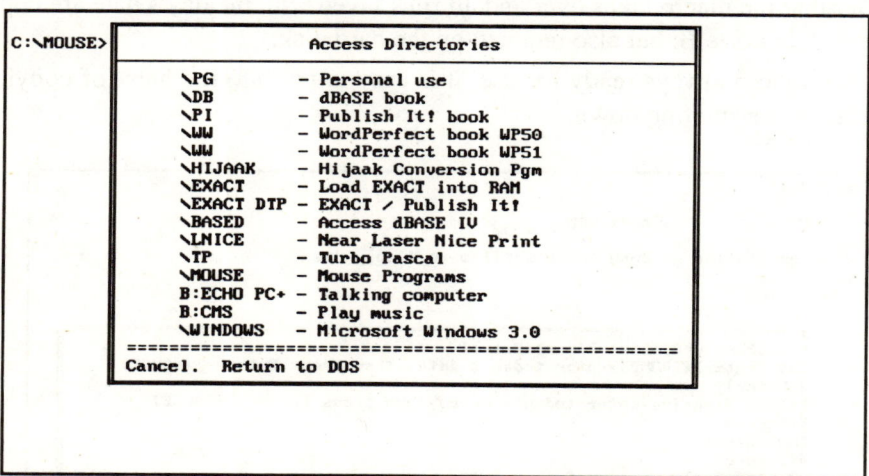

Figure 42-1

When any of the programs using WordPerfect 5.0 are activated, a different menu file is automatically loaded to replace this one.

Fig. 42-2 is the main menu used with WordPerfect 5.0. It offers 17 choices divided into four categories:

**Reload WP**

    **Activate WordPerfect \PG** activates WordPerfect and selects C:\PG as the active directory. It is the directory used for day-to-day miscellaneous purposes.

**Keystrokes**

    **Go to** presses **Ctrl-Home**.

    **Delete to end of Line** presses **Ctrl-End**.

    **Delete to end of Page** presses **Ctrl-PgDn**.

    **Delete to end of Word** presses **Home Del**.

    **Repeat x times** presses **Esc**.

    **Margin Release** presses **Shift-Tab**.

    **Conditional end of page** activates the **EOP.WPM** macro, prompting you to type the number of lines to be kept together.

    **Macro create command (temporary)** presses **Ctrl-PgUp**.

**Utilities**

    **Letter using stationery** activates a macro prompting you for a name to be extracted from a database file. It then places the current date and the name-and-address data on the correct place on the page of stationery.

    **#10 Envelope** activates a macro that places the address in the correct place when a #10 envelope is to be printed.

    **Large envelope, manuscript** does the same and prepares a mailing label for Special Fourth Class Mail - Manuscript.

    **Large envelope, book** does the same and prepares a mailing label for Special Fourth Class Mail - Book.

    **Large envelope, First Class** does the same and prepares a mailing label for First Class.

    **UPS Label** does the same and prepares a label for UPS shipments.

**Other**

    **Time of day** displays the date and the time of day from anywhere within WordPerfect.

    **Exit to DOS (don't save document)** presses **F7 n y** and then loads the main menu file shown in Fig. 42-1 into RAM.

## Chapter 42

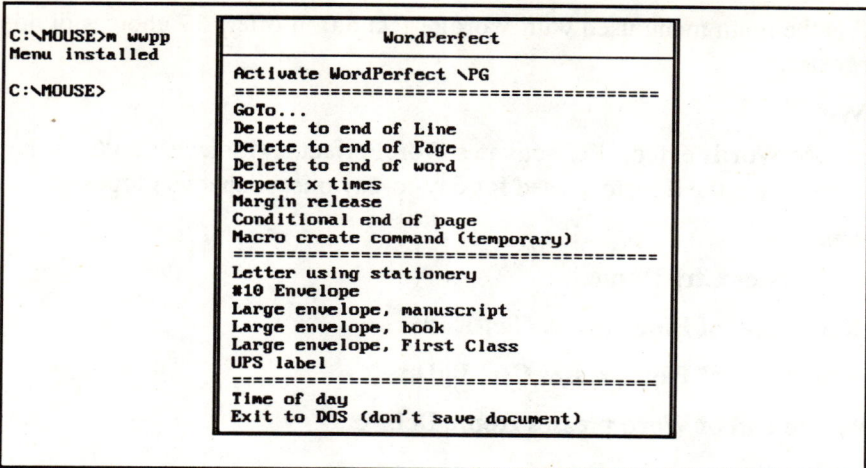

Figure 42-2

The first option comes in handy when you have exited WordPerfect accidentally without using the **Exit to DOS** option. The second group of options performs hard-to-remember keystroke sequences. The third group are utility programs, and the last group is self-explanatory.

Fig. 42-3 is the menu resulting from pressing the middle mouse button. And Fig. 42-4 is the menu resulting from pressing the right button. Each displays 20 of the function-key options in alphabetical order. Highlight any one and the required function keystroke combination is executed.

Figure 42-3

```
              ┌─────────────────────────────────────────────────┐
C:\P          │           Merge R through Underline             │
              │                                                 │
C:\P          │ Merge R         (^R)                       F9   │
              │ Merge/sort                                 C/F9 │
C:\R          │ Move:Sntnce,Pargrph,Pge,Blck,Tblr Col,Rctngl C/F4│
Menu          │ Print:Docmnt,Page,Contrls,Select/Add printer S/F7│
              │ Replace: Confirm Y/N, Search/Replace with  A/F2 │
C:\R          │ Retrieve file                              S/F10│
Menu          │ Reveal Codes                               A/F3 │
              │ Save document                              F10  │
C:\R          │ Screen:  Rewrite, Window, Line draw        C/F3 │
C:\R          │ Search  <---    (backward)                 S/F2 │
              │ Search  --->    (forward)                  F2   │
C:\I          │ Setup      (optional default conditions)   S/F1 │
INSE          │ Shell:    Go to DOS                        C/F1 │
              │ Spell:check word/page/document, Word count C/F2 │
C:\I          │ Style:On/Off,Create,Edit,Delete,Save,Retrve A/F8│
              │ Switch to other screen                     S/F3 │
              │ Tab align: Align char = .                  C/F6 │
C:\M          │ Txt in/out:DOS Text,Psswrd,Gnric,WP4.2,Cmmnt C/F5│
Menu          │ Thesaurus                                  A/F1 │
C:\M          │ Underline                                  F8   │
              └─────────────────────────────────────────────────┘
```

*Figure 42-4*

Following is the source code for the first, second, and third menus. Each OPTION line displays an option and ends with a variable used to perform the appropriate steps.

```
BEGIN LeftB, MidB, RightB

LeftB:  MENU "WordPerfect",1,20,14
        OPTION "Activate WordPerfect \PG              ",pg
        OPTION "======================================"
        OPTION "GoTo...                               ",gt
        OPTION "Delete to end of Line                 ",dl
        OPTION "Delete to end of Page                 ",dp
        OPTION "Delete to end of Word                 ",ew
        OPTION "Repeat x times                        ",zz
        OPTION "Margin Release                        ",ml
        OPTION "Conditional end of Page               ",cep
        OPTION "Macro create command (temporary)      ",mx
        OPTION "======================================"
        OPTION "Letter using stationery               ",let
        OPTION "#10 Envelope                          ",env5
        OPTION "Large envelope, manuscript            ",env4
        OPTION "Large envelope, book                  ",env3
        OPTION "Large envelope, First Class           ",env2
        OPTION "UPS label                             ",env1
        OPTION "======================================"
        OPTION "Time of day                           ",time
        OPTION "Exit to DOS (don't save document)     ",nx
        MEND

MidB:   MENU "Functions Block through Merge Codes",1,5,14
        OPTION "Block                           C/F4  ",bk
        OPTION "Bold                            F6    ",bo
        OPTION "Cancel, Restore Deletions       F1    ",cl
        OPTION "Center                          S/F6  ",ce
        OPTION "Date txt,code,format,Outline,ParaNum,Define S/F5 ",dt
        OPTION "Exit WordPerfect or current screen F7 ",ex
        OPTION "Flush right                     A/F6  ",fr
        OPTION "Font:Size,Appearance,Normal,BaseFont,PrntColrC/F8 ",ft
        OPTION "Footnote, Endnote, Endnote placement C/F7 ",fn
        OPTION "Format: Line, Page, Document, Other  S/F8 ",rp
```

## Chapter 42

```
    OPTION "Graphics:Figure,Table,TextBox,User def,Line  A/F9   ",me
    OPTION "Help   (Press ENTER to exit Help)              F3    ",he
    OPTION "Indent      --->                               F4    ",ni
    OPTION "Indent      <---   --->                        S/F4  ",in
    OPTION "List Files: Dir C:\??\*.*                      F5    ",fl
    OPTION "Macro (Type name to activate)                  A/F10 ",ma
    OPTION "Macro define                                   C/F10 ",md
    OPTION "Mark txt:Auto Ref,Subdoc,Index,ToA,Define      A/F5  ",mt
    OPTION "Math/Columns: on/off/def                       A/F7  ",mc
    OPTION "Merge codes                                    S/F9  ",cm
           MEND

RightB: MENU "Merge R through Underline",1,5,14
    OPTION "Merge R         (^R)                           F9    ",mr
    OPTION "Merge/sort                                     C/F9  ",ms
    OPTION "Move:Sntnce,Pargrph,Pge,Blck,Tblr Col,Rctngl   C/F4  ",mv
    OPTION "Print:Docmnt,Page,Contrls,Select/Add printer   S/F7  ",pr
    OPTION "Replace: Confirm Y/N, Search/Replace with      A/F2  ",re
    OPTION "Retrieve file                                  S/F10 ",rt
    OPTION "Reveal Codes                                   A/F3  ",rc
    OPTION "Save document                                  F10   ",st
    OPTION "Screen:  Rewrite, Window, Line draw            C/F3  ",sc
    OPTION "Search  <---   (backward)                      S/F2  ",sb
    OPTION "Search  --->   (forward)                       F2    ",hs
    OPTION "Setup          (optional default conditions)   S/F1  ",ss
    OPTION "Shell:      Go to DOS                          C/F1  ",sh
    OPTION "Spell:check word/page/document, Word count     C/F2  ",sp
    OPTION "Style:On/Off,Create,Edit,Delete,Save,Retrve    A/F8  ",pf
    OPTION "Switch to other screen                         S/F3  ",sw
    OPTION "Tab align: Align char = .                      C/F6  ",ta
    OPTION "Txt in/out:DOS Text,Psswrd,Gnric,WP4.2,Cmmnt   C/F5  ",tx
    OPTION "Thesaurus                                      A/F1  ",th
    OPTION "Underline                                      F8    ",ul
           MEND
```

Following is the source code for the program execution steps. Each starts with one of the variables and a colon (:), followed by the reserved word TYPE and followed by the steps to be executed. Here many of the extended ASCII codes are used. Appendix A lists all of them, identifying the resulting action.

```
pg:  TYPE "C:",ENTER,"CD\WP50",ENTER,"WP",ENTER,0,63,"=","c:\PG",ENTER,ENTER
let: TYPE 0,113,"C:\PG\LET2",ENTER
env5:TYPE 0,113,"C:\PG\55MAIL",ENTER,ENTER
env4:TYPE 0,113,"C:\PG\33MAIL",ENTER,ENTER
env3:TYPE 0,113,"C:\PG\22MAIL",ENTER,ENTER
env2:TYPE 0,113,"C:\PG\11MAIL",ENTER,ENTER
env1:TYPE 0,113,"C:\PG\44MAIL",ENTER,ENTER
time:TYPE 0,113,"T",ENTER
cep: TYPE 0,113,"C:\WW\EOP",ENTER,ENTER
gt:  TYPE 0,119
nx:  TYPE 0,65,"n","y","CD\RAM",ENTER,"M M",ENTER
dl:  TYPE 0,117
dp:  TYPE 0,118
zz:  TYPE 27
ml:  TYPE 0,15
mx:  TYPE 0,132
ew:  TYPE 0,71,0,83

sh:  TYPE 0,94
ss:  TYPE 0,84
th:  TYPE 0,104
cl:  TYPE 0,59
```

*Mouse Operation with WordPerfect 5.0*

```
sp: TYPE 0,95
sb: TYPE 0,85
hs: TYPE 0,60
re: TYPE 0,105
sc: TYPE 0,96
sw: TYPE 0,86
rc: TYPE 0,106
he: TYPE 0,61
mv: TYPE 0,97
in: TYPE 0,87
ni: TYPE 0,62
bk: TYPE 0,107
tx: TYPE 0,98
dt: TYPE 0,88
mt: TYPE 0,108
fl: TYPE 0,63

ta: TYPE 0,99
ce: TYPE 0,89
fr: TYPE 0,109
bo: TYPE 0,64
fn: TYPE 0,100
pr: TYPE 0,90
mc: TYPE 0,110
ex: TYPE 0,65
rp: TYPE 0,91
ft: TYPE 0,101
pf: TYPE 0,111
ul: TYPE 0,66
ms: TYPE 0,102
me: TYPE 0,112
cm: TYPE 0,92
mr: TYPE 0,67
md: TYPE 0,103
rt: TYPE 0,93
ma: TYPE 0,113
st: TYPE 0,68
```

## CHAPTER 43
# MOUSE OPERATION WITH WORDPERFECT 5.1

This version of WordPerfect can be operated with a mouse. The mouse can position the cursor, block text, call up and select the different functions and features. The Reference Manual covers what can be done with the mouse. There is little to be learned. Just moving the mouse around the work area and clicking here or there tells you how the cursor position can be controlled by the mouse.

The more important advantage is the group of menus you can use to access the different functions and features.

If the mouse cursor, an inverse video rectangle, is not already displayed, click the left mouse button. It appears somewhere in the screen and moves the cursor to that position. Now move it to the left top corner of the screen and click the right mouse button. A banner with a number of menu choices appears across the top of your work area, as in Fig. 43-1.

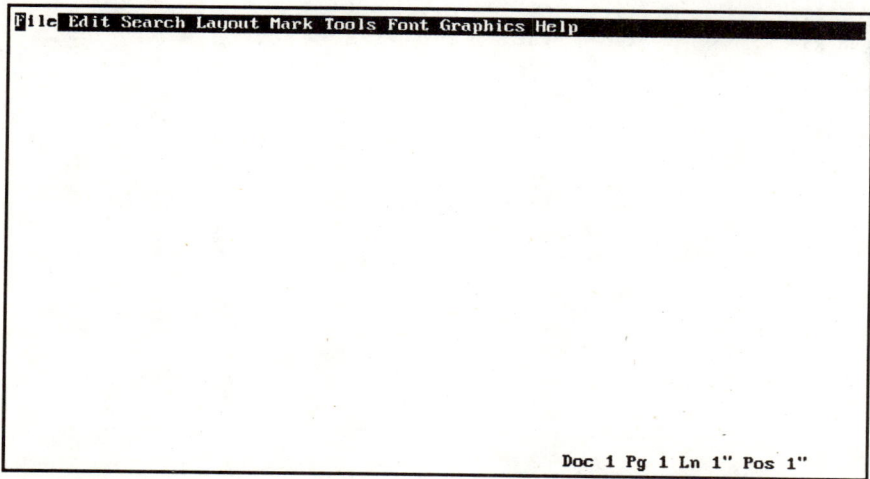

Figure 43-1

With the mouse cursor on **File**, click the left mouse button. The pull-down menu in Fig. 43-2 appears, offering 11 choices. Of those, four also have a solid black triangular marker. Select any of them and additional submenus appear. Figs. 43-3 through 43-6 display the options available with the submenus.

## Mouse Operation with WordPerfect 5.1

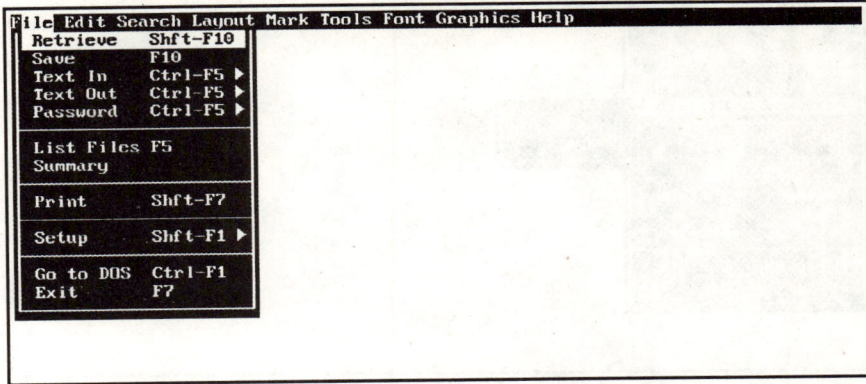

Figure 43-2

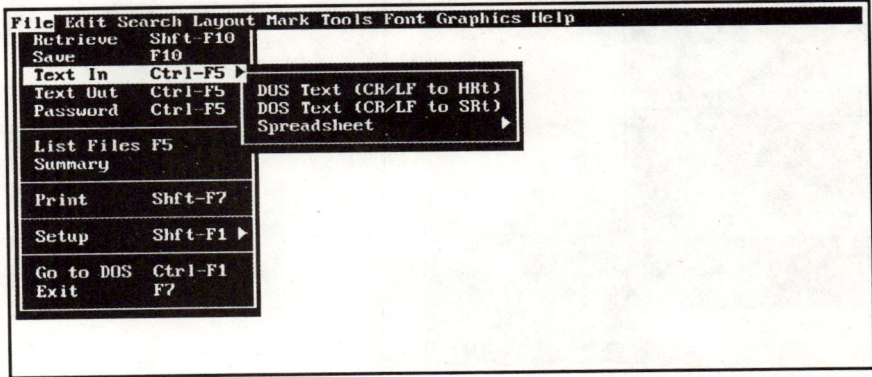

Figure 43-3

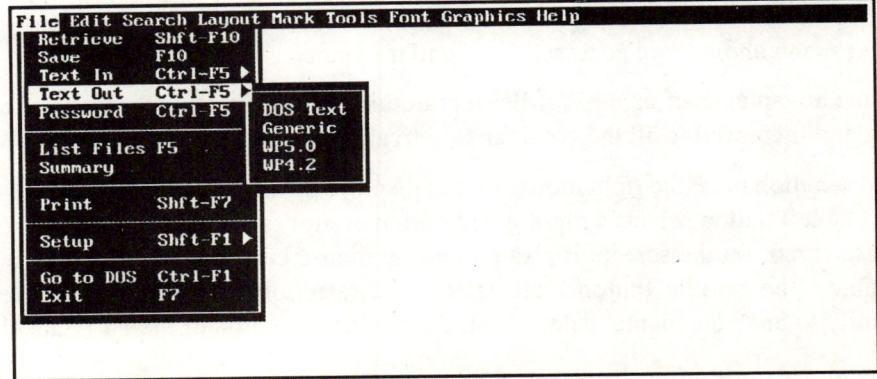

Figure 43-4

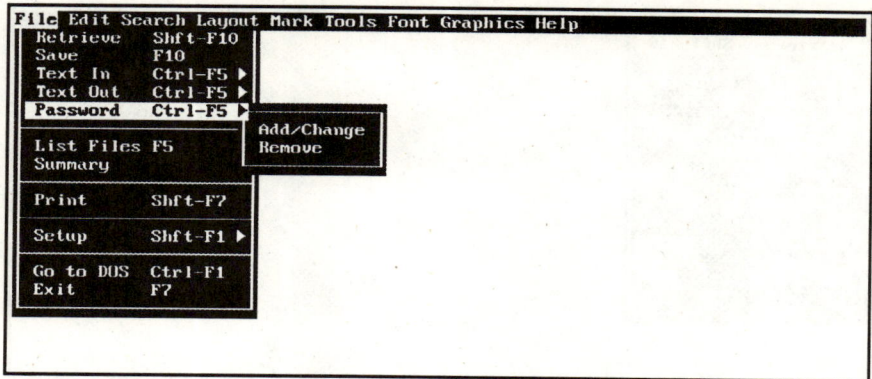

*Figure 43-5*

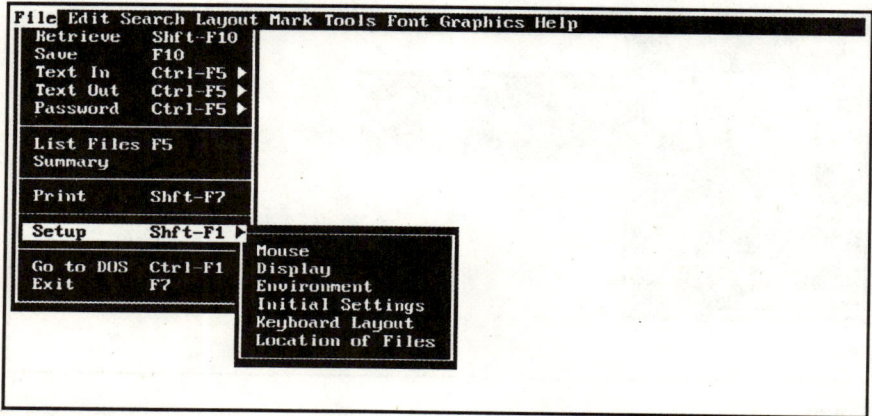

*Figure 43-6*

The other menu choices are accessed in a similar manner.

One of the advantages of using WordPerfect in this menu-driven manner is to eliminate learning and memorizing all the commands activating the different functions.

With three-button mice the right mouse button displays the menu bar across the top of the screen. The left button selects a highlighted option or moves the cursor to the position of the mouse cursor on the screen. It also causes the mouse cursor to be displayed when it is invisible. The middle button cancels the last selection or action, or it offers an opportunity to undo accidental deletions. It duplicates the action of the **F1** (Cancel) key.

## CHAPTER 44
# DRAWPERFECT CLIP ART

DrawPerfect is a full-fledged graphics program designed to be used with WordPerfect 5.0 and 5.1. The program is quite large and powerful and describing it and its features and functions cannot be included in this book.

Part of the program is an extensive clip-art library, in terms of quality as well as subject matter, among the best available today. It consists of these categories: Animals, Arrows, Business, Computer, Flags, Flow Chart, Graphic Devices, Maps, Objects, People, Special Occasions, Sports, Symbols, and Transportation. These categories include a total of 480 images.

You can copy these files to a directory on your hard disk, dividing that directory into subdirectories for each of the categories, or you can copy them to a set of floppy disks. The latter is likely to be the better choice, as the complete collection would use up in excess of a million bytes of available space on your hard disk.

All files are in the .WPG format and can be imported into your WordPerfect document with no difficulty. Fig. 44-1 is the **View document** screen of this manuscript page with one of the images imported into it. Once imported, you can edit and manipulate them in the usual manner. But there are limitations. You cannot place text inside any of the graphic images including white areas for that purpose, such as banners. To be able to do that you need to install the complete DrawPerfect program. With it installed and used in conjunction with WordPerfect, you have a fairly complete desktop publishing setup.

DrawPerfect's picture library is, of course, not the only clip-art library usable with WordPerfect. There is an enormous number of such libraries available, dealing with a literally unlimited variety of general, technical, scientific, and other subjects. As long as the graphics files are in a format WordPerfect can deal with or one convertible to a compatible format, they can be imported into your documents and edited, manipulated, and printed in the usual manner.

Sometimes you may want to view one graphic image after another. Having to enter all those keystrokes time and again can become rather tiresome. Fig. 44-2 is a macro that accesses the graphics mode. It halts execution, waiting for you to enter the drive/path/filename data. Press **Enter**. Macro execution continues, displaying the graphic image in the actual-size **View document** mode.

Chapter 44

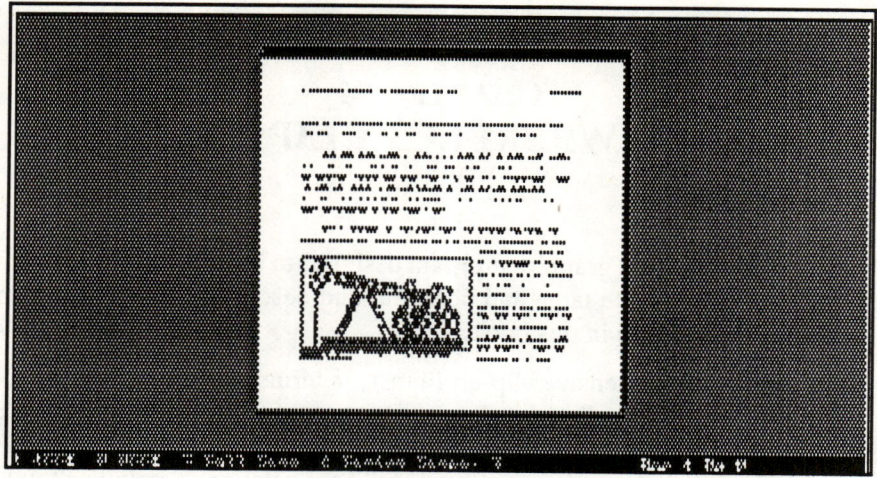

Figure 44-1

```
Macro: Edit

        File            PIC.WPM
  1 - Description       View Graphic
  2 - Action

    ┌─────────────────────────────────────────────┐
    │ {DISPLAY OFF}{Graphics}111{PAUSE}{Enter}    │
    │ 51614{Exit}{Exit}{Print}61                  │
    │                                             │
    │                                             │
    │                                             │
    │                                             │
    └─────────────────────────────────────────────┘

Selection: 0
```

Figure 44-2

# CHAPTER 45
# WRITING PROGRAM SOURCE CODE

The source code for programs, regardless of the language used, is always written in ASCII format. The text editors included with such programs as Turbo Pascal, Turbo C or Turbo BASIC, QuickC, QuickBASIC, and others always produce text files in that format.

There may be times when you would prefer to be able to write source code using WordPerfect to use the many available conveniences. For instance, you can use the automatic line-numbering feature if you want to write source code for BASIC programs. Actually, the newer versions of BASIC no longer require line numbers, but they often do come in handy during debugging sessions.

If that is what you plan to use, create the macro shown in Fig. 45-1. It numbers lines consecutively, starting with 100 and continuing page after page. If you later add lines somewhere in the middle, WordPerfect automatically renumbers all following lines accordingly. Alternately, you can delete or combine lines and the numbering is again adjusted.

```
Macro: Edit
        File            BASIC.WPM
    1 - Description     Automatic line numbering
    2 - Action
        {DISPLAY OFF}{Format}15y1nn4100{Enter}
        5n{Exit}




Selection: 0
```

Figure 45-1

## Chapter 45

Additional advantages of using WordPerfect in this manner are numerous. You can create Alt+digit temporary macros to print all those commands like PRINT, PRINT USING, INPUT, LPRINT, and so on automatically, saving a lot of typing. And you can use the spell-check option to make sure that no typographical errors have crept into the program.

When you're satisfied with your work, print it. Below is a listing of a short Turbo BASIC program that calculates the cost of mortgages. Now save your work as, say, LOAN.PGM representing the WordPerfect version of the code. To make it work as an actual program, take these steps:

```
100     REM Loan Payments
101     111
102     CLS
103     FOR X = 1 TO 5:PRINT:NEXT X
104     COLOR 13
105     PRINT "                         COMPUTING MORTGAGE PAYMENTS"
106     PRINT:PRINT:COLOR 7
107     INPUT "Enter the currently applicable interest rate        ".I
108     III = I:PRINT
109     INPUT "Enter the term of the mortgage in years             ",Y
110     PRINT
111     INPUT "Enter the amount of the loan                       $",L
112     I = I / 12 / 100:Y * 12
113     X = (1+I)^Y:Z = X - 1:P = L * (X * I) / Z
114     PRINT:COLOR 14
115     PRINT "You will have to make ";Y;" payments of ";
116     PRINT USING "$$####,.## each";p
117     PRINT:COLOR 10
118     T = P * Y:II = T - L
119     PRINT "The total cost of the mortgage is ";
120     COLOR 12:PRINT USING "$$######,.##";T
121     COLOR 10:PRINT "                              of which ";
122     COLOR 12:PRINT USING "$$######,.##";II;
123     COLOR 10:PRINT "is interest."
124     PRINT:COLOR 7
125     INPUT "Do you want the results printed?  (Y/N)   ",YN$
126     IF YN$ = "Y" OR YN$ = "y" THEN 222 ELSE 333
127     333
128     PRINT:PRINT:COLOR 9
129     INPUT "Another calculation?   (Y/N)                   ",NY$
130     IF NY$ = "Y" OR NY$ = "y" THEN 111 ELSE CLS:END
131     222
132     LPRINT "At the current interest rate of ";III;"%"
133     LPRINT "a ";Y/12;"-year mortgage totaling ";
134     LPRINT USING "$$######,.##";L
135     LPRINT "will require ";Y;" payments of ";
136     LPRINT USING "$$####,.## each";P
137     LPRINT
138     LPRINT "The total cost of the mortgage is ";
140     LPRINT "                              of which ";
141     LPRINT USING "$$######,.##";II;
142     LPRINT " is interest."
143     GOTO 333
```

1. Press **Ctrl-F5** (Text In/Out).
2. Select **1 DOS Text** and select **1 Save**.
3. When prompted for a filename, change the displayed one to **LOAN.BAS**. In that way you don't lose your original version.
4. Press **F7** (Exit) and type **n y** to exit to DOS.
5. Place the Turbo BASIC Program disk into one of the floppy drives. Type **TB** and press **Enter**. The program is activated.
6. Access the **File** menu and select **Load**.
7. Type **C:\WW\LOAN.BAS** if the file is located on that directory/path.
8. Move the highlighting to **Edit** to look at your file. You notice that the line numbers are missing. They were eliminated during the file conversion to DOS Text.
9. Move the highlighting to **Run** and press **Enter**.

If no errors are found, the program runs as it is supposed to. If errors are found, you can correct them in the Turbo BASIC Edit mode. Later on you can save the corrected program back to its original name and directory/path.

In converting files to the ASCII format, WordPerfect retains the tab stops and similar formatting codes by replacing them with blank spaces and codes ASCII can deal with. For that reason you can just as easily use WordPerfect to write programs in Pascal or C without losing the customary indenting, making such programs relatively easy to read.

If you own the WordPerfect Library program, you can use the **Program Editor** function. It is part of the collection of programs making up the Library, producing ASCII files ready for use with any of the high-level programming language programs. For more on the subject, see Chapter 46.

## CHAPTER 46
## THE LIBRARY SHELL

WordPerfect offers an optional program referred to as the **Library**. It is a collection of utility programs, included here to demonstrate its considerable usefulness.

The WordPerfect Library, usually installed on hard-disk systems on the \LIBRARY subdirectory, consists of six separate programs to be called up from the Shell menu. In addition, you can add other applications programs to that menu.

Shell is really just a menu used to call any one of the other programs or to access WordPerfect or other applications programs you may wish to add to the options automatically provided.

To access the Shell program from DOS:
1. Type **cd\library** and press **Enter**.
2. Type **Shell** (or **shell**) and press **Enter**.

To access the Shell program from WordPerfect:
1. Press **Ctrl-F1** (Shell).
2. Select **1 Go to Shell**. (This prompt is available only when the Library is installed and WordPerfect was activated from it. When not, the prompt is **1 Go to DOS**.)

Either way, the Shell menu in Fig. 46-1 is displayed. By typing any of the letters, the associated program is called up.

```
WordPerfect Library                    Thursday, November 22, 1990, 2:28pm

   A - Appointment Calendar           D - DataPerfect
   B - Beast (game)                   P - PlanPerfect
   C - Calculator                     W - WordPerfect
   E - Edit Macros
   F - File Manager
   G - Go to Dos For One Command
   N - NoteBook
   T - Program Editor
```

*Figure 46-1*

**Appointment Calendar, Calculator,** and **File Manager** are discussed in Chapters 47, 48, and 49. The remaining options are explained here in brief.

**Notebook** might be thought of as a program to organize and manage lists, such as names, addresses, phone numbers, birthdays, and the like. Each notebook you create consists of records and fields, and they can be examined in the form of long lists. They are saved as WordPerfect Merge files and can thus be combined with WordPerfect files. If a modem is available, Notebook can be used to dial telephone numbers automatically.

To access the Notebook from the Shell menu select **N Notebook**. The screen changes to a typical document screen with the legend **Notebook Empty**. The Library software includes a sample notebook file called ART.NB which you can retrieve using **Shift-F10** (Retrieve). Its purpose is to demonstrate how it works. The screen displays a list of names along with home and work phone numbers. You can scroll through the list using the arrow keys as usual or select specific records according to first letters, first and second letters, and so on.

The file contains a great deal more about each person than the name and phone number. Press **Shift-F3** (Switch) and the full record for the person highlighted on the previous list is displayed.

Pressing **F3** (Help) displays all the necessary information on how to edit records, delete or add records, or start a new notebook file.

**Macro Editor** is used to edit macros created in any of the WordPerfect programs. It eliminates the need to redefine large programs after editing changes are made.

To activate the Macro Editor select **E Edit Macros** from the Shell menu. Unlike the screen we've become familiar with when editing macros using WordPerfect, the Macro Editor simply displays all commands and text on the full document screen. The Macro Editor Help screen, invoked by pressing **F3** (Help) from the macro screen, displays all key combinations that are available when using this program to edit macros.

The Library software includes a sample macro called ALTSHFTL.SHM which can be retrieved using **Shift-F10** (Retrieve). It can be used to experiment with the different commands available. The Macro Editor does not automatically wrap long lines into the next line. To activate the word-wrap option to view all commands even on very long lines, move to the head of the macro (**Home Home Up Arrow**), press **Ctrl-F2** (Wrap), and reply to the prompt **Wrap with confirm? (Y/N) N** by typing **n**. This causes all long lines to be wrapped with a comment character and a hard return inserted where the line is broken.

**Program Editor** can be used to edit or create programs or text files. It is the text editor, producing source code in ASCII format, used to write all WordPerfect program code.

When this program is invoked by selecting **T Program Editor** you have access to six help files you might as well look at before going on.

1. Press **F3** (Help). The filenames are **PEHELP.1** a Program Editor keyboard template, **PEHELP.2** cursor keys, **PEHELP.A** an ASCII code chart, **PEHELP.C** character codes, **PEHELP.H** help formatting characters, and **PEHELP.M** Program Editor macros. The first one comes on automatically and the others can be invoked by typing the extension character while the status line reads: **Press any key to continue...**
2. Pressing any key produces a document screen exactly like the document screen used by WordPerfect. Unless you intend to write serious programs in one of the high-level programming languages, it is doubtful you'll use the Program Editor with any degree of frequency.

**Go to DOS for one command** displays the prompt **DOS command:** on the status line. You type a command. It is executed. Afterwards you are returned to the Shell menu.

**Beast** is a game. Fig. 46-2 is the initial screen.

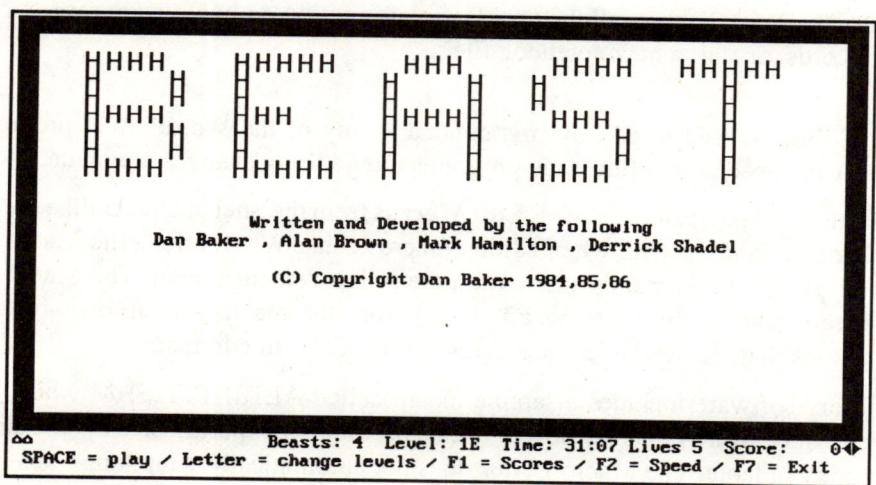

Figure 46-2

## CHAPTER 47
# THE LIBRARY APPOINTMENT CALENDAR

This program displays a monthly calendar along with three windows used to write memos, list appointments by the time of the day, or jot down things to do. It includes an alarm option. Calendar items can be printed and calendar data can be merged into WordPerfect files.

1. From the Shell menu type **A** or **a**. After a moment the Appointment Calendar screen is displayed with the current date highlighted, as in Fig. 47-1.

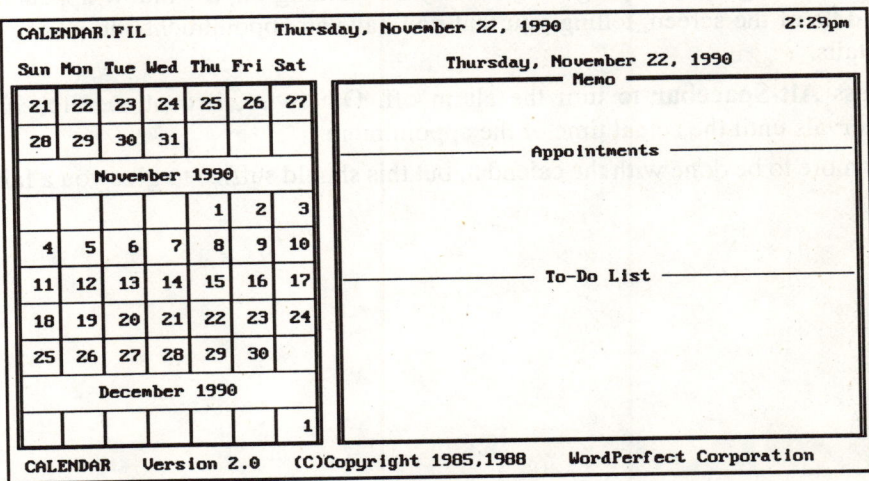

Figure 47-1

2. Press **Tab** and see the cursor moving to the Memo window ready for you to enter data.
3. Press **Tab** again several times and watch the cursor moving from window to window, each time ready to let you type whatever information might be pertinent.
4. Pressing **Shift-Tab** moves the cursor the same way but in reverse order.
5. Press **Tab** or **Shift-Tab** to place the cursor into the **Auto Date** prompt on the status line. Now select **1 Date**, select **1 Go to Date**, type your birth date in mm/dd/yy format, and press **Enter**. The calendar shifts to the appropriate year, month, and date, showing on which day of the week you were born. Use this feature to go to

any date, past or future, for which you want to enter data or examine the days of the week or previously entered data.

6. Move the cursor into the Appointment window and press the **Ins** key. On the status line you're asked to enter a time for the appointment. Use either the 14:15 or 2:15p format. Either way, the time is entered into the Appointment window as 2:15 pm. For this practice session enter a time that is about 15 minutes after the current time.

7. Enter an appointment, just for practice. Press **F7** (Exit) to save the appointment.

8. Press **Tab** a few times to move the cursor away from the appointment window and then back to it. It appears on the first character of the appointment text.

9. Type an asterisk (*) and a musical note character is displayed to the left of the appointment time. This indicates that the alarm has been set and in about five minutes (10 minutes before the time you entered) the computer beeps. Regardless of what you're doing or what program you may be working on, a window appears in the middle of the screen, telling you that you have an appointment and giving all the details.

10. Press **Alt-Spacebar** to turn the alarm off. Otherwise, it continues to chime at intervals until the actual time of the appointment.

There is more to be done with the calendar, but this should suffice to give you a fair idea.

## CHAPTER 48
# THE LIBRARY CALCULATOR

The calculator performs mathematical, trigonometric, financial, statistical, scientific, and programming functions. A tape type of display is used to display calculations on the screen. Calculations can also be printed or saved as a file.

From the Shell menu, type **C** or **c** and the calculator screen is displayed, as in Fig. 48-1. The calculator can be used to perform all kinds of calculations with relative ease, but it takes a bit of learning to make use of its more sophisticated functions. To explore all its capabilities is beyond the scope of this book. To demonstrate, figure compound interest on a certain amount as an example of its more sophisticated capabilities:

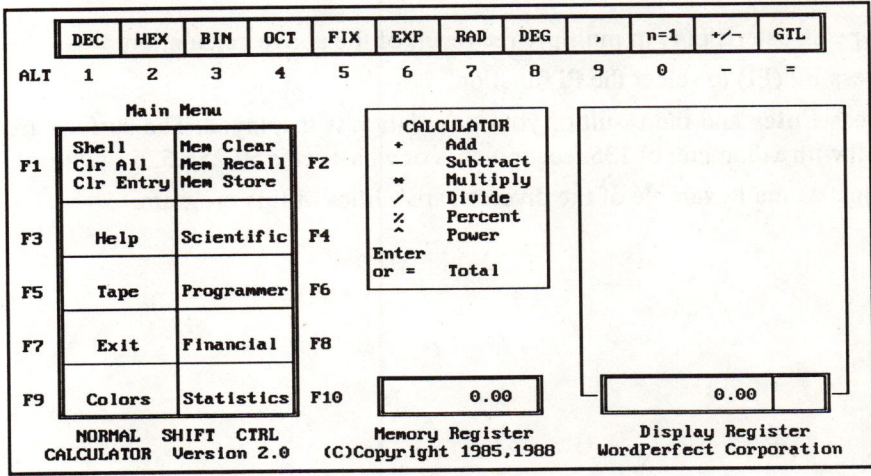

*Figure 48-1*

1. Press **F8** (Financial) which changes the screen to display the financial functions.
2. Press **Shift-F1** (Clear All) just to make sure that there are no old values left from a previous calcuation.
3. Type an amount that represents the present value, say **5000**.
4. Press **F6** (PV) (present value).
5. Type a number for the number of months for which you want the compound interest to be figured, say **12**.
6. Press **F3** (N) (number of periods).

Chapter 48

7. Type **7.25** for the annual interest rate. Type **/12** to produce the interest rate per month. Press **Enter** to produce the result.
8. Press **F4 %i** (percent interest).
9. Press **Shift-F7 Shift-FV** (future value) to cause the calculator to figure the result based on interest compounded monthly after 12 MONTHS.

Now one more example before going on to the next program. This time use the scientific option to calculate the surface area of a ball. The formula is:

**Area = PI * diameter squared**.

1. Press **F4** (Scientific).
2. Press **Shift-F1** to clear away any leftover or forgotten data.
3. Press **Alt-1 DEC** to activate floating point decimal notation.
4. Type the diameter of the ball in any measure, say **135**.
5. Press **Shift-F8** ($X^2$) which calculates the square of the diameter measure that you entered.
6. Type an asterisk (*) to multiply the result of the above calculation.
7. Press **F9** (PI) to select the Pi function.
8. Press **Enter** and the result of your calculation is displayed. The surface area for a ball with a diameter of 135 feet or inches or whatever is 57,255,526 square measures.

This is just a small example of the diverse capabilities of this program.

## CHAPTER 49
# THE LIBRARY FILE MANAGER

The **File Manager** program is used to display selected files in any directory alphabetically by name, extension, date, time or size, displaying date, time and size information. Files can be copied, deleted, moved, renamed, searched in several ways, and displayed.

When this program is called up (from Shell select **F File Manager**) it displays the files on the directory from which Shell was originally invoked. For instance, if you're working on a file in the C:\WP directory and use **Ctrl-F1** (Shell) followed by **1 Go to Shell** to call up Shell, then the C:\WP files are displayed in exactly the same manner as when you press **F5** (List Files) from WordPerfect, and all the available options are displayed on the status line, as in Fig. 49-1.

```
03/05/90  10:53           Directory C:\LIBRARY\*.*
Free Mem:    421104   Disk Space Free: 1775616, Used:   614157     Files:  67

.  <CURRENT>  <DIR>                  ..  <PARENT>   <DIR>
ALTD    .PEM        5  08/24/88 15:32  ALTF    .PEM       27  08/24/88 15:32
ALTM    .PEM       13  08/24/88 15:32  ALTO    .PEM        5  08/24/88 15:32
ALTR    .PEM       26  08/24/88 15:32  ALTSHFTB.SHM       30  08/24/88 15:41
ALTSHFTL.SHM      339  08/24/88 15:41  ALTT    .PEM        6  08/24/88 15:32
ALTU    .PEM        7  08/24/88 15:32  ART     .NB      6653  08/24/88 15:41
ARTCAL  .FIL     1490  08/24/88 15:41  BEAST   .COM    19318  08/24/88 15:34
CALC    .EXE    26624  08/24/88 15:34  CALC    .HLP    25735  08/24/88 15:41
CALENDAR.FIL      532  03/05/90 10:52  CALENDAR.HLP    28065  08/24/88 15:41
CANON   .PRD     1024  08/24/88 15:41  CL      .EXE    68608  08/24/88 15:34
CURSOR  .COM     1451  08/24/88 15:32  DELMARK .PEM        6  08/24/88 15:32
DIABLO  .PRD     1024  08/24/88 15:41  EPSON   .PRD     1024  08/24/88 15:41
FM      .EXE    38912  08/24/88 15:34  FMANAGER.HLP    14923  08/24/88 15:41
FORMLET .MAC      128  08/24/88 15:32  GENERIC .PRD     1024  08/24/88 15:41
HPLASER .PRD     1024  08/24/88 15:32  LECTURE .LTR      320  08/24/88 15:32
LOGREPRT.MRG      647  08/24/88 15:41  MAC     .MEX     6419  08/24/88 15:32
ME      .EXE    65024  08/24/88 15:32  MEHELP  .1       1429  08/24/88 15:32
MEHELP  .2       1063  08/24/88 15:32  MEM     .MEX     6451  08/24/88 15:32
MPM     .MEX     5875  08/24/88 15:32 ▼ NB     .EXE    61952  08/24/88 15:34

1 *Mark; 2 Delete; 3 Move/Rename; 4 Select Files; 5 Lock; 6 Look; (F7 to Exit;
7 Other Dir; 8 Copy; 9 Word Srch; F2 Name Srch; F5 Find Files: 6    F3 for Help)
```

*Figure 49-1*

You can now select files to copy to other disks or directories, to delete, rename, or manipulate in any way indicated.

If you have initially activated WordPerfect without first going through the Library and Shell, then pressing **Ctrl-F1** (Shell) displays **1 Go to DOS** because WordPerfect has no idea that the Library program is available. Type **1** and from the DOS prompt type **C:\LIBRARY\SHELL ENTER** to call up the Shell main menu.

# Chapter 50
# USING EXTERNAL PROGRAMS

WordPerfect can be used in combination with a variety of software, such as desktop publishing programs or various database and spreadsheet programs. It can even make use of a programmable mouse. This chapter takes an abbreviated look, providing sufficient information to let you experiment on your own.

## EXTERNAL GRAPHICS PROGRAMS

WordPerfect can be used in conjunction with a large number of external graphics programs. They produce graphics files with extensions differing from the .WPG extension used by WordPerfect for its graphics programs. Some of these can be imported directly without the need for any conversion. They are:

| *Graphics Programs* | *Filename Extensions* |
| --- | --- |
| AutoCAD | DXF, HPGL |
| Dr. Halo II | DHP |
| GEM Paint | IMG, TIFF |
| GEM Scan | IMG, TIFF |
| Lotus 1-2-3 | PIC |
| Macintosh Paint | PNTG |
| PC Paint Plus | PPIC |
| PC Paintbrush | PCX |
| Publisher's PicturePak | WPG, CGM, PCX |
| Symphony | PIC |
| Windows Paint | MSP |
| VS Software Sled | PCX |

The routine with these files is relatively simple. For instance, Publisher's PicturePak from Marketing Graphics, Inc. offers a very large selection of graphics files available with either the CGM or PCX extension:

1. Place the PicturePak disk containing the graphic file that you want to use into drive B:
2. Press **Alt-F9** (Graphics) and select either **1 Figure** if you want the graphic to be framed by a simple line, or select **4 User Defined** if you want the graphic without a border or with a border designed by you.

3. Select **1 Create** and from the displayed options select **1 Filename**. Type the name of the file along with the appropriate disk/directory/path information. In this case it would be B:FILENAME.CGM. Press **Enter**.
4. Decide on the position on the page where your picture is to be located by using the **4 Vertical Position** and **5 Horizontal Position** options.
5. Decide how large or small you want your picture to be by using the **6 Size** option and selecting either **1 Width**, **2 Height**, or **3 Width and Height** options.
6. Decide whether you want the text to wrap around your picture. You may not if the picture is too large to permit the text in the remaining area to look right.
7. You can use the **8 Edit** option to change the size of the picture inside the frame or designated area. You can move it, rotate it, make it skinnier or fatter, invert it, and so on. Whatever is shown on the screen when you press **F7** (Exit) to save your work is how it is printed or displayed using **Shift-F7** (Print) or **6 View Document**.

When using any of the other graphics programs mentioned above, the routine is the same. But there are quite a few other so-called clip-art programs that produce files not compatible with WordPerfect. Many of these can still be used via WordPerfect's screen-capture facility (GRAB.COM) or any comparable program, such as HiJaak or InSet, which turn a screen into a graphics file convertible to the WordPerfect .WPG format.

On the Conversion disk WordPerfect includes a file called GRAPHCNV.EXE, designed to convert files not compatible with WordPerfect into .WPG files. This works with some, but not with all. When in doubt, try it out:

1. Press **Ctrl-F1** (Shell) and select **1 Go to DOS**.
2. From the DOS prompt, type **GRAPHCVN** and press **Enter**. You are asked for the name of the file to be converted. Type it along with path/directory information and press **Enter**.
3. Next you're asked for the name of the output file. Enter a name with the .WPG extension and press **Enter**.
4. The display either tells you the conversion was successful, or the file is of a format that WordPerfect cannot convert.

If the conversion is successful, you can use the new graphics file in the usual manner. If it is not successful, don't despair. All is not lost.

If you have a scanner (Logitech markets a low-cost hand-held scanner called ScanMan) you can make a print of the graphic image you want to use, using its original program. You can then use the scanner to scan it, producing a TIFF (Tagged Image File Format) file with a .TIF extension. It can be imported directly into WordPerfect using the same procedure described above with regard to PicturePak.

For instance, a company called Micrografx produces a wide selection of truly fine clip-art files, usually run in conjunction with Microsoft Windows. But the file format used by

## Chapter 50

Micrografx is incompatible with WordPerfect and it cannot be converted. On the other hand, you can print any of the images in whatever size you like and you can then use the scanner to produce a .TIF file that WordPerfect can deal with.

It works with various scanners producing TIFF files, such as the Hewlett Packard ScanJet and probably most if not all of the others.

Scanners can be used to scan any kind of black and white or color image including halftone images, regardless of where they were originally reproduced. Then, once they are imported into WordPerfect, the **Edit** option available from the **Graphics** menu can be used to change the size and aspect ratio. What cannot be done is actually to erase something on the image or to add something to it in the graphics format. That can be done by the programs used during the scanning operation such as Microsoft Windows with the Hewlett Packard ScanJet or PaintShow Plus with the Logitech ScanMan. Always remember that care must be taken not to infringe on someone's copyright.

In addition to using graphics from external sources, WordPerfect can deal with fonts produced by other programs. A typical example are the fonts produced by SoftCraft for laser and other printers. Using them involves installing the SoftCraft program (this example assumes a hard disk):

1. From the DOS prompt C> type **MD\WPIP** and press **Enter**. Then type **CD\WPIP** and press **Enter**.

2. Insert Laser Fonts Disk #4 (the WordPerfect Support Disk) into drive A:, type **COPY A:\*.\***, and press **Enter**.

3. Place the Laser Fonts Disk #2 (Utilities Disk) into drive A:, type **COPY A:\*.\***, and press **Enter**.

4. Place any disk(s) containing fonts that you want to use into drive A: and copy the files you want to use onto \WPIP.

5. To use the installed fonts, type **CD\WPIP** and press **Enter** if you're not already in that directory, then type **WPIP** and press **Enter**.

6. The WPIP menu appears with options and directions. Selection can be made with the arrow and tab keys or with the mouse. Once the settings are made, move the cursor to **OK** and either press **Enter** or click the mouse button. All the necessary files are automatically created on the disk/directory on which WordPerfect is located.

To use the fonts and make the best use of this program, read the *SoftCraft User's Manual For WordPerfect* and the other manuals that are part of the program.

There are a great many suppliers of fonts, some of which can be used with WordPerfect while others cannot. Be sure to ascertain the compatibility with WordPerfect and your printer of any font package you're interested in.

If the desktop publishing capabilities of WordPerfect are insufficient for the type of document that is to be created, text files, once converted to the ASCII format, can be imported into such desktop publishing programs as Ventura (from Xerox), PageMaker (from Aldus), Publish It! (from Timeworks, Inc.), First Publisher (from Software Publishing Corporation), and many others.

# PART TWO

# Features and Functions Reference

## CHAPTER 51
# FUNCTION KEYS

In this part of the book all of WordPerfect's functions and features are described. There are 40 function categories, most of which include a number of options, and in many cases these options break down into additional ones.

The available functions and features are grouped with the function categories (the ones activated by pressing a function-key combination), arranged in alphabetical order.

### BLOCK (Alt-F4)

The **Block** command is used to identify a certain section of text or other data. It can move copy, delete it, or format it by changing it to Bold or another attribute. When activated it displays a flashing Block On on the status line, remaining in effect until **Alt-F4** is pressed again, **F1** is pressed to cancel the command, or the block has been manipulated in some other way.

### BOLD (F6)

The **Bold** command causes all text or data to be printed in bold format until **F6** is pressed again, or **Right Arrow** is used to move the cursor past the end code. It produces the [BOLD][bold] codes at the beginning and end of the text or data to be affected by the command.

### CANCEL (F1)

This command displays: **Undelete: 1 Restore; 2 Previous Deletion: 0** on the status line. It is used to:

1. Back out of a WordPerfect menu or remove a message on the status line (which can also be done by pressing Esc). **F1** may have to be pressed more than one time.
2. Cancel a hyphenation request.
3. Recover up to three levels of deleted text or data.
4. Turn off the **Block** feature.
5. Cancel a **Search** or **Macro** operation (It does not turn off a Macro Def message. For that, **Ctrl-F10** (Macro Define) must be pressed again.)
6. It cannot be used to remove the **Reveal Codes** screen. That can be done only by pressing **Alt-F3** (Reveal Codes) again.

## CENTER (Shift-F6)

This command is used to **Center** text on the screen when it is typed after the command has been invoked. It is also centered when printed. It only affects the one line in which it is called. It can also be used to center a **block** of text that has been marked with the **Alt-F4** (Block) command. It inserts a [Cntr] code.

## DATE/OUTLINE (Shift-F5)

When this command is activated it displays on the status line: **1 Date Text; 2 Date Code; 3 Date Format; 4 Outline; 5 Para Num; 6 Define: 0**

**1 Date Text** inserts the current date (like January 1, 1990) at the cursor position in the current document.

**2 Date Code** inserts the date code ^D at the cursor position in the current document.

**3 Date Format** displays the Date Format menu (Fig. 51-1). It includes a large number of options in which date and time data can be displayed. If the date format is to be other than the default, then this option should be used first. The menu is very clear and needs no additional explanation. The code [Date:3 1, 4] or similar is inserted.

```
Date Format
        Character    Meaning
            1        Day of the Month
            2        Month (number)
            3        Month (word)
            4        Year (all four digits)
            5        Year (last two digits)
            6        Day of the Week (word)
            7        Hour (24-hour clock)
            8        Hour (12-hour clock)
            9        Minute
            0        am / pm
            %        Used before a number, will:
                        Pad numbers less than 10 with a leading zero
                        Output only 3 letters for the month or day of the week

        Examples:  3 1, 4         = December 25, 1984
                   %6 %3 1, 4     = Tue Dec 25, 1984
                   %2/%1/5 (6)    = 01/01/85 (Tuesday)
                   8:90           = 10:55am

Date format: 3 1, 4
```

Figure 51-1

**4 Outline** is used to insert paragraph numbers that increment with each new paragraph and are automatically adjusted when paragraphs are either deleted or added. It places the word Outline into the status line as a reminder.

**5 Para Num** places Paragraph Level (Press Enter for Automatic): into the status line. It is used when the starting paragraph number is other than 1. It inserts a [Par Num Def] or a [Par Num:Auto] code.

*Function Keys*

**6 Define** places the Paragraph Number Definition menu into the document screen (Fig. 51-2 for version 5.0 and Fig. 51-2A for version 5.1). This option must be used when the numbering format is to be other than the standard default format.

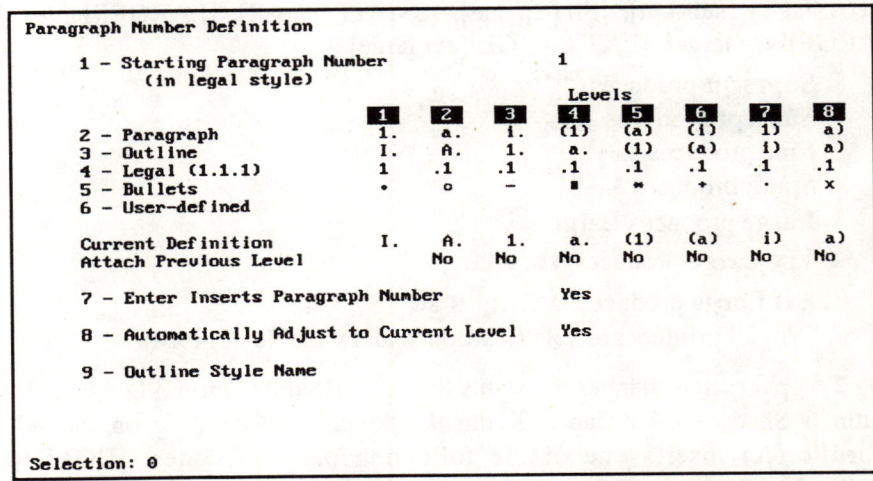

```
Paragraph Number Definition

    1 - Starting Paragraph Number        1
        (in legal style)
                                              Levels
                                1    2    3    4    5    6    7    8
    2 - Paragraph               1.   a.   i.  (1)  (a)  (i)  1)   a)
    3 - Outline                 I.   A.   1.   a.  (1)  (a)  i)   a)
    4 - Legal (1.1.1)           1    .1   .1   .1   .1   .1   .1   .1
    5 - Bullets                 •    o    -    ■    *    +    .    x
    6 - User-defined

    Current Definition          I.   A.   1.   a.  (1)  (a)  i)   a)

        Number Style                Punctuation
        1 - Digits                  #   - No punctuation
        A - Upper case letters      #.  - Trailing period
        a - Lower case letters      #)  - Trailing parenthesis
        I - Upper case roman       (#)  - Enclosing parentheses
        i - Lower case roman        .#  - All levels separated by period
        Other character - Bullet         (e.g. 2.1.3.4)

Selection: 0
```

*Figure 51-2*

```
Paragraph Number Definition

    1 - Starting Paragraph Number        1
        (in legal style)
                                              Levels
                                1    2    3    4    5    6    7    8
    2 - Paragraph               1.   a.   i.  (1)  (a)  (i)  1)   a)
    3 - Outline                 I.   A.   1.   a.  (1)  (a)  i)   a)
    4 - Legal (1.1.1)           1    .1   .1   .1   .1   .1   .1   .1
    5 - Bullets                 •    o    -    ■    *    +    .    x
    6 - User-defined

    Current Definition          I.   A.   1.   a.  (1)  (a)  i)   a)
    Attach Previous Level       No   No   No   No   No   No   No

    7 - Enter Inserts Paragraph Number       Yes

    8 - Automatically Adjust to Current Level   Yes

    9 - Outline Style Name

Selection: 0
```

*Figure 51-2A*

## EXIT (F7)

The **Exit** key is used after many of the commands to accept the selected options. When it is used while in the document screen, it produces Save document? (Y/N) Yes on the status line and after this question has been answered with either **Y** or **N**, it asks Exit Doc 1? (Y/N) No. If this is answered with **Y**, then WordPerfect is exited to DOS or it goes to Document 2 if that was active during this session.

## FLUSH RIGHT (Alt-F6)

This command places the cursor onto the far right column and as text is typed it moves from right to left. It remains in force only for the line in which it has been invoked. It inserts a [Flsh Rt] code.

## FONT (Ctrl-F8)

Selecting this command produces the following status line: **1 Size 2 Appearance 3 Normal 4 Base Font 5 Print Color: 0**

Selecting **1 Size** results in these options on the status line: 1 Suprscpt 2 Subscpt 3 Fine 4 Small 5 Large 6 Vry Large 7 Ext Large: 0. Depending on the selection from these options, any pair of the following codes is inserted [SUPRSCPT][suprscpt], [SUBSCPT] [subscpt], [FINE][fine], [SMALL][small], [LARGE][large], [VRY LARGE][vry large], [EXT LARGE][ext large].

    **Suprscpt** produces $^{superscript}$
    **Subscpt** produces $_{subscript}$
    **Fine** produces Fine
    **Small** produces Small
    **Large** produces Large
    **Vry Large** produces Very large
    **Ext Large** produces Extra large
    (Not all printers are able to produce all available options.)

Selecting **2 Appearance** changes the status line to: 1 Bold 2 Undrln 3 Dbl Und 4 Italic 5 Outln 6 Shadw 7 Sm Cap 8 Redln 9 Stkout: 0. Depending on the selection, WordPerfect inserts one of the following pairs of codes: [BOLD][bold], [UNDRLN][undrln], [DBL UND][dbl und], [ITALIC][italic], [OUTLN][outln], [SHADW][shadw], [SM CAP][sm cap], [REDLN][redln]. [STKOUT][stkout].

    **Bold** produces **Bold type**
    **Undrln** produces <u>Underlined type</u>
    **Dbl Und** produces <u>Double underlined text</u>
    **Italic** produces *Italic text*
    **Outln** produces Outlined text

**Shadw** produces **Shadowed text**
**Sm Cap** produces SMALL CAPITAL LETTERS
**Redln** produces Redlined text
**Stkout** produces ~~Strike-out text~~
(Not all printers can print all available styles.)

When **Normal** is selected, WordPerfect returns to the document screen.

When **Base Font** is selected the "Base Font" appears in the upper left corner of the screen followed by all available font styles and sizes and an asterisk next to the current selection, like *Courier 10 Pitch. A code like [Font:Courier 10 Pitch] is inserted.

When **Print Color** is selected, the Print Color menu is displayed (Fig. 51-3). This menu offers you the choice of mixing colors in many different ways to produce different colors. This choice is only useful if you have a color printer. A code like [Color Black] is inserted.

```
Print Color

                      Primary Color Mixture
                      Red      Green    Blue

       1 - Black      0%       0%       0%
       2 - White      100%     100%     100%
       3 - Red        67%      0%       0%
       4 - Green      0%       67%      0%
       5 - Blue       0%       0%       67%
       6 - Yellow     67%      67%      0%
       7 - Magenta    67%      0%       67%
       8 - Cyan       0%       67%      67%
       9 - Orange     67%      25%      0%
       A - Gray       50%      50%      50%
       N - Brown      67%      33%      0%
       O - Other

       Current Color  0%       0%       0%



Selection: 0
```

Figure 51-3

## FOOTNOTE (Ctrl-F7)

This command places the following options onto the status line: **1 Footnote; 2 Endnote; 3 Endnote Placement.**

**Footnote** creates a footnote that is placed at the bottom of the currently active page. It displays the options **1 Create; 2 Edit; 3 New Number; 4 Options: 0.**

**Create** results in a blank document screen with a number at the top and the code [Note Num] is inserted.

**Edit** places the previously created footnote onto the document screen for editing.

**New Number** asks you to enter a number other than the one automatically produced by WordPerfect.

**Options** produces the Options menu (Fig. 51-4) which includes nine options dealing with formatting your footnote to your own taste.

```
Footnote Options

     1 - Spacing Within Footnotes          1
                 Between Footnotes         0.16"
     2 - Amount of Note to Keep Together   0.5"
     3 - Style for Number in Text          [SUPRSCPT][Note Num][suprscpt]
     4 - Style for Number in Note                 [SUPRSCPT][Note Num][suprscp
     5 - Footnote Numbering Method         Numbers
     6 - Start Footnote Numbers each Page  No
     7 - Line Separating Text and Footnotes 2-inch Line
     8 - Print Continued Message           No
     9 - Footnotes at Bottom of Page       Yes



Selection: 0
```

*Figure 51-4*

**Endnote** works just like footnote, except that the **Endnote Placement** option produces a box with information (Fig. 51-5), and the Options menu is different.

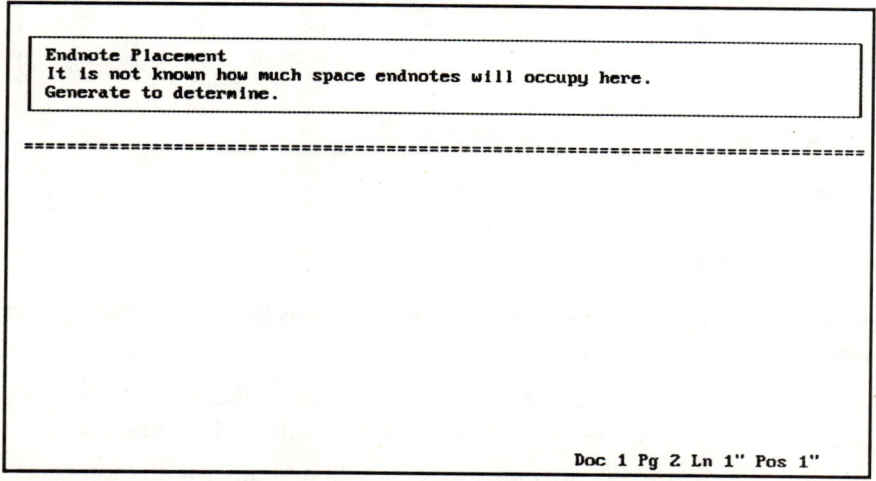

*Figure 51-5*

## FORMAT (Shift-F8)

This is one of the busiest and most frequently used functions, dealing with many different aspects of page and text formatting. Activating **Format** produces its main menu (Fig. 51-6) which offers four major options, each with its own menu and in some cases submenus.

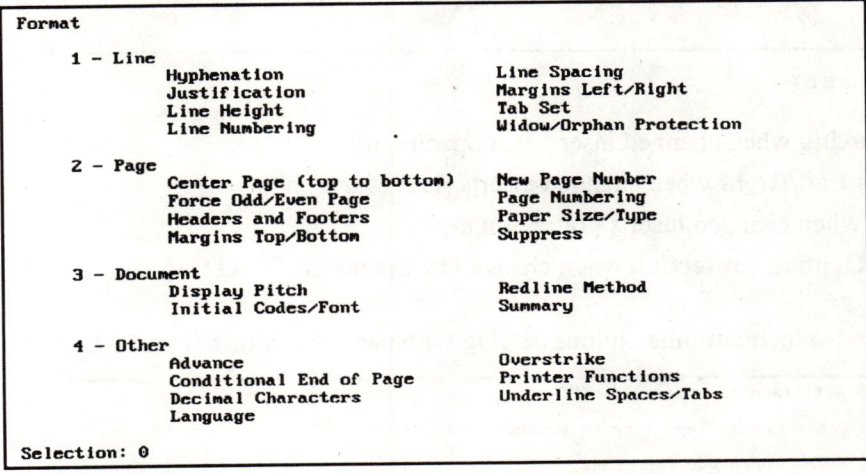

Figure 51-6

**1 - Line** includes nine options dealing with line formatting functions, each displaying the default that was selected by WordPerfect and which can be changed by the user.

**Hyphenation** when changed to **On** inserts [Hyph On]. Options are: **1 Off; 2 Manual; 3 Auto**.

> **Manual** lets you hyphenate each word yourself.
>
> **Auto** hyphenates automatically in accordance with a set of predetermined rules.
>
> **Off** moves words to the next line without hyphenation.
>
> **Hyphenation Zone** when changed inserts [HZone:15%,6%]. It uses whatever values were selected.

**Justification** when changed to **On** inserts [Just On].

**Line Height** when changed inserts [Ln Height: 0.16"] using whatever values were selected.

**Line Numbering** displays its own menu of five choices when it is changed to **Yes** (Fig. 51-7). It inserts [Ln Num:On].

## Chapter 51

```
Format: Line Numbering

    1 - Count Blank Lines                              Yes

    2 - Number Every n Lines, where n is              1

    3 - Position of Number from Left Edge            0.6"

    4 - Starting Number                               1

    5 - Restart Numbering on Each Page               Yes
```

*Figure 51-7*

**Line Spacing** when changed inserts [Ln Spacing:n].

**Margins Left/Right** when changed inserts [L/R Mar:n",n"].

**Tab Set** when changed inserts [Tab Set:n,n].

**Widow/Orphan Protection** when changed to **Yes** inserts [W/O On].

**2 - Page** also includes nine options dealing with page formatting (Fig. 51-8).

```
Format: Page

        1 - Center Page (top to bottom)       No

        2 - Force Odd/Even Page

        3 - Headers

        4 - Footers

        5 - Margins - Top                     1"
                      Bottom                  1"

        6 - New Page Number                   1
            (example: 3 or iii)

        7 - Page Numbering                    No page numbering

        8 - Paper Size                        8.5" x 11"
            Type                              Standard

        9 - Suppress (this page only)

Selection: 0
```

*Figure 51-8*

**Center Page (top to bottom)** when changed to **Yes** inserts [Center Pg]. This has no effect on the screen display. It centers the page vertically when printed. It can be examined using **Shift-F7** (Print) **6 View Document**.

**Force Odd/Even Page** displays **1 Odd; 2 Even: 0** on the status line. It renumbers the current and subsequent pages based on the user selection. It inserts either [Force:Odd] or [Force:Even].

*Function Keys*

**Headers** and **Footers** display **1 Header A; 2 Header B: 0** or **1 Footer A; 2 Footer B: 0**. The command places Header text at the top of the page and Footer text at the bottom of the current page. When a selection is made, the status line displays: **1 Discontinue; 2 Every Page; 3 Odd Pages; 4 Even Pages; 5 Edit: 0**. When 2, 3, or 4 are selected, a code like [Header A:2] is inserted.

**Margins Top/Bottom** when changed inserts [T/B Mar:n",n"].

**New Page Number** changes the page number automatically generated by WordPerfect to one of your choice. It inserts [Pg Num:n].

**Page Numbering** first produces its own menu (Fig. 51-9) and when a selection has been made, it inserts [Pg Numbering:Top Right] or whatever the user selects.

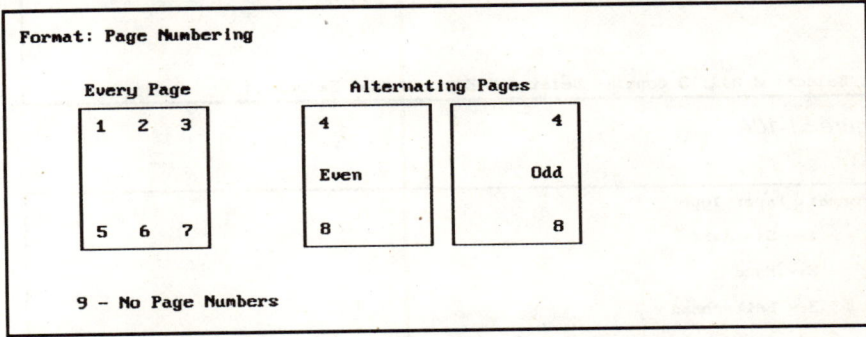

*Figure 51-9*

**Paper Size/Type** displays a menu of 10 choices for the paper size (Fig. 51-10 for version 5.0 and Fig. 51-10A for version 5.1) and another menu of eight choices for paper type (Fig. 51-11). It inserts [Paper Sz/Type:8.5" x 14",Letterhead] depending on the choices selected by the user.

```
Format: Paper Size

    1 - Standard              (8.5" x 11")
    2 - Standard Landscape    (11" x 8.5")
    3 - Legal                 (8.5" x 14")
    4 - Legal Landscape       (14" x 8.5")
    5 - Envelope              (9.5" x 4")
    6 - Half Sheet            (5.5" x 8.5")
    7 - US Government         (8" x 11")
    8 - A4                    (210mm x 297mm)
    9 - A4 Landscape          (297mm x 210mm)
    0 - Other
```

*Figure 51-10*

```
Format: Paper Size/Type
                                                       Font  Double
Paper type and Orientation      Paper Size   Prompt Loc  Type Sided  Labels
Standard                        8.22" x 12"   No    Contin Port  No
Standard                        8.5" x 11"    No    Contin Port  No
[ALL OTHERS]                    Width ≤ 15"   Yes   Manual       No




















1 Select; 2 Add; 3 Copy; 4 Delete; 5 Edit; N Name Search: 1
```

*Figure 51-10A*

```
Format: Paper Type
        1 - Standard
        2 - Bond
        3 - Letterhead
        4 - Labels
        5 - Envelope
        6 - Transparency
        7 - Cardstock
        8 - Other








Selection: 1
```

*Figure 51-11*

**Suppress (this page only)** displays a menu of 8 choices (Fig. 51-12) and after a choice has been made it inserts a code like [Suppress:HA, HB,FA,FB].

```
Format: Suppress (this page only)

    1 - Suppress All Page Numbering, Headers and Footers

    2 - Suppress Headers and Footers

    3 - Print Page Number at Bottom Center    No

    4 - Suppress Page Numbering               No

    5 - Suppress Header A                     No

    6 - Suppress Header B                     No

    7 - Suppress Footer A                     No

    8 - Suppress Footer B                     No




Selection: 0
```

*Figure 51-12*

**3 - Document** displays a menu of five options which include the default selections.

**Display Pitch** can be used to adjust the amount of horizontal space that is used by each character. Depending on the capabilities of your printer, it may have no effect at all.

**Initial Codes** activates the Reveal Codes screen and displays the default codes currently in effect such as [Just:Off].

**Initial Font** displays the default font.

**Redline Method** depends on the printer being used and may have no effect at all.

**Summary** displays a template for developing a document summary (Fig. 51-13 for version 5.0 and Fig. 51-13A for version 5.1). The filename is added when the

```
Document Summary
          System Filename         (Not named yet)
          Date of Creation        November 9, 1990
    1 - Descriptive Filename
    2 - Subject/Account
    3 - Author
    4 - Typist
    5 - Comments
  ┌─────────────────────────────────────────────────┐
  │                                                 │
  │                                                 │
  └─────────────────────────────────────────────────┘
```

*Figure 51-13*

## Chapter 51

summary and/or document are being saved. The current date is entered automatically and the other data can be entered by the user or be left blank. Comments calls for some descriptive copy. Creating document summaries is a good idea as Word Search commands work much faster when they are restricted to the document summaries.

```
Document Summary
        Revision Date
    1 - Creation Date   11-09-90 02:32p
    2 - Document Name
        Document Type
    3 - Author
        Typist
    4 - Subject
    5 - Account
    6 - Keywords
    7 - Abstract



Selection: 0                    (Retrieve to capture; Del to remove summary)
```

*Figure 51-13A*

**4 - Other** menu (Fig. 51-14) offers 7 choices.

**Advance** displays **1 Up; 2 Down; 3 Line Left; 4 Line; 5 Right; 6 Position: 0** on the status line, all of which can be used to change the position of certain text. It often has no effect on the screen display but does affect the way a document is printed.

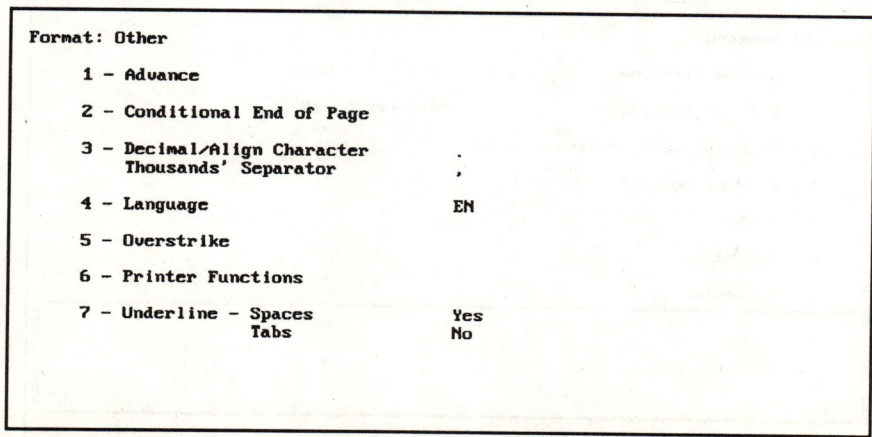

*Figure 51-14*

**Conditional End of Page** displays Number of Lines to Keep Together: on the status line and it controls the manner in which page breaks are entered by WordPerfect.

**Decimal/Align Character** controls the manner in which decimal figures and figures in excess of 999.99 are displayed (1,000.50).

**Language,** when changed, includes special characters used by other languages. The available languages and their language codes are:

| | | | |
|---|---|---|---|
| CA | Canadian French | NE | Dutch |
| DA | Danish | NO | Norwegian |
| DE | German | PO | Portugese |
| EN | English | SU | Finnish |
| ES | Spanish | SV | Swedish |
| FR | French | UK | British English |
| IC | Icelandic | US | United States |
| IT | Italian | | |

The Thesaurus and Speller may be ordered in more than one language.

**Overstrike** is used to print more than one character in the same position. It offers **1 Create; 2 Edit: 0** and when **Create** is selected the characters to be combined should be typed. It inserts [Ovrstk].

**Printer Functions** displays its own menu (Fig. 51-15 for version 5.0 and Fig. 51-15A for version 5.1) with four options (five with 5.1).

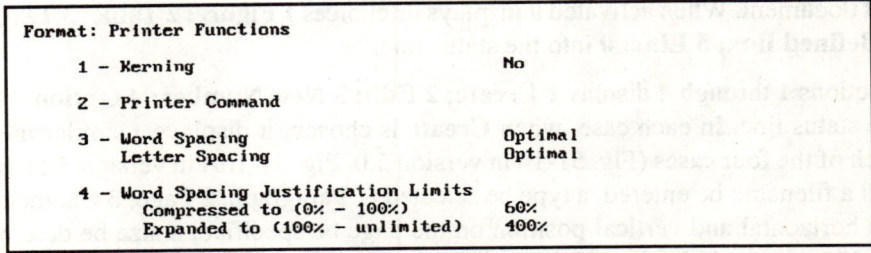

Figure 51-15

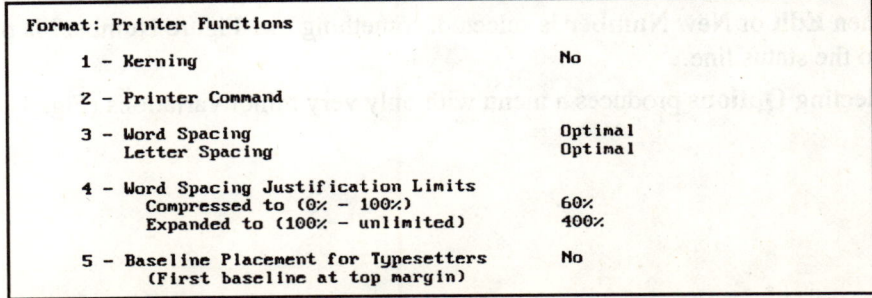

Figure 51-15A

**Kerning** can be used to reduce space between certain letters like i, l, etc. It depends on the ability of your printer to perform proportional printing.

**Printer Command** is used to enter commands for your printer. It displays 1 Command; 2 Filename: 0. If **Command** is selected you enter commands in a format that your printer can accept. These commands are not displayed but can be shown by using Reveal Codes. Command codes can be written as a BASIC file in which case WordPerfect sends the entire file to the printer. To do this, select **Filename** and enter the filename used when saving the BASIC file.

**Word Spacing** and **Letter Spacing** place Word Spacing: or Letter Spacing: 1 Normal; 2 Optimal; 3 Percent of Optimal; 4 Set Pitch: 0 into the status line. **Normal** uses the spacing that is considered best by the manufacturer of the selected printer. **Optimal** is the spacing thought best by WordPerfect. **Percent of Optimal** permits you to enter a width of your choice. **Set Pitch** asks that you enter the number of characters per inch. The printed results depend on the capabilities of the printer.

**Word Spacing Justification Limits** is used to set the limit for spaces that is allowed when Right Justification is On. The default is perfectly fine, though when narrow columns of text are used, it might need adjustment.

## GRAPHICS (Alt-F9)

This feature is used to produce and insert graphic images from a variety of sources into your text document. When activated it displays its choices **1 Figure; 2 Table; 3 Text Box; 4 User-defined Box; 5 Line: 0** into the status line.

The selections **1** through **4** display **1 Create; 2 Edit; 3 New Number; 4 Options: 0** into the status line. In each case, when **Create** is chosen, it displays a similar menu in each of the four cases (Fig. 51-16 in version 5.0, Fig. 51-16A in version 5.1). It asks that a filename be entered, a type be selected (1 Paragraph; 2 Page; 3 Character: 0), the horizontal and vertical position on the page be specified, a size be determined (1 Width (auto height); 2 Height (auto width); 3 Both Width and Height: 0), text wrap around the box be determined, and any needed editing is done.

When **Edit** or **New Number** is selected, something like Figure Number? is placed into the status line.

Selecting **Options** produces a menu with only very minor variations (Fig. 51-17).

```
Definition: Figure

    1 - Filename
    2 - Caption
    3 - Type                     Paragraph
    4 - Vertical Position        0"
    5 - Horizontal Position      Right
    6 - Size                     3.25" wide x 3.25" (high)
    7 - Wrap Text Around Box     Yes
    8 - Edit
```

*Figure 51-16*

```
Definition: Figure

    1 - Filename
    2 - Contents                 Empty
    3 - Caption
    4 - Anchor Type              Paragraph
    5 - Vertical Position        0"
    6 - Horizontal Position      Right
    7 - Size                     3.25" wide x 3.25" (high)
    8 - Wrap Text Around Box     Yes
    9 - Edit
```

*Figure 51-16A*

```
Options:    Figure

    1 - Border Style
            Left                       Single
            Right                      Single
            Top                        Single
            Bottom                     Single
    2 - Outside Border Space
            Left                       0.16"
            Right                      0.16"
            Top                        0.16"
            Bottom                     0.16"
    3 - Inside Border Space
            Left                       0"
            Right                      0"
            Top                        0"
            Bottom                     0"
    4 - First Level Numbering Method   Numbers
    5 - Second Level Numbering Method  Off
    6 - Caption Number Style           [BOLD]Figure 1[bold]
    7 - Position of Caption            Below box, Outside borders
    8 - Minimum Offset from Paragraph  0"
    9 - Gray Shading (% of black)      0%
```

*Figure 51-17*

## Chapter 51

When **Line** is selected, **1 Horizontal; 2 Vertical: 0** is placed into the status line. When **Horizontal** is selected, it displays a menu with four or five choices (Fig. 51-18 in version 5.0, Fig. 51-18A in version 5.1) which are self-explanatory. When **Vertical** is selected, it displays a menu with five choices (Fig. 51-19) which are also self-explanatory.

```
Graphics: Horizontal Line
    1 - Horizontal Position          Left & Right
    2 - Length of Line
    3 - Width of Line                0.01"
    4 - Gray Shading (% of black)    100%
```

*Figure 51-18*

```
Graphics: Horizontal Line
    1 - Horizontal Position          Full
    2 - Vertical Position            Baseline
    3 - Length of Line
    4 - Width of Line                0.013"
    5 - Gray Shading (% of black)    100%
```

*Figure 51-18A*

```
Graphics: Vertical Line
    1 - Horizontal Position          Left Margin
    2 - Vertical Position            Full Page
    3 - Length of Line
    4 - Width of Line                0.01"
    5 - Gray Shading (% of black)    100%
```

*Figure 51-19*

## HELP (F3)

WordPerfect stands ready with a huge selection of **Help** screens that vary in content with the particular stage in the work during which **F3** was pressed. When it is pressed while text is being typed, it displays the basic Help screen (Fig. 51-20) asking that a letter be typed to display all features and functions starting with that letter. There is a total of 20 such lists from A through W which represent a useful shortcut when a specific explanation is needed. In addition, once **F3** has been pressed, pressing any key other than a letter key produces additional help screens. Furthermore, there is a Help screen for each and every feature and function.

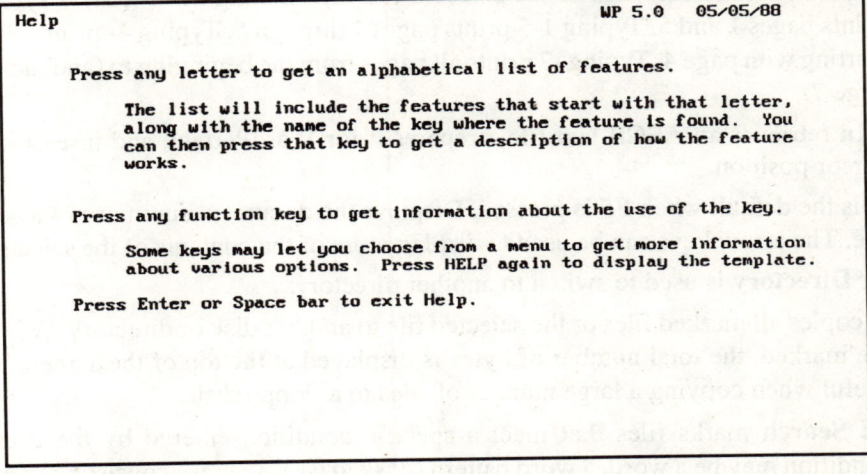

Figure 51-20

## INDENT <—> (Shift-F4)

This feature indents the left margin to the next tab stop and the right margin an equal amount. Pressing **Enter** cancels the effect. It inserts the **[<indent>]** code.

## INDENT —> (F4)

This feature indents to the next tab stop each time it is pressed, and that position becomes the left margin for all succeeding lines until **Enter** is pressed or a hard page break **(Ctrl-Enter)** is used.

## LIST FILES (F5)

This option lists all files on the currently logged disk or directory in alphabetical order. Files can be selected by using the arrow keys and they can be marked by typing an asterisk (*). At the bottom a list of options is displayed:

**1 Retrieve** places the selected file into the currently active document screen.

**2 Delete** deletes all marked files or the selected file after asking Delete? (Y/N) No.

**3 Move/Rename** renames a file and if complete disk/directory and path information is included, it moves the renamed file to that location.

**4 Print** prints all marked files or the selected file after asking Print (All)?. Typing 1,5 prints pages 1 and 5. Typing 1-5 prints pages 1 through 5. Typing 4- prints all pages starting with page 4. Typing -7 prints all pages from the beginning to (and including) page 7.

**5 Text In** retrieves an ASCII text file, prepares it for WordPerfect, and inserts it at the cursor position.

**6 Look** is the default when **F5** is pressed. Displays the document summary of a selected file. The arrow keys can be used to display more of the contents of the selected file.

**7 Other Directory** is used to switch to another directory.

**8 Copy** copies all marked files or the selected file to another disk or directory. When files are marked, the total number of bytes is displayed at the top of the screen. This is useful when copying a large number of files to a floppy disk.

**9 Word Search** marks files that meet a specific condition entered by the user. The condition may be a word, a word pattern (d*sk, d?sk), a phrase consisting of several words or conditional statements in which ; = AND, , = OR, ? matches one letter, * matches one or more letters.

**10 Name Search** highlights the file or files the name(s) of which most closely resembles the letters typed by the user.

## MACRO (Alt-F10)

This feature asks for a macro name and then executes that macro, assuming it has been previously defined. Permanent Alt macros (Alt-A, Alt-B, etc.) and temporary Alt macros (Alt-1, Alt-2, etc.) can be executed without this command by pressing **Alt** and the letter or digit in question.

## MACRO DEFINE (Ctrl-F10)

This function records each and every keystroke until **Ctrl-F10** (Macro Define) is pressed again. It first prompts Define a Macro: which expects that you enter a name. You have two choices: type **Alt** and a letter from **A** to **Z** to create a permanent Alt macro, or you can enter a name consisting of one to eight characters (no extension). You're then prompted for a Description. It is a good idea to enter one because it is displayed when the **Macro Edit** option is used, making it a lot easier to see what the macro is designed to accomplish. It then displays Macro Def flashing on the status line while any number of commands and keystrokes are entered. If **Merge** is used, it must be at the end. If **Ctrl-PgUp** is pressed, you may choose from four options: **1 Pause** stops macro execution to allow user input until **Enter** is pressed; **2 Display** turns the display on or off during macro execution; **3 Assign** assigns a user-defined value or block to a macro variable. **4 Comment** enters comments that are ignored during macro execution.

When editing a previously named macro, the keystrokes are displayed. In this mode, pressing **Ctrl-F10** activates the macro editing mode. It permits including such keystrokes as **Enter** or **F7** (Exit) that are otherwise not available. Pressing **Ctrl-PgUp** in this mode produces a display of available macro commands that can be scrolled using the cursor keys.

## MARK TEXT (Alt-F5)

Activating this option places **1 Auto Ref; 2 Subdoc; 3 Index; 4 ToA Short Form; 5 Define; 6 Generate: 0** into the status line. **Auto Ref** is a fairly complicated feature that adjusts automatic references. For details use **F3 Alt-F5 1** which displays the appropriate Help screen. **Subdoc** is another complicated feature. For details use **F3 Alt-F5 2**, displaying the appropriate Help screen. **Index** is used to select words and phrases from the document for use in an index. For details use **F3 Alt-F5 3** which places the appropriate Help screen into display. **ToA Short Form** is used to generate a Table of Authorities. For details use **F3 Alt-F5 4** to display the appropriate Help screen. **Define** defines tables of contents, lists, and tables of authorities. For details use **F3 Alt-F5 5** which places the appropriate Help screen into display. **Generate** can be used to remove certain commands such as strikeout text from document, redline, compare documents for redline and strikeout, expand or condense master documents, generate tables, indexes, automatic references, and endnote placements.

## MATH/COLUMNS (Alt-F7)

This feature deals with **Math** and with individual **Columns**. When activated it places **1 Math On; 2 Math Def; 3 Column On/Off; 4 Column Def: 0** into the status line. The **Math** mode permits having WordPerfect perform mathematical calculations. For details use **F3 Alt-F7 1** which places the appropriate Help screen into display. **Math Def** produces up to 24 columns and instructs WordPerfect how to handle the data in those columns. Again, for details use **F3 Alt-F7 2** to view the appropriate Help screen.

**Column On/Off** turns previously defined columns on or off.

**Column Def** is used to create text columns of various types. Again, for details use **F3 Alt-F7 4** for the appropriate Help screen.

## MERGE R (F9)

In the process of creating a secondary merge file, **F9** places a ^R code in version 5.0 and {END FIELD} in version 5.1 into the document at the cursor position, followed by a hard return. During merge execution, **F9** indicates that the user has finished entering text or data.

## MERGE CODES (Shift-F9)

This option displays all merge codes (except ^R or {END FIELD}) and asks for a selection to be typed. For a complete list of the available codes and their functions, press **F3 Shift-F9**. The codes differ between version 5.0 and 5.1.

## MERGE/SORT (Ctrl-F9)

This feature includes three options: **1 Merge; 2 Sort; 3 Sort Order: 0**. **Merge** is used for form letters, mail-merge, etc. It incorporates data from a secondary file into the primary file that represents the format of the document. **Sort** is used to sort lists alphabetically or numerically in ascending or descending order. It also includes a **Select** option used to extract selected items from a list. To see an explanation of the various options and suboptions, use **F3 Ctrl-F9 2** which displays the appropriate Help screen. **Sort Order** displays the options **US/European** and **Scandinavian**.

## MOVE (Ctrl-F4)

This option can be used to move, copy, or delete text. It places **Move: 1 Sentence; 2 Paragraph; 3 Page; 4 Retrieve: 0** into the status line. Selecting **1, 2,** or **3** changes the status line to **1 Move; 2 Copy; 3 Delete; 4 Append: 0**. Text to be moved, copied, deleted, or appended must first be highlighted. If **Block** is **Off** then the sentence, paragraph, or page on which the cursor is located is highlighted automatically. If **Block** is **On** then the marked block must be highlighted before an action is selected. Selecting **4** changes the status line to **Retrieve: 1 Block; 2 Tabular Column; 3 Rectangle**. After text has been marked as a **Block**, a complete block, a tabular column, or a rectangle can be highlighted. For more details use **F3 Ctrl-F4 2** which displays the appropriate Help screen.

## PRINT (Shift-F7)

When this feature is selected, WordPerfect displays the Print menu consisting of a number of options (Fig. 51-21).

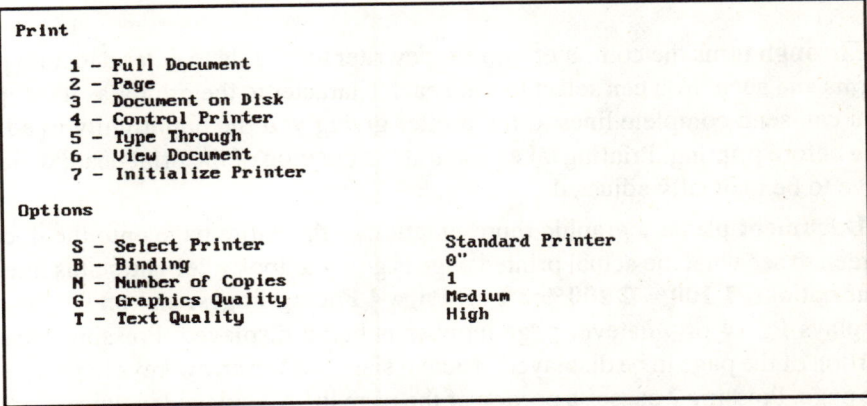

Figure 51-21

**1 Full Document** prints the document currently located on the selected document screen.

**2 Page** prints the page on which the cursor is currently located.

**3 Document on Disk** asks for the document filename to be typed along with disk/directory and path information (if other than the currently logged drive or directory). Pressing **Enter** prints the entire document. Typing 5,8 prints pages 5 and 8. Typing 5-8 prints pages 5 through 8. Typing -8 prints pages 1 through 8.

**4 Control Printer** causes a new menu to be displayed (Fig. 51-22). When **1 Cancel Job(s)** is selected, all print jobs are canceled. When **2 Rush Job** is selected, the order in which print jobs are executed is changed. When **3 Display Jobs** is selected, the various print jobs are displayed. **4 Go** starts the printer when it has been stopped or when it has waited for some action. **5 Stop** stops the print job.

## Chapter 51

```
Print: Control Printer

Current Job

Job Number:  None                           Page Number:  None
Status:      No print jobs                  Current Copy: None
Message:     None
Paper:       None
Location:    None
Action:      None


Job List

Job  Document                Destination         Print Options




Additional Jobs Not Shown: 0



1 Cancel Job(s); 2 Rush Job; 3 Display Jobs; 4 Go (start printer); 5 Stop: 0
```

*Figure 51-22*

**5 Type Through** turns the computer into a typewriter to be able to enter data into printed forms and such. You can select to send each character to the printer as it is typed, or you can send complete lines to the printer giving you the opportunity to edit each line before printing. Printing takes place at the position of the print head, which may have to be manually adjusted.

**6 View Document** places a graphic representation of the entire page onto the document screen to see what the actual printed page is going to look like. The status line offers four options: **1 100% 2 200% 3 Full Page 4 Facing Pages:** and on the far right it displays Pg 14 or whatever page number is being displayed. Pressing **1** causes a portion of the page to be displayed in actual size. Use the arrow keys to move around the page. Pressing **2** causes a portion of the page to be displayed in twice actual size. In this stage, text can actually be read. Again, use the arrow keys to move around the page. Pressing **3** displays the entire page with the text greeked (not readable) to show what the printed page looks like. You can use PgUp and PgDn to look at other pages. Pressing **4** places facing pages into view. Again, using PgUp or PgDn displays other pages.

**7 Initialize Printer** removes any soft fonts from the printer's memory.

**S Select Printer** is used to change to another printer, selecting the printer from the printers that are listed on the four Printer Disks.

**B Binding** moves the text to the right on odd-numbered pages and to the left on even-numbered pages when double-sided pages are to be bound.

**N Number of copies** permits entering the number of copies of the document or page to be printed.

**G Graphics Quality** and **T Text Quality** place **1 Do Not Print; 2 Draft; 3 Medium; 4 High** into the status line. **Draft** can be used to print rough drafts. In this mode printing is speeded up. **Do Not Print** is used if you want to print only text and no graphics or vice versa.

## REPLACE (Alt-F2)

This feature is used to replace a word, phrase, or WordPerfect code with a different word, phrase, or code. When the feature is activated, it places w/Confirm? (Y/N) No into the status line. If **No** is accepted, all occurrences of the word, phrase, or code are replaced. If **Yes** is chosen, WordPerfect stops at each occurrence, asking whether or not the word, phrase, or code is to be replaced. In either case, the status line changes to **-> Srch** and WordPerfect is waiting for you to enter the word, phrase, or code to be replaced. Then press **F2** (Search). The status line changes to **Replace with:** and you now type the new word, phrase, or code and press **F2** (Search) again. You can use **Home Alt-F2** (Replace) which extends the search into headers, footers, footnotes, endnotes, etc.

## RETRIEVE (Shift-F10)

This function is used to retrieve a file from disk and place its contents onto the document screen. The text is inserted at the cursor position and any text below the cursor position is moved down.

## REVEAL CODES (Alt-F3)

Every editing command such as bold, center, soft and hard returns, and just about everything else causes an invisible WordPerfect code to be inserted in the document. Using this function displays the text along with all codes at the bottom half of the screen. All typing and editing functions are available in this stage and codes can be deleted or added. To return to the document screen, press **Alt-F3** (Reveal Codes) again.

## SAVE (F10)

This saves the document to disk. The filename to be used can have up to eight characters and you may add an optional up-to-three-letter extension (FILENAME.EXT). If the filename already exists, then WordPerfect asks **Replace (Y/N) No** and if you type **Y**, the old file is replaced with the new one. Even though WordPerfect can be programmed to perform automatic saves into a backup file every few minutes, it is a good idea to use Save often to avoid inadvertent loss of data.

## SCREEN (Ctrl-F3)

When activated, it places **0 Rewrite; 1 Window; 2 Line Draw** into the status line.

**0 Rewrite** rewrites the entire screen. It is useful if you want to see the effects of certain changes in the format.

**1 Window** splits the screen into two windows, both of which can be used independently for editing. Enter the number of lines to retain for the current document, and the other screen uses the balance (typing 12 produces two even-sized windows). To move back and forth between the two windows, use **Shift-F3** (Switch).

**2 Line Draw** is used for drawing boxes, graphs, etc., using the arrow keys. It produces a number of options on the status line: **1 |; 2 ||; 3 \*; 4 Change; 5 Erase; 6 Move: 1**. The first three indicate the line style used. **4 Change** displays a large number of additional line styles plus an **Other** option letting you enter a character to be used as a line (such as ^ or + for instance). Use the **Repeat** function (**Esc**) and a number to determine the length of the line.

## SEARCH <— (Shift-F2)

This function searches backward in the current document for an indicated word, phrase, or code. When activated **<- Srch** is placed into the status line. Type the combination of characters or codes that you want WordPerfect to find and press **Shift-F2** again. To continue the search after the first find, repeat the process except that the word, phrase, or code to be found does not need to be entered again. Pressing **Home Shift-F2** extends the search into headers, footers, footnotes, etc. While lowercase letters match lowercase as well as uppercase letters, uppercase letters match only uppercase.

## SEARCH —> (F2)

This functions exactly like the foregoing, except that the search is performed forward rather than backward.

## SETUP (Shift-F1)

This group of functions is used to control the various settings on a permanent basis. Everything selected using **Setup** remains in effect permanently or until changed using Setup again. To make temporary changes, use the **Format** feature. When **Setup** is selected, it displays the Setup menu (Fig. 51-23 in version 5.0, Fig. 51-23A in version 5.1).

*Function Keys*

```
Setup

    1 - Backup
    2 - Cursor Speed              30 cps
    3 - Display
    4 - Fast Save (unformatted)   No
    5 - Initial Settings
    6 - Keyboard Layout
    7 - Location of Auxiliary Files
    8 - Units of Measure
```

*Figure 51-23*

```
Setup

    1 - Mouse
    2 - Display
    3 - Environment
    4 - Initial Settings
    5 - Keyboard Layout
    6 - Location of Files
```

*Figure 51-23A*

**1 Backup** displays a second menu (Fig. 51-24) explaining the options available to cause WordPerfect to create backup files automatically.

```
Setup: Backup
    Timed backup files are deleted when you exit WP normally.  If you
    have a power or machine failure, you will find the backup file in the
    backup directory indicated in Setup: Location of Auxiliary Files.

        Backup Directory

    1 - Timed Document Backup            No
        Minutes Between Backups          30

    Original backup will save the original document with a .BK! extension
    whenever you replace it during a Save or Exit.

    2 - Original Document Backup         No
```

*Figure 51-24*

241

*Chapter 51*

**2 Cursor Speed** controls the number of characters per second that WordPerfect can accept. It places **Characters per second: 1 15; 2 20; 3 30; 4 40; 5 50; 6 Normal: 3** into the status line.

**3 Display** places another menu into display (Fig. 51-25 in version 5.0, Fig. 51-25A in version 5.1).

```
Setup: Display
        1 - Automatically Format and Rewrite     Yes
        2 - Colors/Fonts/Attributes
        3 - Display Document Comments            Yes
        4 - Filename on the Status Line          Yes
        5 - Graphics Screen Type                 IBM EGA 640x350 16 color
        6 - Hard Return Display Character
        7 - Menu Letter Display                  BOLD
        8 - Side-by-side Columns Display         Yes




Selection: 0
```
*Figure 51-25*

```
Setup: Display
        1 - Colors/Fonts/Attributes
        2 - Graphics Screen Type                 EGA 640x350 16 color
        3 - Text Screen Type                     Auto Selected
        4 - Menu Options
        5 - View Document Options
        6 - Edit-Screen Options







Selection: 0
```
*Figure 51-25A*

**1 Automatically Format and Rewrite** reformats your work as you type and edit or, if **No** is selected, reformats when scrolling forward or backward.

242

**2 Colors/Fonts/Attributes** displays **1 Screen Color; 2 Fast Text Yes**, and when **1** is selected, it displays a new menu (Fig. 51-26) which can be used to change the color combinations used on the screen. **Fast Text** should be **Yes** unless it created snow on the screen, in which case it should be changed to **No**.

```
Setup: Colors/Fonts

Attribute           Font   Foreground   Background   Sample
Normal              N      H            B            Sample
Blocked             N      B            H            Sample
Underline           Y      H            B            Sample
Strikeout           N      C            B            Sample
Bold                N      G            B            Sample
Double Underline    N      F            B            Sample
Redline             N      E            B            Sample
Shadow              N      A            D            Sample
Italics             N      B            D            Sample
Small Caps          N      E            D            Sample
Outline             N      F            D            Sample
Subscript           N      G            D            Sample
Superscript         N      H            D            Sample
Fine Print          N      B            A            Sample
Small Print         N      C            A            Sample
Large Print         N      D            A            Sample
Very Large Print    N      E            A            Sample
Extra Large Print   N      F            A            Sample
Bold & Underline    N      A            C            Sample
Other Combinations  N      A            G            Sample

Switch to switch; Move to copy settings    Doc 1
```

*Figure 51-26*

**3 Display Document Comments** refers to the comments in boxes and should be left at **Yes**.

**4 Filename on the Status Line** should also remain at **Yes**.

**5 Graphics Screen Type** is based on what WordPerfect has sensed relative to your installed graphics adapter and monitor. It might have to be changed if you change graphics adapters or monitors or if you use more than one monitor with your computer.

**6 Hard Return Display Character** is left blank and might as well remain so.

**7 Menu Letter Display** is set up as **Bold**. It can be changed to **Normal** or you can select **Size** or **Appearance** and make changes in accordance with the options that are presented on the status line.

**8 Side-by-side Columns Display** if retained as **Yes** displays columns in that manner. If changed to **No** it displays columns as one column per screen. Columns are always printed side-by-side.

**4 Fast Save (unformatted)** is set to **No** and should stay that way. Documents saved with the Fast Save option cannot be printed until they go through a formatting routine.

**5 Initial Settings** produces another menu (Fig. 51-27 in version 5.0, Fig. 51-27A in version 5.1).

```
Setup: Initial Settings
    1 - Beep Options
    2 - Date Format              3 1, 4
    3 - Document Summary
    4 - Initial Codes
    5 - Repeat Value             8
    6 - Table of Authorities
```

*Figure 51-27*

```
Setup: Initial Settings
    1 - Merge
    2 - Date Format              3 1, 4
                                 November 9, 1990
    3 - Equations
    4 - Format Retrieved Documents   No
        for Default Printer
    5 - Initial Codes
    6 - Repeat Value             8
    7 - Table of Authorities
    8 - Print Options




Selection: 0
```

*Figure 51-27A*

**1 Beep Options** are Beep on Error, Beep on Hyphenation, Beep on Search Failure all of which should probably remain at **No**.

**2 Date Format** produces its own menu (Fig. 51-28) which explains how to set up the kind of date and time format you like best.

**3 Document Summary** offers Create on Save/Exit Yes and Subject Search Text Subject:.

**4 Initial Codes** displays the codes in effect when WordPerfect is activated.

**5 Repeat Value** is the number that appears as the default when **Esc** is pressed. Enter any number you like.

**6 Table of Authorities** offers Dot Leaders Yes; Underlining Allowed No; Blank Line Between Authorities Yes. All three default setting can be reversed if called for.

```
Date Format

      Character    Meaning
          1        Day of the Month
          2        Month (number)
          3        Month (word)
          4        Year (all four digits)
          5        Year (last two digits)
          6        Day of the Week (word)
          7        Hour (24-hour clock)
          8        Hour (12-hour clock)
          9        Minute
          0        am / pm
          %        Used before a number, will:
                      Pad numbers less than 10 with a leading zero
                      Output only 3 letters for the month or day of the week

      Examples:  3 1, 4        = December 25, 1984
                 %6 %3 1, 4    = Tue Dec 25, 1984
                 %2/%1/5 (6)   = 01/01/85 (Tuesday)
                 8:90          = 10:55am

Date format: 3 1, 4
```

*Figure 51-28*

**6 Keyboard Layout** can be used if you want to change the effects resulting from pressing certain keys. For detailed instructions, use F3 Shift-F1 6 which places the appropriate **Help** screen into display.

**7 Location of Auxiliary Files** produces its own menu (Fig. 51-29 in version 5.0, Fig. 51-29A in version 5.1). It identifies the disks, directories, and subdirectories used for different types of files. Where nothing is indicated, no special disks or directories were set up.

```
Setup: Location of Auxiliary Files

      1 - Backup Directory

      2 - Hyphenation Module(s)

      3 - Keyboard/Macro Files

      4 - Main Dictionary(s)

      5 - Printer Files                    C:\WP50

      6 - Style Library Filename

      7 - Supplementary Dictionary(s)

      8 - Thesaurus
```

*Figure 51-29*

Chapter 51

```
Setup: Location of Files
     1 - Backup Files
     2 - Keyboard/Macro Files          C:\WP51
     3 - Thesaurus/Spell/Hyphenation
                       Main
                       Supplementary
     4 - Printer Files                 C:\WP51
     5 - Style Files
             Library Filename
     6 - Graphic Files                 C:\WP51
     7 - Documents
```

*Figure 51-29A*

**8 Units of Measure** also produces its own menu (Fig. 51-30) which can be used to change the units of measure used on the status line and elsewhere to whatever format you like best.

```
Setup: Units of Measure
     1 - Display and Entry of Numbers    "
         for Margins, Tabs, etc.
     2 - Status Line Display             "

Legend:
     " = inches
     i = inches
     c = centimeters
     p = points
     u = WordPerfect 4.2 Units (Lines/Columns)
```

*Figure 51-30*

### SHELL (Ctrl-F1)

This function returns you to DOS so you can enter a DOS command. When activated, it places **1 Go to DOS: 0** into the status line. Typing **1** returns you to DOS while WordPerfect remains in the resident memory. You can execute any number of DOS commands. To return to WordPerfect, type **EXIT** or **exit** (the actual letters, not the F7 (Exit) key) and press **Enter**. Do not turn off the computer without first returning to WordPerfect.

If you have the WordPerfect Library, you can retrieve the clipboard or use other library programs and functions, assuming they are on the logged disk/directory.

*Function Keys*

## SPELL (Ctrl-F2)

This function activates the spelling checker. It places a number of choices into the status line: **Check: 1 Word; 2 Page; 3 Document; 4 New Sup.Dictionary; 5 Look Up; 6 Count: 0.**

**1 Word** checks the single word on which the cursor is located and if it is not found, it displays suggested alternatives.

**2 Page** checks all words on the page on which the cursor is located, highlighting any questioned words and suggesting alternatives.

**3 Document** checks the entire document in the same way.

**4 New Sup. Dictionary** permits also using a supplementary dictionary if one was created. It asks for the filename for it.

**5 Look Up** looks for and displays words that match a word pattern or a phonetic spelling. Word patterns can include wild cards where * stands for any number of characters and ? stands for one character. As for phonetic spelling, let's take *awry* which is pronounced "ary" or "arye" and use Look Up. The speller produces several screens full of suggestions which in this case include awry under U on the first screen (Fig. 51-31).

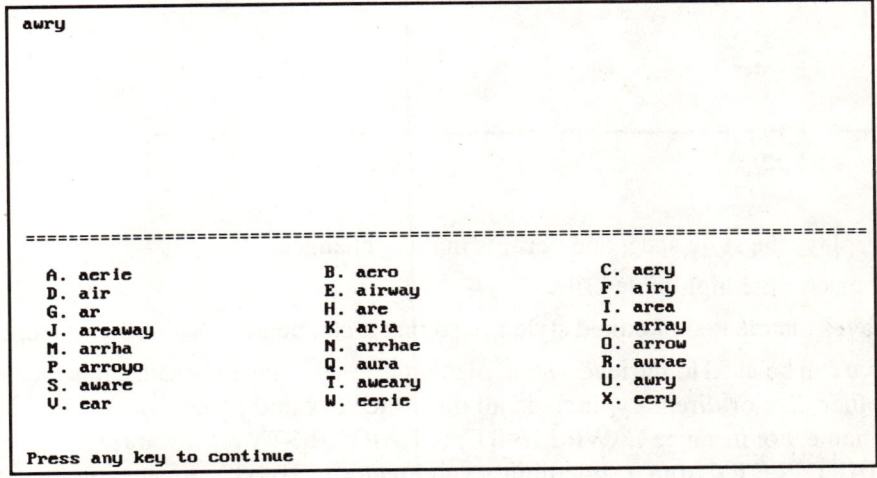

Figure 51-31

**6 Count** simply counts the number of words in the document.

247

Chapter 51

## STYLE (Alt-F8)

When this function is activated, it displays **Styles** at the top left corner and on the line beneath **Name Type Description** plus the names of any style files that may have previously been created. The status line displays the available options: **1 On; 2 Off; 3 Create; 4 Edit; 5 Delete; 6 Save; 7 Retrieve; 8 Update: 1**.

**1 On** formats the document to be created with the styles represented by the highlighted filename.

**2 Off** turns those formatting codes off.

**3 Create** produces a menu (Fig. 51-32) which asks for a file **Name** and for a **Type** which may be **Paired** or **Open**. Paired means that it includes a beginning and end in the same manner as such functions as Bold or Underline, while Open means that it has a beginning and no end. All style sheets that are used during the creation of a document are saved with that document.

```
Styles: Edit
    1 - Name
    2 - Type          Paired
    3 - Description
    4 - Codes
    5 - Enter         HRt
```

*Figure 51-32*

**4 Edit** displays the style sheet and permits making changes.

**5 Delete** deletes the highlighted file.

**6 Save** saves the created or edited style file so that it can be used with other documents.

**7 Retrieve** can be used to retrieve a style file that is not displayed because it is located on another disk or directory. Include all disk/directory and path information with the filename. For instance C:\WP\LIB.STY\CHAPTER.STY retrieves a style file called CHAPTER.STY from a style library subdirectory LIB.STY, located on the C:\WP directory.

**8 Update** retrieves a defined style library if one exists.

## SWITCH (Shift-F3)

This function is used to toggle back and forth between Document 1 screen and Document 2 screen. If both are to be displayed in split-screen fashion, use the **Ctrl-F3** (Screen) function.

## TAB ALIGN (Ctrl-F6)

This function aligns columns of data vertically in accordance with the align character, which is set initially to period (.) because such alignment is done most often with numerical data that include decimal spaces. It can be changed by using the **Other** option in the **Shift-F8** (Format) function. When this function is active, the cursor moves to the next tab stop, and characters typed ahead of the align character are pushed to the left. Those typed after the align character move to the right.

## TEXT IN/OUT (Ctrl-F5)

The options available with this feature are displayed on the status line: **1 DOS Text; 2 Password; 3 Save Generic; 4 Save WP; 5 Comment: 0**.

**1 DOS Text** offers three choices: **Save** saves the document as a DOS text file. **1 Retrieve** retrieves a DOS text file. Any text files can be safely retrieved with this option. **2 Retrieve** is the same except that carriage return and line-feed combinations are changed to [SRt].

**2 Password** is used to protect or lock a document. Nobody can access the file without first entering the Password. The **Add** option asks that you type a password and then type it again for verification. There is absolutely no way of unlocking the file if you forget the password. So don't. The **Remove** option removes the password from the file. It can be used only after the file has been retrieved using the password.

**3 Save Generic** saves the document with all WordPerfect codes removed.

**4 Save WP** saves the file in the WordPerfect 4.2 format.

**5 Comment** is used to enter comments into the documents. Comments are displayed but not printed. The **Create** option is used to create a comment. The **Edit** option is used to edit a comment. It searches backward from the cursor position to the first comment it finds and displays it for editing. The **Convert to Text** option searches backward from the cursor position to the first comment it finds and changes it to text, regardless of whether or not it is displayed.

## THESAURUS (Alt-F1)

This feature displays lists of synonyms and antonyms for the word on which the cursor is located. By placing the cursor on a word such as "display" and pressing **Alt-F1**, a long list of words is displayed along with a series of options in the status line (Fig. 51-33). **1 Replace Word** asks that the letter that identifies the replacement word in the list be typed. **2 View Doc** asks that **Exit** be pressed when done. **3 Look Up Word** works in a similar way to that option in the Speller. **4 Clear Column** clears away the suggested word list, leaving the boxes on the screen.

Chapter 51

```
display-(n)
  1 A  ·array                     ·flash
    B  ·demonstration             ·flaunt
    C  ·exhibit                   ·parade
    D  ·presentation
    E  ·show                  5   ·expose
                                  unfold
  2 F   fanfare                   unfurl
    G   fireworks                ·unveil
    H   panoply
    I  ·pomp                 display-(ant)
    J  ·spectacle             6   ·conceal
                                  ·hide
display-(v)
  3 K  ·demonstrate
    L  ·exhibit
    M  ·show

  4 N  ·brandish
1 Replace Word; 2 View Doc; 3 Look Up Word; 4 Clear Column: 0
```

*Figure 51-33*

## UNDERLINE (F8)

This option underlines all text typed after it is selected until **F8** is pressed a second time. If a block of text is marked using **Alt-F4** (Block) followed by pressing **F8**, the entire block is underlined.

# Chapter 52
# ADDITIONAL FUNCTIONS AND FEATURES

## ADVANCED MACROS

Advanced Macros can be useful but are only *temporary* because they are lost when the computer is turned off.

1. Press **Ctrl-PgUp.**
2. When asked for a variable, type any digit from 0 to 9.
3. When asked for a value, type the word(s) or phrase(s) you want to see on the document screen when Alt-0 (or whatever number you used) is pressed.

## CAPITAL LETTERS

Capital letters are typed when CapsLock is on or Shift is pressed. To change blocks of text to uppercase or lowercase, use the Block command to identify the block of text, then:

1. Press **Shift-F3** (Switch).
2. Select **1 UPPER CASE** or **2 lower case**.

When lowercase is selected, WordPerfect does not change the first words in sentences or the I followed by an apostrophe (I'll, I'm, etc.) to lowercase. Always include the ending period (.) of the sentence preceding the block to be changed to lowercase in the block identification. Otherwise, WordPerfect has no way of knowing that the first letter of the first word in a sentence is to remain a capital letter.

## CENTER TEXT

Center Text is used to center text between margins, headings over columns, or each line in a block of text:

1. Press **Home Left Arrow** or mark a block in which all lines are to be centered.
2. Press **Shift-F6** (Center), type text to be centered, and press **Enter** to end centering; or, in case of centering a marked block of lines, answer the displayed question [Cntr] (Y/N) No with **Y**.

To center a heading over a column that was created with the Column feature, use the left margin of the column rather than the left margin of the page and then:

1. Press **Shift-F6** (Center) and press **Down Arrow**.

To center a heading over a column that was created with tabs or indents:

1. Move cursor to center of column.
2. Press **Shift-F6** (Center) and type the heading text.

## CHARACTERS (SPECIAL)

Special characters can be created using a special WordPerfect function:

1. Press **Ctrl-V** which produces the prompt Key = on the status line.
2. Type the first character and then type the second character and the desired symbol appears at the cursor position.

   What follows is a list of some of the character combinations that can be used:

   | Type | Result |
   |------|--------|
   | AE   | Æ      |
   | ae   | æ      |
   | ss   | ß      |
   | -L   | £      |
   | "a   | ä      |
   | 'E   | É      |
   | "o   | ö      |
   | ,c   | ç      |
   | ~n   | ñ      |
   | ^u   | û      |

Or you can access the eleven WordPerfect character sets by typing the set number, followed by a comma, and then the character number. For instance:

1. Press **Ctrl-V** and type **1,23** to get ß.
2. Press **Ctrl-V** and type **4,6** to get §.

   Depending on your printer, you may not be able to access all characters in those character sets, and some printers print only a few or none. To see which characters your printer can handle, attempt to print the CHARMAP.TST file on the Conversion diskette.

## CODES

Codes are commands used to tell WordPerfect and the printer how to treat, display, and/or print the text or other data contained in a given file. These codes remain hidden unless, and until, you decide that you want to get a look at them. To do that press **Alt-F3** (Reveal Codes), which divides the screen horizontally into two windows where the top window is part of the currently active document while the bottom portion displays that same text, along with the editing codes that were used during text generation.

*Additional Functions and Features*

What follows is a list of all WordPerfect codes that might appear on the Reveal Codes (Alt-F3) screen.

| | |
|---|---|
| [ ] | Hard Space |
| [-] | Hyphen |
| - | Soft Hyphen |
| / | Cancel Hyphenation |
| [Adv] | Advance |
| [Align] | Tab Align |
| [BLOCK] [Block] | Block beginning, ending |
| [Block Pro] | Block Protection |
| [BOLD] [bold] | Bold beginning, ending |
| [Box Num] | Caption in Graphics Box |
| [C/A/FlRt] | End Tab Align or Flush Right |
| [Center Pg] | Center Page, top to bottom |
| [Cntr] | Center |
| [Cndl EOP] | Conditional End of Page |
| [Col Def] | Column Definition |
| [Col On] [Col Off] | Beginning, End of Text Column |
| [Comment] | Document Comment |
| [COLOR] [Color] | Print Color, begin, end |
| [Date] | Date/Time Function |
| [DBL UND] [Dbl Und] | Double underline, begin, end |
| [Decml Char] | Decimal Character, Thousands Separator |
| [Def Mark:Index] | Index Definition |
| [Def Mark:Listn] | List Definition |
| [Def Mark:ToC] | Table of Contents Definition |
| [DSrt] | Detectable Soft Return |
| [End Def] | End Definition (any type) |
| [End Opt] | Endnote Options |
| [Endnote] | Endnote |
| [Endnote Placement] | Endnote Placement |
| [Ext Large] | Extra Large Print |
| [Figure] | Figure Box |
| [Fig Opt] | Figure Box Option |
| [Fine] | Fine Print |
| [Flsh Rt] | Flush Right |
| [Footnote] | Footnote |
| [Font] | Base Font |
| [Footer] | Footer |
| [Force] | Force Odd/Even Page |
| [Form] | Form (Printer Selection) |

253

## Chapter 52

| Code | Description |
|---|---|
| [FtnOpt] | Footnote/Endnote Options |
| [Full Form] | Table of Authorities, Full Form |
| [HLine] | Horizontal Line |
| [Header] | Header |
| [HPg] | Hard Page Break |
| [HRt] | Hard Return |
| [Hyph] | Hyphenation |
| [HZone] | Hyphenation Zone |
| [-Indent] | Indent |
| [-Indent-] | Left/Right Indent |
| [Index] | Index Entry |
| [ISRt] | Invisible Soft Return |
| [ITAL] [Ital] | Italics, begin, end |
| [Just] | Right Justification |
| [Just Lim] | Word/Letter Spacing Justification Limits |
| [Kern] | Kerning |
| [L/R Mar] | Left/Right Margins |
| [Lang] | Language |
| [Large] | Large Print |
| [Line Height] | Line Height |
| [Ln Num] | Line Numbering |
| [-Mar Rel] | Left Margin Release |
| [Mark:List] | List Entry |
| [Mark:ToC] | Table of Contents Entry |
| [Math Def] | Definition of Math Columns |
| [Math Off] | End of Math |
| [Math On] | Beginning of Math |
| ! | Formula Calculation |
| t | Subtotal Entry |
| + | Calculate Subtotal |
| T | Total Entry |
| = | Calculate Total |
| * | Calculate Grand Total |
| [Note Num] | Footnote/Endnote Reference |
| [Outln] | Outline Attribute |
| [Ovrstk] | Overstrike |
| [Paper Sz/Typ] | Paper Size and Type |
| [Par Num] | Paragraph Number |
| [Par Num Def] | Paragraph Numbering Definition |
| [Pg Num] | New Page Number |
| [Pg Numbering] | Page Number Position |
| [Ptr Cmnd] | Printer Command |

*Additional Functions and Features*

| Code | Description |
|---|---|
| [RedLn] | Redline |
| [Ref] | Automatic Reference |
| [Set End Num] | Set New Endnote Number |
| [Set Fig Num] | Set New Figure Box Number |
| [Set Ftn Num] | Set New Footnote Number |
| [Set Tab Num] | Set New Table Box Number |
| [Set Txt Num] | Set New Text Box Number |
| [Set Usr Num] | Set New User-Defined Box Number |
| [Shadw] | Shadow |
| [Sm Cap] | Small Caps |
| [Small] | Small Print |
| [SPg] | Soft New Page |
| [SRt] | Soft Return |
| [StkOut] | Strike Out |
| [Style] | Styles |
| [Subdoc] | Subdocument (Master Documents) |
| [SubScrpt] | Subscript |
| [SuprScrpt] | Superscript |
| [Suppress] | Suppress Page Format |
| [T/B Mar] | Top and Bottom Margins |
| [Tab] | Tab |
| [TblOpt] | Table Box Options |
| [Tab Set] | Tab Set |
| [Table] | Table Box |
| [Target] | Target (Auto Reference) |
| [Text Box] | Text Box |
| [TxtOpt] | Text Box Options |
| [UND] [und] | Underline on, off |
| [UNDRLN] [undrln] | Underline Spaces/Tabs on, off |
| [Usr Box] | User-Defined Box |
| [UsrOpt] | User-Defined Box Options |
| [VLine] | Vertical Line |
| [Vry Large] | Very Large Print |
| [W/O] | Windows/Orphans |
| [Wrd/Ltr Spacing] | Word and Letter Spacing |

All of these codes are produced automatically by WordPerfect when the specific commands are entered from any menu.

## CONDITIONAL END OF PAGE

Conditional End of Page is an option that can be used to prevent a given number of lines from being separated by a page break:

1. Move the cursor to the line above the lines to be protected.
2. Press **Shift-F8** (Format) and select **4 Other**.
3. Select **2 Conditional End of Page**.
4. Enter number of lines to be protected.
5. Press **F7** (Exit).

WordPerfect keeps these lines together and treats the page breaks accordingly. In some cases the Block Protect feature can be used instead. Widows and orphans can also be avoided using the Widow/Orphan Protection option.

## CURSOR MOVEMENT AND SHAPE

Basically the cursor is a short, blinking underline, but its shape can be changed by using the DOS program CURSOR.COM and following the on-screen instructions.

The cursor can be moved to any place in a document but it cannot be moved beyond the limits of the currently active document. The means by which the cursor can be positioned are:

**Arrow Keys** are used to move the cursor one space (horizontally) or one line (vertically) at a time.

**Ctrl-Left Arrow** moves the cursor one word to the left.

**Ctrl-Right Arrow** moves the cursor one word to the right.

**Home Left Arrow** moves the cursor to the beginning of the line.

**End** moves the cursor to the end of the line.

**Home Home Up Arrow** moves the cursor to the beginning of the document.

**Home Home Down Arrow** moves the cursor to the end of the document.

**Home Home Home Up Arrow** or **Left Arrow** moves the cursor to the beginning of the document ahead of any codes or to the extreme left edge of the document ahead of any codes.

To use **Go To** press **Ctrl-Home**. It can be used to move the cursor to specified positions.

**Ctrl-Home Ctrl-Home** moves the cursor to the previous position.

**Ctrl-Home Left Arrow/Right Arrow** moves the cursor from one text column to another.

**Ctrl-Home Home Left Arrow/Right Arrow** moves the cursor to the first or last text column on the page.

**Ctrl-Home Up Arrow/Down Arrow** moves the cursor to the top or bottom of a column or page.

**Ctrl-Home Block** moves the cursor to the beginning of a currently marked block. If Block is accidentally turned off, press Ctrl-Home Ctrl-Home to rehighlight it.

**Ctrl-Home Character,** where character stands for any letter, digit or symbol, moves the cursor forward to the immediate right of the first occurrence of that character. In this function, lowercase letters match lowercase as well as uppercase letters but uppercase letters match only uppercase letters.

**Ctrl-Home Page Number** moves the cursor to the top of that page.

**PgUp, PgDn** move the cursor to the first line of the previous or next page, not the top or bottom of the current document screen.

Use the plus and minus (+, –) keys on the number pad with Num Lock off to move the cursor to the first or last line on the current document screen. When pressed repeatedly it scrolls up or down, one screen at a time.

**Esc** is used as a **Repeat** feature which asks that a number be typed, followed by a character or one of the cursor-movement commands. That character is typed that many times or the cursor-movement command is executed as many times as indicated by the number (Esc 6 Left Arrow moves the cursor six spaces to the left).

## DATE

The Date can be inserted into the active document as text or a function code. The function code updates automatically each time the document is retrieved and/or printed. There are a number of different formats in which the date can be displayed.

To insert the date as **Text**:
1. Move the cursor to the place where the date is to be inserted.
2. Press **Shift-F5** (Date/Outline) and select **1 Date Text**.

To insert the date as a WordPerfect **code**:
1. Move the cursor to the place where the date is to be inserted.
2. Press **Shift-F5** (Date/Outline) and select **2 Date Code**.

To change the **format** in which the date is displayed:
1. Press **Shift-F5** (Date/Outline), select **3 Date Format**, and select your choice from the displayed options:

| *Format typed* | *Display* |
| --- | --- |
| 3 1,4 | October 15, 1990 |
| 3 1,4 - - 8:90 | October 15, 1990 - - 10:55am |
| DATE: 2/1/5(6) | DATE: 10/20/90 (Saturday) |
| %2/%1/5 | 02/07/90 |
| %7:90 | 09:06am |
| %3.1,4(%6) | Oct.20, 1990 (Sat) |

To enter the current date during a **merge**:

1. Move the cursor to the place where the date is to be inserted.
2. Press **Shift-F9** (Merge Codes) and type **d** (to insert the ^D code into the file).

## DELETE TEXT

Deleting text can be accomplished in a number of ways:

**Backspace** (←) deletes the character to the left of the cursor.

**Delete (del)** deletes the character at the cursor.

**Delete Block** requires that a block be designated after which pressing the **Del** key and typing **Y** in answer to the displayed Delete Block? (Y/N) No erases the block. You can also press **Ctrl-F4**, select **1 Bock,** and select **3 Delete**.

**Delete Word (Ctrl-Backspace)** deletes the word at the cursor.

**Delete to End of Line (Ctrl-End)** deletes text and codes from the cursor position to the end of the line.

**Delete to End of Page (Ctrl-PgDn)** deletes text and codes from the cursor position to the end of the page.

**Delete to Word Boundary (Home-Backspace or Home-Del)** deletes all characters from the cursor position to the beginning or end of the word on which the cursor is located.

## ERROR MESSAGES

Error messages are displayed to alert you to some type of problem. Most of the error messages displayed by WordPerfect are self-explanatory. What follows are a few that tend to represent common errors:

**File Not Found** is displayed when the file that you're trying to retrieve does not exist on the currently logged disk or directory, or the filename was misspelled. If the file is to be retrieved from another disk or directory, include the path information in a format like C:\WP\LEARN\FILENAME.EXT or B:FILENAME.EXT.

**Not Enough Memory** is displayed if less than 512K of RAM is available. In such a situation some WordPerfect features, such as "Compare Documents" or "Retrieve Graphic Files," may not be usable.

**WP Disk Full — Press any Key to Continue** is a fairly mysterious message that results from trying to retrieve a document that filled up the available memory and is overflowing onto the WordPerfect diskette without room on that diskette for the text in the overflow files.

**Extended Search** and **Extended Search and Replace** which includes headers, footers, footnotes, endnotes, and tables of authority in the search is accomplished by preceding the code with **Home. (Home F2, Home Shift-F2,** or **Home Alt-F2)**.

## HARD SPACE

Hard spaces are used to keep words together, preventing the word wrap feature from splitting them:

1. Type the first word (**January**).
2. Press **Home Spacebar** which inserts a [ ] code.
3. Type the next word (**1,**).
4. Press **Home Spacebar** which inserts another [ ] code.
5. Type the next word (**1990**).

January 1, 1990 is not split if it happens to fall on the end of a line.

## HYPHENATION

Hyphenation can be used in different ways by WordPerfect. There are **Hard Hyphens** represented by the minus sign (–) (not from the number pad) and there are **Soft Hyphens** that are created by pressing **Ctrl –**. The difference is that hard hyphens remain in place regardless of whatever editing is done, while soft hyphens are inserted when word wrap needs to split a word into two-syllable groups. Soft hyphens disappear when editing causes the position of the hyphenated word to be moved away from the end of a line.

## INVISIBLE SOFT RETURN

WordPerfect offers an Invisible Soft Return function that is automatically inserted when a word extends from the left margin to the right margin. To manually enter an invisible soft return press **Home-Enter**. This function is useful for en-dashes and em-dashes or words that are separated by slashes (/).

## MARGIN RELEASE

Margin release is accomplished by moving the cursor to the beginning of a line and pressing **Shift-Tab**, which moves the cursor one tab stop to the left. To effect margin release for the right end of a line, press **Shift-F8** (Format), select **1 Line**, select **7 Margins**, and type **0** for the right margin. (You can also type **0** for the left margin if you want a line to start at the left edge of the paper.) To turn off this type of margin release, repeat the above step and reenter the previous margin values.

## NEW PAGE

New Page is produced by pressing **Ctrl-Enter** which inserts a hard-page code **[HPg]** into the document at the cursor position, while inserting a double line (========) on the document screen.

## PAGE NUMBERING/NEW PAGE NUMBER

Page Numbering and New Page Number offer a number of useful options:

1. Press **Shift-F8** (Format).
2. Select **7 Page Numbering**, and from the 13 displayed options select the one that appeals to you.

To start page numbering with a number other than 1:

1. Press **Shift-F8** (Format).
2. Select **6 New Page Number** and enter the number in whatever style you like (6, VI, vi, or whatever). WordPerfect increments the number, page after page, starting with the number you selected.

The **New Page Number** feature is useful if a document is made up of several files such as a book, each chapter of which is saved as a separate file.

You can automatically insert the current page number anywhere in the text by pressing **Ctrl-B**, which inserts a ^B code that prints the page number. When editing changes the page number it is also updated by the code.

## REPEAT

The Repeat command is used by pressing **Esc** and adding a number and then typing the character or command to be repeated. For instance:

1. **Esc 10 -** produces - - - - - - - - - -.
2. **Esc 5 Spacebar** moves the cursor five spaces to the right.
3. **Esc 3 PgUp** moves the cursor to the top of the third preceding page.

# PART THREE

## Macro and Style Libraries

## Chapter 53
# UTILITY MACRO LIBRARY

Asterisk (*)     **{DISPLAY OFF}{Font}11*{Right}**

Prints an asterisk (*) that is superscript.

Characters per line     **{Setup}81p2p{Exit}{Format}17{Enter}{PAUSE}{Enter}{Exit}{CHAIN}linenum.wpm~**

Changes units of measure to picas and stops execution for you to enter a value for the right margin (according to the chart in Chapter 20). Then activates the LINENUM.WPM macro that activates line numbering. (See **Return to normal** for the macro that reverses this action.)

COMMENT box     **{Text In/Out}51{PAUSE}**

Creates a comment box at the cursor position and waits for data input.

DATE & TIME display     **{DISPLAY OFF}{Bold}{Underline}{Date/Outline} 33 1, 4 8:90{Enter}2{Exit}{Enter}{Enter}{Cancel}{Underline}{Bold}**

Displays the current date and time from anywhere within the system. Press **F1 Cancel** to continue working.

Degree (°)     **{DISPLAY OFF}{Font}11o{Right}**

Prints the letter **o** in superscript.

Delete to EOL     **{DISPLAY OFF}{Del to EOL}{Down}{CHAIN}ALTY.WPM~**

Deletes to the end of the line on the page or inside a column, moves down one line and repeats until F1 Cancel is pressed. Macro is named ALTY.WPM.

Delete word     **{DISPLAY OFF}{Del Word}{Down}{CHAIN}ALTZ.WPM~**

Deletes word to the right of the cursor, moves down one line, and repeats until F1 Cancel is pressed. Macro is named ALTZ.WPM.

| | |
|---|---|
| Dingbat (¤) | {DISPLAY OFF}{^V}4,24{Enter} |
| | Prints a small dingbat character. |
| Double spacing | {DISPLAY OFF}{Format}162{Exit}{Exit} |
| | Activates double spacing anywhere in the document. |
| Envelope, address | {DISPLAY OFF}{Format}174{Enter}{Enter}{Exit} {Format}252{Enter}{Enter}{Exit}{Merge/Sort} 2ADDRESS.LST{Enter}{Enter}734{Del to EOL}keyg= {PROMPT}Type the name. Then press F7 (Exit) and 1 ~ |
| | Prompts you to type the name of the addressee, retrieves it from the ADDRESS.LST file, and prints it on a #10 envelope. |
| Fraction $1/2$ | {DISPLAY OFF}{Font}111{Right}/{Font}122{Right} |
| | Prints the fraction in superscript/subscript format. |
| Fraction $1/4$ | {DISPLAY OFF}{Font}111{Right}/{Font}124{Right} |
| | Prints the fraction in superscript/subscript format. |
| Graphic, view | {DISPLAY OFF}{Graphics}111{PAUSE}{Enter} 51614{Exit}{Exit}{Print}61 |
| | Accesses the graphics mode, stops for you to enter the name and path data for the graphics file to be retrieved, then causes it to be displayed in the View document format. |
| LABELS, 3 across | {DISPLAY OFF}{Format}170.25{Enter}0.25{Enter}{Exit} {Format}250.2{Enter}0.2{Enter}{Exit}{Math/Columns} 41223{Enter}30.25{Enter}{Exit}3 |
| | Sets up three parallel columns. Enter complete name and address data. Then press Ctrl-Enter to move to the next column in the same line. After three labels on one line have been entered, press Ctrl-Enter to move down to the next row of labels. |
| Letter | {DISPLAY OFF}{Enter}{Enter}{Enter}{Enter}{Enter} {Enter}{Enter}{Enter}{Enter}{Date/Outline}2 {Enter}{Enter}{Merge/Sort}2c:\add\address.lst{Enter} {Enter}734{Del to EOL}keyg= {PROMPT} Type the name. Then press F7 Exit and 1 ~ |
| | Designed to be used with preprinted stationery, the current date is printed and you are prompted to key in the name of the person to be addressed. |

## Utility Macro Library

| | |
|---|---|
| Letterhead | **{Retrieve}lethed.wpg{Enter}{Enter}{Enter}{Enter}{Enter} {Enter}{Date/Outline}2{Enter}{Enter}{Enter}{Enter} {Merge/Sort}2 c:\add\address.lst{Enter}{Enter}4keyg= {Format}171** |
| | Retrieves a graphics file representing a company logo and letterhead (lethed.wpg). Prints the current date. Accesses a database (c:\add\address.lst) and waits for you to key in the name of the person to be addressed. |
| Merge Codes | **{DISPLAY OFF}(Press F9){Merge Codes}O {Merge Codes}C{Merge R}{Merge Codes}O** |
| | Prints (Press F9)^O^C ^R^O |
| Percent | **{DISPLAY OFF}{Font}11o{Right}/{Font}12o{Right}** |
| | Prints percent sign (°/o) made with superscript and subscript. |
| Personalized letters | **{Merge/Sort}1RECORD.PF{Enter}RECORD.SF{Enter}** |
| | Combines format data in the primary file RECORD.PF with data in the secondary file RECORD.SF. |
| Return to normal | **{DISPLAY OFF}{Setup}81"2"{Exit}** |
| | Reverses result of using the Characters per line macro, restoring default conditions. |
| Single spacing | **{DISPLAY OFF}{Format}161{Exit}{Exit}** |
| | Activates single spacing anywhere in the document. |
| Spreadsheet | **{DISPLAY OFF}{Center}{Font}15SPREADSHEET{Font} 15{Enter}{Esc}78={Enter}{Enter}{Math/Columns}412220 {Enter}{Exit}3A{Hpg}B{Hpg}C{Hpg}D{Hpg}E{Hpg} F{Hpg}G{Hpg}H{Hpg}I{Hpg}J{Hpg}K{Hpg}L{Hpg} M{Hpg}N{Hpg}O{Hpg}P{Hpg}Q{Hpg}R{Hpg}S{Hpg} T{Hpg}** |
| | Creates 20 parallel columns, each headed with a letter of the alphabet from A through T. Enter data into column after column, pressing Ctrl-Enter to move from one column to the next or from one row to the next. |

*Chapter 53*

Vertical line          **{DISPLAY OFF}{Graphics}5214{Exit}{Exit}**

Draws a vertical line from page top to page bottom at the horizontal cursor position.

Vertical line, short   **{DISPLAY OFF}{Graphics}5214{Exit}25{Exit}{Exit}**

Draws a vertical line from the cursor position to the bottom of the page.

# CHAPTER 54
# UTILITY STYLE LIBRARY

Memo format

> [Center][BOLD]INTER[-]OFFICE MEMO[C/A/Flrt][HRt]
> [HRt]
> Date: [Date:3 1, 4][HRt]
> [HRt]
> From:[HRt]
> [HRt]
> To: [HRt]
> [HRt]
> [-][-][-][-][-][-][-][-][-][-][-][-][-][-][-][-]
> [-][-][-][-][-][-][-][-][-][-][-][-][-][-][-][-]
> [HRt]
> **Subject:**[bold]

Prints the format for an inter-office memo.

Restaurant Menu

> [L/R Mar:0",0"][Tab Set:2.3"][AdvToLn:1.5"][Cntr]
> [OUTLN][EXT LARGE]The Brasserie[C/A/Flrt][HRt]
> [AdvToLn:1"][Figure:1;;][AdvToLn:2.5"][Cntr][SM CAP]
> Dinner Menu[C/A/Flrt][HRt][HRt][HRt][SHADW]MEAT
> [Indent][HRt][HRt][HRt][HRt]FISH[Indent][HRt][HRt]
> [HRt][HRt]SALADS[Indent][HRt][HRt][HRt][HRt]DESSERT
> [Indent][HRt][HRt][HRt][HRt]BEVERAGES[Indent][HRt]
> [HRt][HRt][HRt][HLine:Center,7.5",0.08",80%]
> [AdvToLn:9.5"][ext large][shadw][sm cap][Cntr][BOLD]
> 1127 Monterey Drive, Los Angeles, California 90021
> 213 555 1234

Prints the menu in Fig. 54-1.

## Chapter 54

---

**The Brasserie**

DINNER MENU

**MEAT**

**FISH**

**SALADS**

**DESSERT**

**BEVERAGES**

―――――――――――――――――――――

1127 Monterey Drive, Los Angeles, California 90021   213 555 1234

---

*Figure 54-1*

Letterhead

[HRt][HRt][HRt][HRt][LARGE][BOLD]Henry W. Smith
[large][bold][Flsh Rt][Date:3 1, 4][C/A/Flrt][HRt]
President[HRt][HRt][HRt][Footer A:3;[Cntr]
XYZ Company, Inc. 55 Main Street, Anytown, XX
12345-6789][HRt][Comment]

Prints the letterhead in Fig. 54-2.

20-column spreadsheet

[Cntr][LARGE]SPREADSHEET[large][C/A/Flrt][HRt]
=================================================
==============================[HRt][HRt]
[Col Def:20,1",1.23",1.33",1.56",1.66",1.89"
1.99",2.22",2.32",2.55",2.65",2.88",2.98",3.21",
3.31",3.54",3.64",3.87",3.97",4.2",4.3",4.53",
4.63",4.86",4.96",5.19",5.29",5.52",5.62",5.85",
5.95",6.18",6.28",6.51",6.61",8.84",6.94",7.17",
7.27",7.5"][Col On]A[HRt]
B[HRt]
C[HRt]
D[HRt]
E[HRt]
F[HRt]
G[HRt]
H[HRt]
I[HRt]
J[HRt]
K[HRt]
L[HRt]
M[HRt]
N[HRt]
O[HRt]
P[HRt]
Q[HRt]
R[HRt]
S[HRt]
T[Col Off]
[HRt][Col On][HRt]

Prints the 20-column spreadsheet heading in Fig. 54-3, ready for data entry. Use only Ctrl-Enter to move from column to column and row to row.

*Chapter 54*

```
Henry W. Smith                                    March 14, 1990
President
```

```
              XYZ Company, Inc. 55 Main Street, Anytown, XX 12345-6789
```

*Figure 54-2*

*Utility Style Library*

```
                    S P R E A D S H E E T
==================================================================
  A   B   C   D   E   F   G   H   I   J   K   L   M   N   O   P   Q   R   S   T
```

*Figure 54-3*

# APPENDIX A
# EXTENDED ASCII CODES

| Code | Result | Code | Result | Code | Result |
|---|---|---|---|---|---|
| 1 | Ctrl-A | 0,19 | Alt-R | 0,67 | F9 |
| 2 | Ctrl-B | 0,20 | Alt-T | 0,68 | F10 |
| 3 | Ctrl-C BREAK | 0,21 | Alt-Y | 0,71 | Home |
| 4 | Ctrl-D | 0,22 | Alt-U | 0,72 | Cursor Up |
| 5 | Ctrl-E | 0,23 | Alt-I | 0,73 | PgUp |
| 6 | Ctrl-F | 0,24 | Alt-O | 0,75 | Cursor Left |
| 7 | Ctrl-G | 0,25 | Alt-P | 0,77 | Cursor Right |
| 8 | Ctrl-H | 0,30 | Alt-A | 0,79 | End |
| 9 | Ctrl-I | 0,31 | Alt-S | 0,80 | Cursor Down |
| 10 | Ctrl-J | 0,32 | Alt-D | 0,81 | PgDn |
| 11 | Ctrl-K | 0,33 | Alt-F | 0,82 | Ins |
| 12 | Ctrl-L | 0,34 | Alt-G | 0,83 | Del |
| 13 | Ctrl-M ENTER | 0,35 | Alt-H | 0,84 | Shift-F1 |
| 14 | Ctrl-N | 0,36 | Alt-J | 0,85 | Shift-F2 |
| 15 | Ctrl-O | 0,37 | Alt-K | 0,86 | Shift-F3 |
| 16 | Ctrl-P | 0,38 | Alt-L | 0,87 | Shift-F4 |
| 17 | Ctrl-Q | 0,44 | Alt-Z | 0,88 | Shift-F5 |
| 18 | Ctrl-R | 0,45 | Alt-X | 0,89 | Shift-F6 |
| 19 | Ctrl-S | 0,46 | Alt-C | 0,90 | Shift-F7 |
| 20 | Ctrl-T | 0,47 | Alt-V | 0,91 | Shift-F8 |
| 21 | Ctrl-U | 0,48 | Alt-B | 0,92 | Shift-F9 |
| 22 | Ctrl-V | 0,49 | Alt-N | 0,93 | Shift-F10 |
| 23 | Ctrl-W | 0,50 | Alt-M | 0,94 | Ctrl-F1 |
| 24 | Ctrl-X | 0,59 | F1 | 0,95 | Ctrl-F2 |
| 25 | Ctrl-Y | 0,60 | F2 | 0,96 | Ctrl-F3 |
| 26 | Ctrl-Z | 0,61 | F3 | 0,97 | Ctrl-F4 |
| 27 | Esc | 0,62 | F4 | 0,98 | Ctrl-F5 |
| 0,15 | Shift-Tab | 0,63 | F5 | 0,99 | Ctrl-F6 |
| 0,16 | Alt-Q | 0,64 | F6 | 0,100 | Ctrl-F7 |
| 0,17 | Alt-W | 0,65 | F7 | 0,101 | Ctrl-F8 |
| 0,18 | Alt-E | 0,66 | F8 | 0,102 | Ctrl-F9 |

## Appendix A

| Code | Result | Code | Result | Code | Result |
|------|--------|------|--------|------|--------|
| 0,103 | Ctrl-F10 | 0,113 | Alt-F10 | 0,123 | Alt-4 |
| 0,104 | Alt-F1 | 0,114 | Ctrl-PrtSc | 0,124 | Alt-5 |
| 0,105 | Alt-F2 | 0,115 | Ctrl-Cursor-Left | 0,125 | Alt-6 |
| 0,106 | Alt-F3 | 0,116 | Ctrl-Cursor-Right | 0,126 | Alt-7 |
| 0,107 | Alt-F4 | 0,117 | ^End | 0,127 | Alt-8 |
| 0,108 | Alt-F5 | 0,118 | Ctrl-PgDn | 0,128 | Alt-9 |
| 0,109 | Alt-F6 | 0,119 | Ctrl-Home | 0,129 | Alt-0 |
| 0,110 | Alt-F7 | 0,120 | Alt-1 | 0,130 | Alt-– |
| 0,111 | Alt-F8 | 0,121 | Alt-2 | 0,131 | Alt-= |
| 0,112 | Alt-F9 | 0,122 | Alt-3 | 0,132 | Ctrl-PgUp |

# APPENDIX B
# LIST OF MACROS

| Chapter | Action |
|---|---|
| 1  | A Umlaut (ä) |
| 1  | Activate Italics |
| 2  | Address a #10 envelope, using address data stored in the ADDRESS.LST file |
| 53 | Asterisk. Prints superscript asterisk (*) |
| 18 | Automatic Reference with prompt for input |
| 13 | Business cards, six to a page |
| 11 | Chapter or article Page 1 format with prompt for font selection |
| 53 | Characters per line. Limits the number of characters per line |
| 53 | Comment boxes. Creates comment boxes, waits for data input |
| 53 | Date and time is displayed anywhere at any time |
| 53 | Degree. Prints ° |
| 26 | Delete one word, line after line, until F1 Cancel is pressed |
| 26 | Delete to end of line, line after line until F1 Cancel is pressed |
| 53 | Dingbat. Prints ¤ |
| 53 | Double spacing |
| 17 | Endnote defined with prompt for input |
| 17 | Endnote placed based on input |
| 53 | Envelope. Addresses #10 envelopes from database records |
| 40 | Files, copy today's work to floppy |
| 16 | Footer for any kind of use |
| 17 | Footnote. Prompt for input |
| 53 | Fraction $^1/_2$ |
| 53 | Fraction $^1/_4$ |
| 53 | Graphic. Select graphic to be viewed in the View document format |
| 16 | Header for chapter or article (can be for other uses) |
| 21 | Horizontal graphics line with prompt length and parameters |
| 21 | Horizontal graphics line, five inches $^1/_2$ inch wide, 50% shading |
| 34 | Index created |
| 34 | Index generated |
| 34 | Index styled and created |

Appendix B

| Chapter | Action |
|---|---|
| 7 | Invoice format |
| 7 | Invoice format with codes for data |
| 53 | Labels. Prints labels three across |
| 6 | Letter format including a letterhead prompts for data input |
| 2 | Letter with preprinted letterhead, address data stored in the file |
| 21 | Line draw, double line |
| 21 | Line draw, single line |
| 20 | Line numbering including blank lines on next pages |
| 6 | Memorandum form with codes and text prompting for input |
| 53 | Merge codes. Prints (Press F9)^O^C ^R^O |
| 53 | Percent. Prints % |
| 53 | Personalized letters. Merges data from two files |
| 31 | Redline codes removed |
| 53 | Return to normal after using the characters-per-line macro |
| 53 | Single spacing |
| 27 | Slide show using graphic text slides |
| 27 | Slide show using View Document text |
| 4 | Sorting address data in any database by state two-letter ID and city |
| 4 | Sorting address data in any database by company names |
| 4 | Sorting address data in any database by zip codes |
| 4 | Sorting address data in any database file by last names |
| 4 | Sorting ADDRESS.LST data by key word |
| 53 | Spreadsheet, 20 columns |
| 31 | Strikeout codes removed |
| 21 | Vertical graphics line with prompt |
| 53 | Vertical line, top to bottom, at cursor position |
| 53 | Vertical line, from cursor position to bottom of page |

# APPENDIX C
# GLOSSARY

| Term | Definition |
|---|---|
| ASCII | American Standard Code for Information Interchange. One of the standard formats for text files, making it possible to move files between programs. |
| Bit | The smallest binary storage unit. |
| Buffer | A temporary data storage area used by computers and printers. |
| Byte | The amount of storage area capable of storing one character, digit, or symbol. One byte consists of eight bits. 1024 bytes represent one kilobyte (KB). |
| Card | A printed circuit board that is plugged into one of the extension slots in the computer. |
| Default | The initial setting used by programs such as WordPerfect. WordPerfect defaults can be changed temporarily, using Shift F8 (Format) and certain other functions, or permanently, using Ctrl F1 (Setup). |
| DOS | Disk Operating System. It is the software controlling the transfer of data between the computer and storage devices such as floppy or hard disks. |
| Driver | A set of commands contained in a program and used to run peripheral devices such as printers. |
| Font | A type face, point size, and weight such as 10-point Times Roman Bold. |
| Kilobyte (KB) | 1024 bytes. |
| Megabyte (MB) | 1024 kilobytes or 1,048,576 bytes. |
| Memory | A data storage area. See RAM, ROM. |
| Parallel Interface | An interface permitting the transmission of information simultaneously in two directions. |
| Parallel Printer | A printer using parallel interface. |

| Term | Definition |
|---|---|
| Path name | Information telling the computer where to look for a file: B:FILENAME or C:\WP\FILENAME where B: and C: represent the disk drives and \WP represents a directory. C:\WP\LIB\FILENAME includes a subdirectory called \LIB. |
| Port | The connector or outlet that is used to connect the computer to an external peripheral device such as a printer, monitor, scanner, etc. |
| RAM | Random Access Memory. The working space used by the computer to temporarily store data. All data in RAM are lost if the computer is turned off. |
| RAM Resident Programs | Programs activated when the computer is turned on. They remain active in RAM until the computer is shut down. |
| ROM | Read Only Memory. The storage area containing permanent information used by the computer to run the system. It remains unaffected by power interruptions. |
| Serial Interface | The interface that transmits data one bit at a time. |
| Serial Printer | A printer using a serial interface. |
| TSR | Terminate and Stay Resident program. Same as RAM resident programs. |
| Typeface | Type style such as Times Roman. |
| Weight | The appearance of a character such as bold, normal, etc. |

# INDEX

**Address list, database**, 5
    hard page breaks, 5
Advanced macros, 251
ASCII codes, extended, 271 - 272
Automatic references, 87 - 89
    macro, 89

**Base fonts for different printers**, 19
Block protect feature, 174 - 175
Block, 217
Block, saving, 177
Bold, 217
Book, chapter, first page format, 52 - 54
Business cards, print six, 59 - 62

**Cancel**, 217
Capital letters, 251
Center, 218
Center text, 251
Chapter, first page format, 52 - 54
Characters per line, number of, 96 - 97, 99
Characters, special, 252
City and State, receiving data by, 17
Clip art, DrawPerfect, 199 - 200
    macro, 200
    sample page in view document mode, 200
Codes, 252 - 255
Columns, 41
    calculate numeric data, 48
    calculate percentages, 50 - 51
    column definition screen, 42
    editing parallel columns, 129 - 133
    newspaper type, 41
    parallel type, 45
    spreadsheet type, 47
    three column format, 42
    two column format, 41
Comment boxes, 105 - 113
    business form document, 109 - 114
    letter, used with, 105
    macro, 109
    parallel columns, 111 - 114

Compare documents, 156 - 158
    redline, add, 156
    redline, remove, 157
    strikeout, add, 156
    strikeout, remove, 157
    macros, 158
Conditional end of page, 174, 256
Contents, Tables of, 163 - 165
    levels, 164
Converting word processing files, 184 - 187
    from WordPerfect, 185 - 186
    to WordPerfect, 186 - 187
    wild cards (* and ?), 184
Cursor movement, shape, 256

**Database, address list**, 5
    form letters, 12
    retrieving selected data, 10 - 11
    sort option, 6
    use with envelopes, 5
Date/outline, 218
Date/Outline option to insert current date, 7
Date, 257
Delete text, 258
Disk labels, 62 - 65
DOS programs from inside WordPerfect, 176 - 177
    size limits, 176 - 177

**Endnotes**, 84 - 86
    placement, 84
Error message, 258
Exit, 220
External graphics programs, 212 - 215
    conversion (GRAPHCVN.EXE), 213
    scanners (.TIF files), 214

**Flush right**, 220
Font, 220
Footers, 80 - 81
Footnotes, 82 - 83, 221
Foreign characters, 4
Form letters, 12

277

# Index

Format, 223
Function keys (alphabetical listing), 217 - 250
    block, 217
    bold, 217
    cancel, 217
    center, 218
    date/outline, 218
    exit, 220
    flush right, 220
    font, 220
    footnote, 221
    format, 223
    graphics, 230
    help, 233
    indent <—>, 233
    indent —>, 233
    list files, 234
    macro, 234
    macro define, 235
    mark text, 235
    math/columns, 236
    merge R, 236
    merge codes, 236
    merge/sort, 236
    move, 237
    print, 237
    replace, 239
    retrieve, 239
    reveal codes, 239
    save, 239
    screen, 240
    search <—, 240
    search —>, 240
    setup, 240
    shell, 246
    spell, 246
    style, 247
    switch, 248
    tab align, 248
    text in/out, 248
    thesaurus, 249
    underline, 250
Functions and features, additional, 251 - 260
    advanced macros, 251
    capital letters, 251

Functions and features (additional) Cont.
    center text, 251
    characters, special, 252
    codes, 252 - 255
    conditional end of page, 256
    cursor movement, shape, 256
    date, 257
    delete text, 258
    error message, 258
    hard space, 259
    hyphenation, 259
    invisible soft return, 259
    margin release, 259
    new page, 259
    pagenumbering/new page number, 260
    repeat, 260

**Glossary**, 275 - 276
Graphics, 140 - 149, 230
    edit graphic image, 144
    empty box, 140 - 141
    external programs, imported, 212 - 215
    image with caption, 141
    table, 143
    text box, 146
    text box with shading, 147
    user-defined box, 148

**Hard space**, 259
Headers, 78 - 79
Help, 233
Hyphenation, 159, 259

**Indent —>**, 233
Indent <—>, 233
Indenting, 90 - 94
Indexes, 166 - 172
    combine several indexes, 170
    concordance files, 171, 172
    define, 166
    format for page numbers, 167
    generate, 168
    macros, 168 - 169
Invisible soft return, 259

# Index

Invoice, 31
    basic format, 32
    data added to preprinted form, 40
    entering data, 35
    merge option to position cursor, 37
    printing into basic format, 34

**Labels, three in a row**, 55 - 58
Letter format, 28
    Style sheet, 74 - 77
    with prompt lines, 30
Library, 204 - 211
    Appointment calendar, 207 - 208
    Beast, 206
    Calculator, 209 - 210
    Calendar, 207 - 208
    File manager, 211
    Shell, 204
Lines, drawing, 100 - 104
    graphic format, 102 - 104
List of macros, 273 - 274
List files, 117 - 123 - 234
    asterisk to select files, 188
    macro, 189
    backup files, timed, 122
    expanded summary, 120
    summaries, 118 - 119
    word search, 120

**Macro define**, 235
Macros, three types, 1
    editing mode, 5
    view existing macro, 2
Macros, 234, 261 - 264
    asterisk (*), 261
    characters per line, 261
    comment box, 261
    date & time display, 261
    degree (°), 261
    delete EOL, 261
    delete word, 261
    dingbat (✄), 262
    double spacing, 262
    envelope, address, 262
    fraction $^1/_2$, 262
    fraction $^1/_4$, 262
    graphic view, 262
    labels, 3 across, 262
    letter, 262
    letterhead, 263
    merge codes, 263
    percent %, 263
    personalized letters, 263
    return to normal, 263
    single spacing, 263
    spreadsheet, 263
    vertical line, 264
    vertical line, short, 264
Macros, listed, 273 - 274
Margin release, 259
Mark text, 235
Master document, 160
    expand master document, 161
    generate, 161
    size of (limits), 162
    subdocument, 160
Math/columns, 236
Mathematic symbols, 178 - 183
    compose function (Ctrl-V), 178
    Equation option (5.1 only), 181 - 183
    Exact program, 178 - 179
    WordPerfect 5.0, 178 - 180
    WordPerfect 5.1, 181 - 183
Memorandum format, 24 - 25
    date code, 25
    multiple users, 25
    printing multiple copies, 25
    style sheet, 72 - 73
Merge codes, 9
Merge/sort, 236
Merge R, 236
Merge codes, 236
Mouse operation, 190 - 198
    Logitech mouse program for 5.0, 190 - 192
    menu bar (5.1), 196
    sample menus, 197 - 198
    source code, 193 - 195
    WordPerfect 5.0, 190 - 195
    WordPerfect 5.1, 196 - 198
Move, 237

*Index*

**New page**, 259
Numbering lines, 95
    characters per line, 96 - 97, 99
    resorting, 95
Line numbering, 95
    characters per line, 96 - 97, 99
    resorting, 95

**Orphans**, 173
Outdenting, 90 - 94

**Page Numbering/New Page Number**, 260
Preprinted documents, printing into, 34
Print, 237

**References, automatic**, 87 - 89
    macro, 89
Repeat, 260
Replace, 239
Retrieve, 239
Reveal codes, 239

**Save**, 239
Screen capture programs, 150 - 155
    GRAB.COM, 150 - 153
    HiJack, 154 - 155
    InSet, 155
Screen, 240
Screens, two, 115 - 116
Search, 240
Setup, 240
Shell, 246
Source code, writing, 201 - 203
    line numbering, automatic, 201
    macro, 201
    source code sample, 202

Special characters, foreign, 4
Spell, 246
State and City, retrieving data by, 17
Style, 66 - 77, 247
    books format, 68
    change formats, 69 - 70
    edit screen, 67
    letter format, 74 - 77
    line spacing, 71
    memo format, 72 - 73
    reveal codes screen, 67
    screen to create styles, 66
    underline, 70
Styles, 265 - 270
    letterhead, 267 - 268
    memo format, 265
    restaurant menu, 265 - 266
    twenty-column spreadsheet, 267, 269
Switch, 248

**Tab align**, 248
Text in/out, 248
Thesaurus, 249
Today's work, save to floppy disk, macro, 189
Two screens, 115 - 116
Typewriter option, 34

**Umlaut, uppercase and lowercase**, 3
Underline, 250

**Windows**, 173
Word processing files, converting, 184 - 187

**Zip code, retrieving data by**, 17